The Hillsborough Disaster

In Their Own Words

Mike Nicholson

Foreword by the Hillsborough Family Support Group

AMBERLEY

*All of the proceeds received by the author will be donated to
the Alder Hey Children's Hospital, Liverpool.*

First published 2016

Amberley Publishing
The Hill, Stroud
Gloucestershire, GL5 4EP

www.amberley-books.com

British Library Cataloguing in Publication Data.
A catalogue record for this book is available from the British Library.

ISBN 978 1 4456 3486 9 (print)
ISBN 978 1 4456 3507 1 (ebook)

Typesetting and Origination by Amberley Publishing.
Printed in the UK.

Contents

Diagram of Leppings Lane end of Hillsborough Stadium

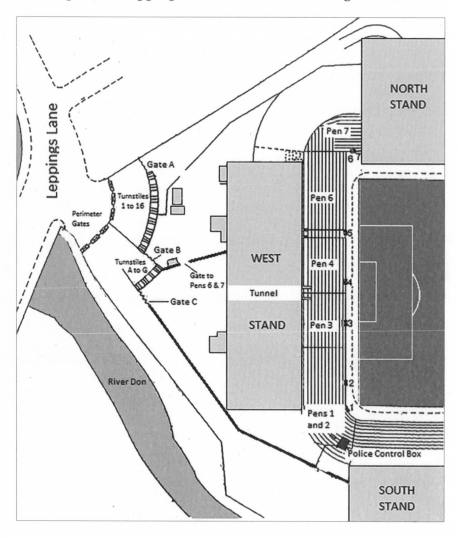

Foreword

The book is an excellent account of one of the most harrowing days in British history. The author, Mike Nicholson, is able to bring the story to life in a thoughtful and intelligent way by using first-hand accounts of survivors and families, interspersed with known facts and witness testimony. This book is a must read for anyone who wants to understand the true story of Hillsborough and it gives an insight into the reasons why the families and survivors have maintained their incredible fight for justice in the face of overwhelming odds and adversity.

Without survivors' accounts and statements we would not have been able to get to the truth. It is through the support of all our fans and survivors and indeed our city that believed in the families from the very beginning that the truth came out. There are so many people nationwide, and indeed globally who believed and understood why we've kept our fight going and there are so many people that we should thank, some who we might never have even have met, people like Mike who can put our message out so articulately.

We still have a long way to go, and sadly on our harrowing journey we have lost many dear family members and also some survivors, who fought for so long and hard alongside us. They all passed away tormented, some without even seeing the truth, all without seeing any justice and accountability. If we win this battle, we will have won it not only for the 96 but for all who have passed and all those who are still fighting.

From the very beginning right up to the present day and whatever the outcome may be we have done this together, it is not just the families, it is everyone who has supported us in the past, present and hopefully in the future. On behalf of the Hillsborough Family Support Group I thank all of you – God bless you all – we never walked alone.

Margaret Aspinall, Chairman
Hillsborough Family Support Group

Preface

Explaining how the Hillsborough disaster happened to a forty-year-old football fan who used to attend football matches in the 1980s has always been a far easier job than trying to explain it to a twenty-year-old fan who has only ever enjoyed the beautiful game in today's comparative luxury. It must be hard for the younger fan to comprehend how it is even physically possible for ninety-six people to be crushed to death at a football match, when their only experience of top-flight football has been inside safe, all-seater stadia, and at football matches that are generally well managed by stewards and police.

Misinformation about the cause of the disaster was spread far and wide through the media in the immediate aftermath, so it will require an open mind to revisit this subject today. The families and survivors of the disaster have had to endure over a quarter of a century of lies and accusations that blamed the victims for causing the disaster, when the real truth is very different. That battle for the truth and 'justice for the 96' was at least partly won in September 2012, when the Hillsborough Independent Panel (HIP) released their report. After years of painstaking research, which included looking through over 450,000 documents from organisations such as the South Yorkshire Police, the South Yorkshire Ambulance Service, the South Yorkshire Fire Service, the coroner, Sheffield City Council, and solicitors representing all of these bodies, the truth of Hillsborough was finally told and put on public record.

Within an hour of the report being released to the media (which only happened once the families had been told), the apologies started to arrive. The Prime Minister, David Cameron, stood up in Parliament to make an unreserved apology. He spoke of 'the double injustice' that the families had suffered, explaining that it was 'the injustice of the appalling events, the failure of the state to protect their loved ones and the indefensible wait to get to the truth. Then the injustice of the denigration of the deceased; that they were somehow at fault for their own deaths. So on behalf of the Government, and indeed our country, I am profoundly sorry that this double injustice has been left uncorrected for so long.' Mr Cameron went on to talk about how 'a narrative about hooliganism on the day was created, which led many in the country to accept that somehow it was a grey area. Today's report is black and white. Liverpool fans were not the cause of the disaster.'

The report was a catalyst for a chain of events that saw apologies surface from many of the bodies involved in the disaster. It was the Football Association who booked the Hillsborough Stadium for their showpiece event, and David Bernstein offered an apology: 'This fixture was played in the FA's own competition, and on behalf of the Football Association I offer a full and unreserved apology and express sincere condolences to all of the families of those who lost their lives, and to everyone connected to the City of Liverpool and Liverpool Football Club.'

Sheffield Wednesday Football Club also released a statement, part of which read, 'The current board of directors have adopted a policy of complete compliance with the requests of the Hillsborough Independent Panel and on behalf of the club would like to offer our sincere condolences and an apology to all the families who have suffered as a consequence of the tragic events of 15 April 1989.'

David Crompton, the current Chief Constable of the South Yorkshire Police, added to the wave of apologies: 'In the immediate aftermath, senior officers sought to change the record of events. Disgraceful lies were told, which blamed the Liverpool fans for the disaster. These actions have caused untold pain and distress for over twenty-three years. I am profoundly sorry for the way the force failed.'

The verdicts of accidental death were also quashed, with fresh inquests ordered.

'Justice for the 96' is a chant heard from the supporters at almost every game that Liverpool Football Club play, but what does justice mean? Margaret Aspinall of the Hillsborough Family Support Group says, 'I don't believe in the word "justice". There can be no justice for the loss of one life, never mind 96 lives. However, I'm a great believer in accountability. Those responsible for the deaths of the 96 need to be held accountable, named and shamed.'

Twenty-three years after Britain's worst sporting disaster, the Hillsborough Independent Report, and the subsequent apologies, might have helped the country realise what Liverpool fans have always known, and in doing so helped set the record straight. What the report couldn't do was legally hold any organisation or individual responsible. One might say that the battle for the truth has been won through the excellent work of the Hillsborough Independent Panel, but the war for justice has only just started. At the time of writing this book, just a few months before the twenty-fifth anniversary of the disaster, new inquests are imminent; the Independent Police Complaints Commission is undertaking the biggest investigation in its history and a criminal investigation is underway.

Twenty-five years ago, 24,256 Liverpool supporters set off to watch a football match. 96 lost their lives and never returned home. The eldest was sixty-four and the youngest was just ten years old. They were fathers, sons, mothers, daughters, brothers, sisters ... they are known collectively as the 96, but they are individual people who were loved and lost on a bright, sunny day in Sheffield.

This book tells the story of those who know best what happened – it's the story of those who were there. The majority of quotations from Liverpool fans were taken in face-to-face interviews by me; the quotations from Leeds fans were submitted to me via email, after I appealed for witnesses, and the police quotations are taken from their own witness statements, which are freely available to all on the Hillsborough Independent Panel website at http://hillsborough.independent.gov.uk/.

1

Before Hillsborough

Football in the seventies and eighties was blighted by football-related violence, and although only a very small proportion were guilty of such behaviour, many fans of the era recall an atmosphere of being viewed as 'guilty until proven innocent', just because you were a football supporter. Policing seemed to place the emphasis on the containment and control of supporters, and as a result safety seemed to fall down the pecking order of importance. In short, the football fan was viewed through a lens of suspicion just because they were at a football match. Liverpool fan Ed Critchley recalls trips as an away fan back in the eighties: 'I remember going to places like Old Trafford in the eighties and being treated like absolute scum by the police. We were pushed around, sworn at, kicked up the arse, and generally treated like second-class citizens. My mate got run over by a police horse. Football in the eighties was not a pleasant place to be, but you got used to being treated that way. When you're a die-hard Liverpool fan, you just rough it and put up with it.'

Supporters of the away team were often met at the station and frogmarched to the ground by the local police force. On arrival, spectators were corralled into the away terraces, into pens made from tall fences at the front and often at the sides. Richie Greaves is another football supporter who remembers how differently he was treated as a fan back in those days: 'It's interesting that they call them pens, isn't it? I mean, you keep animals in pens. I think in those days that was how football fans were thought of by the police. They just herded you in, and I don't think there was much thought for our safety.'

There is no doubt that the Hillsborough disaster acted as a wake-up call for the footballing world. The perimeter fences that used to pen fans in like animals were pulled down. The old, and often dangerous, football stadia in the United Kingdom started to be modified and, after the Taylor Report into the disaster, all-seater stadia became mandatory in the top two divisions of British football. Today, football fans can watch football in well-maintained stadia, with good amenities and, most importantly, in safety. This is about the only bright spot to come out of the darkest day in British football history. It is, however, hard not to come to the conclusion that this wake-up call came too late. If Hillsborough was the alarm call that finally woke football from its slumber, then the beautiful game had surely been guilty of hitting the snooze button too many times. Disaster followed disaster, and opportunities to learn vital lessons were at best only partly learned. There is a quotation by George Bernard Shaw that reads, 'We learn from history that we learn nothing from history', and that statement seems very fitting when looking at the history of football disasters in the UK.

On 9 March 1946, a quarter-final second-leg match between Bolton Wanderers and Stoke City was played at Burnden Park, which was the home of Bolton Wanderers at the time. In those days, you weren't asked to buy a ticket in advance of attending a football match, you simply turned up at the turnstiles and paid your money on the day. At Burnden Park that day, far more fans attended than anticipated, and the turnstiles kept admitting them onto the banked terrace at the Bolton end of the ground until about twenty to three. Once the turnstiles were closed, more fans climbed over the walls to gain entry and somebody picked a lock in a perimeter exit gate, which allowed even more fans to enter. The already packed crowd became fatal as a crush barrier collapsed and the people at the front collapsed on top of one another. Thirty-three people died that day. The subsequent Moelwyn Hughes Report was commissioned to look into the causes, and made recommendations on how football could stop incidents like this from happening again. Those recommendations included the introduction of counting systems on turnstiles so that clubs could monitor how many people have been admitted, a review of safety barriers, and a mechanical means to ascertain when a certain enclosure had reached its capacity.

On 16 September 1961, two people died in a crush on stairway thirteen at the Ibrox Stadium in Glasgow. The large, open stairway allowed thousands of tightly packed people to travel down a steep stairwell towards the exit gate, and a barrier collapsed under the weight. This was not the event that has become known as the Ibrox disaster, but it can most certainly be considered a disaster that two fans went to watch a football match and ended up losing their lives.

On 24 August 1968, a fire broke out at the City Ground in Nottingham during a match between Nottingham Forest and Leeds United. It is thought that the fire started somewhere around the dressing room area at half-time. Despite there being over 30,000 supporters in attendance, amazingly nobody was killed. Fans managed to escape out of the front of the stand and onto the pitch. A wooden stand and a flame came together to devastating effect, and the entire stand burned to the ground.

On 2 January 1971, Rangers played Celtic at the Ibrox Stadium in Glasgow. Sixty-six people were crushed to death on stairway thirteen. Rangers fans had started to leave down the packed stairway towards the exit gates below, but the roar of the crowd in reaction to a late equaliser caused some to turn around and try to get back up the stairs to the terraces. The sheer weight of tightly packed supporters travelling down a steep stairwell meant that, when somebody lost their footing, people behind fell over them, and the people behind those fell over them like dominoes. The crowd had no way of pushing back against the heavy flow of people behind. At the time, this was the worst sporting disaster in British history, and sixty-six people were killed, with hundreds more injured.

On 11 May 1985, Bradford City played Lincoln City at Valley Parade. It should have been a joyous occasion, as Bradford City had already secured promotion by winning the Third Division, and the trophy was paraded in front of the home crowd before kick-off. The main stand had been condemned to be demolished, and work was due to start just days later, but on this windy day in West Yorkshire it was full of celebrating, happy Bradford City supporters. Just before half-time, a small fire was reported, but in the windy conditions it quickly spread and, within minutes, the entire stand was ablaze. One supporter told the BBC that 'the fire spread as fast as a man can run'. Julian Gratton is a Bradford City supporter, and he and his family used to sit in the main stand for home matches, but for some reason that day he had an overwhelming desire to go to the Kop end instead:

'All I remember about the fire is that it started where we would normally sit. I didn't understand what was going on. From what I remember, people were under the impression it was some kind of smoke bomb, as all there was at first was smoke, but then you saw the flames. It was then that some people began to start shouting across the pitch for people to "get out of there". The flames soon spread and in no time at all it was probably a 3-metre-square patch of fire … and that's when people began to realise something was wrong. The flames spread, people began to move away from that side of the stadium and then the flames hit the ceiling of the stand. I've never seen fire like it. The heat generated from that ball of flames as the old lead paint that lined the ceiling got lit up caused an almighty panic. People were screaming, shouting … to my right, where the Kop met the stand, you could see people being helped over to safety. I remember seeing people rushing to the ground level. There was a high concrete wall that blocked access to the pitch, and you could see people struggling to get over. You could see people helping each other, smoke pouring off their clothes… further up the stand I saw a guy dragging someone over the seats to safety. My mum grabbed me to turn me away, but I pulled away, telling her, "I want to watch." The stadium was fully ablaze, and it was at this point I saw something that has haunted me since that day. There was a man fully on fire. I remember at this point that screams of panic, desperation and sheer helplessness filled the air. "Get him out, get him out" – that's all I can remember hearing … then a ball of flames shot across him and he disappeared. More than twenty-five years later, that day still haunts me. It wasn't until the season before we got into the Premiership that I dared visit the stadium again for a game. I still find it hard now going back. And I still see him. That man all in flames … people screaming, the ball of flames taking him. The heat. The smell. The helplessness.'

Decades of rubbish at Bradford had fallen between the gaps in the wooden stand and it had accumulated underneath. Discarded waste piled many feet high. All it took was a dropped cigarette to set the whole thing ablaze like a giant tinderbox. The disaster killed fifty-six people, and injured hundreds more. In the enquiry chaired by Sir Oliver Popplewell, a British judge, it was found that Bradford City Football Club had been warned by the county council about the safety risk posed by the rubbish under the stand. The Bradford fire was absolutely nothing to do with crowd unrest, of course, but on the same day as the Bradford disaster, fans fought at Birmingham City Football Club and a teenage boy died as a wall collapsed. As a result, instead of focusing solely on the safety of football supporters post-Bradford, Sir Oliver Popplewell was asked to review 'safety' and 'control' in his report. How difficult it must have been for Sir Popplewell to reconcile the use of high, overhanging perimeter fences at football grounds with both safety and control benchmarks.

The Popplewell Report made many recommendations after the Bradford disaster. Chillingly, Popplewell noted that, had there been perimeter fences at the front of the main stand, 'casualties would have been on a substantially higher scale'. The fences were undoubtedly good at containing supporters, but could they be deemed safe? Anybody who has seen video footage of the Bradford fire unfolding would have to agree with Popplewell, because the only real means of escape from the fire (with the turnstiles at the back locked) was forwards and onto the pitch. It wouldn't be unreasonable, having seen the television images from Valley Parade, to estimate that the death toll would have been in the thousands had there been a 10-foot-high steel fence between the stand and the pitch. However, perimeter fences remained at many grounds after the Bradford disaster – including the Hillsborough Stadium in Sheffield.

On 11 May 1981, Tottenham Hotspur and Wolverhampton Wanderers were drawn to play each other in the semi-final of the FA Cup. The Football Association selected the Hillsborough Stadium in Sheffield to host the match. Despite having the largest average home support, Tottenham were allocated the smaller end of Sheffield Wednesday's Hillsborough Stadium, known as the

Leppings Lane end. As kick-off approached, the tightness of the crowd on the Leppings Lane terraces increased. Neil Irving was there to support Spurs that day, and he describes what he calls 'the scariest two hours of my life': 'I took my position behind a barrier that nobody was standing near. I watched the players come out to warm up as they do before kick-off. Gradually, more and more people would come in behind me and around me. The pressure was slowly building as time moved on towards kick-off and more and more people were pressed into me from behind. It was a gradual feeling of pressure built up over thirty to thirty-five minutes before kick-off, and as that pressure reached the point where I found it difficult to breathe, I elevated myself up so the crush barrier was pressed against my legs, rather than my chest. That is how I remained for the next two hours. The pressure was so great from the number of people that I was pinned into the air with my feet off the ground. It was the scariest two hours of my life.'

Perimeter fences of the day were approximately 10 feet high, made of steel, and at their very top they bent inwards, pointing back towards the supporters they were designed to contain. In each of those fences was a small gate that allowed access from the terraces to the pitch. On that day in 1981, when Neil Irving and Tottenham Hotspur fans were housed on the Leppings Lane terraces, an officer on the pitch side of that gate opened it to allow those being crushed to escape onto the pitch side. Neil is convinced that the quick actions of that officer were the reason that people weren't killed that day.

'I distinctly remember that there was a lot of conversation between the Spurs fans at the front and the policeman on the perimeter track. He [the officer] seemed to be letting out ten to fifteen people at a time, and then shutting the gate. But more and more people were being crushed, and he would realise this and then let another ten or fifteen people out until a point when there were hundreds of people on the side of the pitch. It was an age that was perhaps rife with hooliganism, so it could have been easier for him to say this is a hooligan situation, but he could tell the difference. He could see this wasn't crowd trouble, and acted accordingly.'

Disaster was averted, in Neil Irving's opinion, by a South Yorkshire Police officer recognising the crushing and opening the exit gate quickly. But despite swift action, there were still many injuries, including broken bones, and afterwards Hillsborough was not selected as a semi-final venue by the Football Association for six years.

Between 1981, when Spurs fans sustained crushing injuries, and 1987, when the Football Association decided to use the stadium as an FA Cup semi-final venue once more, the stadium reverted to its usual purpose, which was as the home of Sheffield Wednesday Football Club. The Leppings Lane end of the ground, the away end, would not experience crowds anywhere near as large as they did for semi-finals during this period, yet South Yorkshire Police still had concerns about access for away fans.

Inspector Calvert had a long working relationship with Sheffield Wednesday Football Club and the Hillsborough Stadium because he had spent around eight years working as the liaison officer between the club and South Yorkshire Police. Inspector Calvert said in his witness statement: 'In 1984, I (and other officers) realised that after Sheffield Wednesday Football Club's return to Division One, problems were evident at Leppings Lane turnstiles due to an increase in away fans. I suggested with a rough sketch that the whole of Leppings Lane turnstiles – then a crescent shape – should be demolished, with new ones built parallel to and near the rear of stand with access to individual pens and to the stands.'

In 1946, after the Burnden Park disaster in which thirty-three people died from crushing injuries, the Moelwyn Hughes report suggested 'a mechanical means to ascertain when a certain enclosure had reached its capacity'. In 1984, Inspector Calvert of the South Yorkshire Police was effectively making the same suggestion. Inspector Calvert continued: 'This was discussed with then senior officers – Chief Superintendent Moseley and Superintendent Lock – agreed should be put to club. Then Secretary Mr Chester came forward with a compromise as turnstiles are laid out now – new turnstiles A/G built – in the light of climate then prevailing on spending at football grounds accepted on basis that anything is better than nothing. The intention was twofold (1) on the practice then operating to allow different sets of supporters into different pens and (2) to give greater space at the turnstiles.'

This was not, however, the last time that Inspector Calvert had felt moved to voice his concerns about the inadequacies of access at the Leppings Lane end. After the turnstiles had been modified, access for any large crowd was still problematic. In June 1986, he wrote a memo to senior officers that read: 'One of the greatest problems we have is access to the ground, particularly at the Leppings Lane end. The redesigned turnstiles do not give anything like the access to the ground, either on the Leppings Lane terraces or in the West Stand, needed by away fans. On occasions last season when large numbers attended, we had away supporters who were justifiably irate because of the inefficiency of the system, which was turned on the police and could have resulted in public disorder.'

As there were no FA Cup semi-finals played at Hillsborough during this period, we must assume that the problems that Inspector Calvert speaks of had occurred at a League match, with a significantly smaller crowd than the 24,256 spectators that were scheduled to enter the stadium via the Leppings Lane end on semi-final days.

By the time Hillsborough had been reintroduced as a FA Cup semi-final venue in 1987, the Leppings Lane terraces at the west side end of the stadium had undergone some modifications. The most notable of these was the introduction of lateral fences that now ran from the wall at the back of the terraces down to the high perimeter fence at the front. These lateral fences split the width of the Leppings Lane terrace into individual pens and prevented supporters in the central two pens from moving sideways along the terrace. The introduction of these lateral fences had a potentially dangerous consequence. As supporters entered at the back of the West Stand through turnstiles A–G, which were the turnstiles allocated to those with standing tickets, they entered a courtyard. Once in that courtyard, there was only one obvious way to go: a tunnel directly in front of them, which ran underneath the West Stand and into the Leppings Lane terraces. This dark tunnel had the word 'standing' printed above it, and was the entrance that the majority of supporters would take if no direction was given. However, with lateral fences now splitting the terraces into individual pens, the tunnel only fed the central two pens and not the entire terrace, as originally designed. Also, the safety certificate had not been updated after the changes. The report into the disaster by Lord Justice Taylor was to find that, 'The performance by the City Council of its duties in regard to the Safety Certificate was inefficient and dilatory. The failure to revise or amend the certificate over the period of three years preceding this disaster, despite important changes in the layout of the ground, was a serious breach of duty. There were, as a result, no fixed capacities for the pens. The certificate took no account of the 1981 and 1985 alterations to the ground.'

There is a West Midlands Police video, found on the Hillsborough Independent Panel website, which visualises this perfectly. The video was taken by the West Midlands Police after the disaster, in an empty ground, and presumably as evidence for the Taylor Enquiry into the disaster. The video starts as the cameraman initially enters the ground through exit gate C, which is next to turnstiles A–G, and the tunnel is clearly visible straight ahead. Slightly to the left of the view, the insides of turnstiles A–G are in view. As the camera pans left further still, there is a wall with a gap in it. The camera walks the viewer through that gap in the wall and over to the far left of the West Stand, where the narrator tells you there is access to wing pens five and six, which are at the North Stand side of the Leppings Lane terrace. There are no signs directing you to pens five and six, however, and it is still not entirely obvious from that view, in an empty ground, that you can walk around the brick wall at the far corner to gain access.

The camera then goes back and shows you what supporters would have seen had they entered through exit gate C and turned right instead of heading for the tunnel straight ahead. To the right there is no wall blocking your vision, and when the camera reaches the far end of the West Stand there is a sign on a post that reads 'standing' and points to an area behind the wall at the far right of the stand. Before the camera moves towards the sign from gate C, you can't read what that sign says, and it would appear on the video to be a significantly smaller sign than the one that reads 'standing' above the central tunnel. It is, of course, much further away from the fans as they enter the ground as well, which would have further reduced its likelihood of being noticed. So there were no signs whatsoever directing fans who were looking to the left (pens five and six) and just one, smaller sign some distance away for supporters looking to the right, offering access to pens one and two. Directly in front of supporters entering via the turnstiles or gate C, there was a large, dark tunnel. The 'standing' sign was larger, nearer and was placed directly in front of supporters as they entered the turnstiles and gate C. There was one more thing that made it seem like the correct way to go, as supporter Grant Walker explained as he entered through gate C: 'When you looked down the tunnel, you could see the top of the goal.' Many other fans also recall seeing a glimpse of the pitch and the top of the goal, and in the absence of any other obvious route, they walked down a long, dark tunnel.

The Leppings Lane terraces were situated below the West Stand. They were steeply banked, running from the back, where the tunnel led, right down towards the pitch, where there was a tall, steel fence blocking access to the pitch. If you were in those central pens and became uncomfortable, it would have been necessary for you to force your way back up the terrace through the crowd, and back up the tunnel to the concourse, before you could elect to turn left or right to find the entrances to the wing pens. Fences blocked your progress to the front, to the left and to the right, so the tunnel was the only obvious way to get in and out of the central pens. There were, however, small gates right at the back of the lateral fences, which, when unlocked, allowed spectators to leave the central pens.

The entire standing Leppings Lane terrace had a capacity of 10,100, but pens three and four in the centre were only safe to hold a combined 2,100 spectators. The redesigned terraces, with lateral fences, meant that the only obvious entrance, which was likely to attract the majority of supporters if no direction was given, was now only suitable for around 20 per cent of the ground's capacity. In 1987, forty-one years after the Burnden Park disaster, there was still no mechanical means to measure the fill of each enclosure, despite the recommendations of the Moelwyn Hughes Report. The turnstiles counted people through, but their movement after that needed to be monitored by those in charge of managing the match. The entrance to the central pens had to be managed in order to keep the crowd safe.

In 1987, it was Leeds United who were allocated the Leppings Lane end of the ground for their FA Cup semi-final match versus Coventry City. Many Leeds United supporters told of their bad experiences at the first FA Cup semi-final to be held at Hillsborough since the day that over thirty Tottenham Hotspur fans were injured in 1981. Richard Jones wasn't long out of hospital when he travelled to watch Leeds take on Coventry in the FA Cup semi-final at Hillsborough: 'I was twenty-five years old and played amateur football myself, and had just had just left hospital a week earlier after an operation on my knee. A mate of mine was fortunate enough to get me a ticket for the game. On the day, I remember hobbling through the turnstiles on my one crutch and a copper saying to me "you must be bloody mad son". Only when entering the Leppings Lane terrace did I realise what he meant! It was bloody heaving with swaying fans and I was struggling to keep my knee from popping its stitches. My mate suggested tying a Leeds Utd pillowcase (the nearest thing we could find to a flag!) to the end of my crutch, and holding it aloft so we might see it on the telly later! By now, the crowd seemed to have swelled even more and the crushing and swaying was quite alarming, especially for the kids I saw struggling to hold on to their dads' hands. The poor little buggers looked petrified and couldn't even see the pitch! When we scored the first goal it went mental, my stitches popped, and my crutch was never seen again! I think I was carried about 30 yards without my feet touching the floor. I was getting nearer the fencing at the front and didn't like the look of it one bit, especially seeing the young ones that were squashed right up against it. After we had lost 3-2, it took us half an hour just to get out.'

Richard Monroe arrived at Hillsborough a few hours before kick-off in 1987, and remembers the police cordons that checked tickets away from the ground: 'I attended the match, and had a ticket for the Leppings Lane terracing. The match was on a Sunday with a 12.15 kick-off. I arrived with a friend in Sheffield early, probably around 10.00. We parked near Middlewood Road and set off to walk the half mile or so to Hillsborough. As we reached Hillsborough Park, about a quarter of a mile from the ground, we were stopped by police and asked to show our tickets. Without a ticket we would not have been allowed to get any closer to the ground. We then walked the rest of the distance to the ground and arrived at the turnstile behind the Leppings Lane stand.'

Andy Peterson went to Hillsborough that day, hoping to see his team get to an FA Cup final: 'With a £5 standing ticket secured for £30 on the black market, I was ready to go that morning, Sunday April 12th. Being as I was the only one of the regulars who had secured one, I travelled on my own, on one of the four specially procured trains that ran from City station at regular intervals. Right from the off it was clear that this was a major police operation. All of those queuing for the train were checked for possession of a legitimate ticket. No ticket? No travel, we were told emphatically. Once off the train, there were at least two, but maybe three, concentric circles of police on our route, at which point tickets were checked again.'

These 'concentric circles of police' in the lead-up to the ground were to take on added significance in 1989. Many Leeds United supporters who attended the semi-final that day remember having to walk through two or three police roadblocks, where they were asked to show their ticket. These barriers also slowed the flow of people moving towards the turnstiles, which was of paramount importance because there were only twenty-three turnstiles available to admit over 24,000 fans. The standing terrace had a capacity for 10,100 supporters, and they only had seven turnstiles through which to enter.

The flow of Leeds fans towards the turnstiles in 1987 was slowed down by the police roadblocks. Their journey was staggered towards the turnstiles, which prevented a build-up of supporters becoming compressed in the tight concourse outside the ground. Significantly, because of traffic problems that day, kick-off was delayed by fifteen minutes to allow those affected to get to the stadium safely and enter before the match kicked off. However, once Leeds United supporters went through the turnstiles into the concourse area, the only obvious way to go was through the tunnel, which only fed the central two pens. Lloyd was there that day, and tried to avoid going down the tunnel, but because of a lack of signage directing people to the virtually hidden entrances to the side pens, he ended up following the crowd: 'I was never one for going behind the goals, with all the hurly-burly, even though I was a fit twenty-four-year-old. I had been to Hillsborough once before and I hoped to again go to the left of the central pens, where the high corner terrace was. I was with one friend, and we went towards that area, but the gate to the covered stairway was locked. We had a dilemma. I didn't know how to get to the end pens at the other corner: was it down the central tunnel and turn right? Or could you walk along the holding pen at the back of the stand and enter in the corner itself? If there had been a sign pointing the way that would have been my preference, but there wasn't. At this point, because of the steady flow of people following behind me, I knew any delay to walk the 40 or so yards to check the corner could lose us precious and scarce space inside the centre pen, so reluctantly I headed down the tunnel. There was not a single steward or policeman to be seen on the courtyard at the rear of the stand; everyone was in position for the kick-off, so asking for help wasn't a possibility. Once getting to the terrace it was extremely full, but me and my friend were able to squeeze in and we managed to get under a crash barrier and stay there so that the barrier was eliminating any pressure from behind. It was uncomfortable but bearable. Our arms were constricted with our hands clenched under our chins.'

John South, a Leeds fan who had been to many matches by the time the 1987 semi-final came around, remembers how the tunnel seemed the obvious route to get to the terraces: 'I used to go to lots of away matches in the seventies and eighties to watch Leeds. In those days, crowd control was poor and stadiums were packed, so I talk through experience. I had never been in the Leppings Lane end until the semi-final in '87. On entering through the turnstiles, my brothers and I saw the tunnel, the goalposts and the pitch. There seemed to be no filtering of the fans so we went through the tunnel behind the goal. It was like an obvious choice. This was about 1½ hours before kick-off. Having been in crush situations before, like at Wolverhampton Wanderers in 1977 for one, I was aware of the potential danger. I noted that the fences creating "pens" on the terraces would prevent lateral movement and the perimeter fencing would prevent forward movement. The pen behind the goal by this time was starting to fill up, but the areas near the corner flags were not crowded. I told my brothers that we should get back out through the tunnel and go to the corner section to the right, while we had chance to do so. I said if we left it until later we wouldn't be able to make our way back through the tunnel. We did so, with a bit of difficulty. About half an hour before kick-off, the pen behind the goal was packed and supporters were being lifted up to the seats above (just like '89). Where we were now stood was not packed. I thought at the time that the pen and tunnel was a potential danger and couldn't believe that the police, council safety inspectors, the club, etc., didn't see the potential for danger themselves. After all, if I had, why had the so-called experts not?'

David Rice, a Leeds supporter who was at Hillsborough that day, remembers how tightly packed it was in the central pens: 'I was at Hillsborough and stood on the middle terraces on the Leppings Lane against Coventry in the '87 FA Cup semi-final. It was scary, believe me – we were packed in so tight it was difficult to breathe. We should have been allocated the other side of the ground – it was madness how we were given the Leppings Lane … it was a huge relief to get out safely at the end. I felt exhausted and dehydrated and grateful that I was not hurt that day.'

Karl Skirrow remembers the songs of Wembley and the carnival atmosphere before seeing the panic and the sheer helplessness in the central pens: 'It wasn't that bad when I first got in; I remember just walking down towards the back of the goals, then moving became harder and harder. I remember looking back while I still could and thinking there's no more room, but it didn't stop. It got to the stage where I couldn't look around anymore, and at one stage my arms were down my sides and I couldn't move them. Looking in front of me, I could see so many people having difficulty in standing up and moving. It was like when you're on a plane – I always look at the stewardesses' faces to see if they're worried or not, and if they're not, I feel okay and start enjoying my flight. But it wasn't like that; people were worried and a lot seemed to panic. When the goals were scored, I had no control of my body at all and that was the scary part, not having control. You went to the left, everybody went to the left and vice versa.'

Leeds fan David Hall was only young in 1987, but he still vividly remembers the uncomfortable experience of being packed into the Leppings Lane central pens: 'I was there watching Leeds v. Coventry and it was unbelievably packed. As a fifteen-year-old, I was in the middle pen and for the first ninety minutes we just got carried where the crowd took us. Then, at full-time we had to take one of our mates out before extra time as he was white as a sheet and had fainted from being continuously thrown about. When the Liverpool disaster happened it deeply saddened Leeds fans, as most who went to the Coventry game knew it could have been us but for the grace of God. RIP the 96.

The central position of the tunnel made it by far the most obvious entrance to the terraces, and understandably it had caused the majority of supporters to head towards pens three and four that day. While Leeds United fans remember it being overcrowded, thankfully the police closed off access to the tunnel in time to prevent any serious injury. The fact that the tunnel was the only obvious entrance, with poor signage to other entrances, was still a potential risk, however, that needed to be managed to keep it safe. The green of the pitch and the glimpse of the crossbar was drawing the majority of supporters towards the tunnel, and only effective management could stop those central pens from becoming overfilled. In 1987, nobody was seriously hurt, but the stories of Leeds fans show that it was extremely uncomfortable. The flow of fans down the tunnel was only as fast as the turnstiles would allow, and was eventually stemmed by the police that day. The South Yorkshire Police deemed the match to have been a success from a management point of view, but many Leeds fans will tell you that on a big match day, those central pens were a potential hazard, or as some Leeds fans described it, 'an accident waiting to happen'.

In 1988, Liverpool Football Club drew Nottingham Forest in the semi-final of the FA Cup, and the Football Association chose the Hillsborough Stadium as the venue. At that time, Liverpool had a far higher average crowd than their opponents, Nottingham Forest. But in line with South Yorkshire Police strategy, they insisted that Liverpool supporters were to be accommodated in the far smaller Leppings Lane end of the ground. The rationale for this decision was that the vast majority of Liverpool fans would be arriving in Sheffield from the north and therefore would arrive at the Leppings Lane (west) end of the Hillsborough Stadium, and that the Nottingham Forest supporters would be travelling mainly from the south of Sheffield, and would therefore arrive at the Spion Kop (east) side of the Hillsborough Stadium. It was the opinion of the South Yorkshire Police that to swap the teams around would risk the two sets of supporters crossing paths, with a possible risk of disorder. The 1988 match was policed by the experienced Chief Superintendent Brian Mole, who had also been in overall command of the 1987 semi-final between Leeds United and Coventry City the year before.

Liverpool supporters walking towards the Leppings Lane end of the ground in 1988 remembered police roadblocks at certain points, at which some fans were searched and all fans were asked to produce a ticket. John Joynt, a Liverpool supporter who attended the semi-final in 1988 remembers the roadblocks: 'In 1988, we got a coach to Hillsborough, parked up a mile or so away from the ground and we starting walking down. When we got to the top of Leppings Lane there were barriers, which is not something I had noticed before. There were ticket searches, basically, and two or three more times down the road there were more barriers. It was a steady flow of people towards the turnstiles.'

Many fans remembered these police cordons checking for tickets. The consequence, intentional or not, was that they slowed the flow of fans arriving at the small concourse area outside the turnstiles.

As fans entered the turnstiles in '88 they were confronted with a tunnel directly in front of them, with the word 'standing' above it and a glimpse of the pitch at the very end. As with the Leeds fans in 1987, once fans walked down that tunnel, the only way out again was back the way you came. Under the management of Chief Superintendent Brian Mole (although not necessarily because of him), officers remember standing in the mouth of the tunnel once they estimated the central pens to be full and directed fans to the far less conspicuous entrances to the side pens. Liverpool won the match, beating Nottingham Forest 2-1, and the South Yorkshire Police considered the match to have been a success from a policing standpoint.

However, as with Leeds in 1987, there were a number of Liverpool fans who reported extremely overcrowded conditions in the central pens, which prompted some fans to write to the Football Association. Kevin Morland was at the '88 semi-final, also supporting Liverpool: 'We had all been to the fixture the year before and we had stood in the Leppings Lane end right behind the goal, near the back and behind a crush barrier. In 1988, about five minutes before kick-off, I remember the crush starting to get like something I'd never experienced before. I had always stood on the Kop and had been to many away games and been uncomfortable, but never as scared as I was in 1988. The barrier bent slightly under the weight of bodies; luckily, once the game kicked off the crowd seem to settle and although being packed like sardines we watched the game. In the days after the semi-final in '88 my dad was saying how lucky we were no one was seriously injured or killed on Leppings Lane, and he told my Mum that it was a death trap because of the high fences right round it and the tunnel at the back.'

In a statement that can be viewed on the Hillsborough Independent Panel website, one fan wrote to the FA to complain about the conditions in the central pens: 'I attended the above football match on Saturday April 9th 1988, and write to protest in the strongest possible terms at the disgraceful overcrowding that was allowed to occur (in an all ticket match) in the Leppings Lane Terrace area. The whole area was packed solid to the point where it was impossible to move and where I, and others around me, felt considerable concern for personal safety (as a result of the crush an umbrella I was holding in my hand was snapped in half against the crush barrier in front of me). I would emphasise that the concern over safety related to the sheer numbers admitted, and not to crowd behaviour, which was good. My concern over safety was such (at times it was impossible to breathe) that at half time when there was movement for toilets, refreshments etc. I managed to extricate myself from the terrace, having taken the view that my personal safety was more important than watching the second half.'

Another fan wrote, 'It was impossible to move sideways as the momentum of the crowd continued to push us forward. We were forced to duck under metal barriers or suffer even more crushing. Finally we were forced right up against the barriers that prevent the fans from getting on to the pitch. During the match we had to constantly bear the crushing force of the crowd swaying forward from behind. It would not have been so bad if we had been able to move sideways, away from this central part, but it was so packed, and the constant pushing, jostling and surging of the fans made this prospect appear even more dangerous. During the game some fans actually collapsed or fainted and were passed over people's heads towards the front of this section of the ground. Some fans tried to open this gate but it had been padlocked. Some fans attracted the attention of a policeman or steward, I can't remember which, but he appeared to be totally unaware of the situation. During the whole of this game, we were very concerned for the safety of our youngsters but the police were only allowing injured fans through the gate. After the match finished we all vowed never to enter the Leppings Lane end ever again. As far as I am concerned, when there is a large crowd entering this part of the ground, it will always be a death trap.'

After the disaster a year later, the FA said that they could find no record of having received either of these letters, but their content speaks volumes about the cramped conditions that supporters at big semi-final matches were enduring in Hillsborough's Leppings Lane central pens. As fans entered through turnstiles A–G, poor signage, proximity and a glimpse of the pitch was leading a high percentage of people towards the tunnel, and only human intervention directed fans elsewhere. The 'design imbalance' of having one, main entrance that actually only allowed access to 20 per cent of the space was causing over-crowding in the central pens. As Liverpool fans exited the central pens at full-time, walked up the dark tunnel, out into the light and onto the street via exit gate C, they were celebrating a 2-1 victory and savouring a trip to Wembley in May. Some of the Liverpool fans who were in the central pens that day complained, and others vowed never to enter that area ever again. Once again, the match was considered to be a success by the South Yorkshire Police and the 'accident waiting to happen', as many Leeds fans called it in 1987, was apparently neither recognised nor rectified.

A year later, on 20 March 1989, Liverpool Football Club was once again drawn to play Nottingham Forest in the semi-final of the FA Cup, and once again the Hillsborough Stadium in Sheffield was selected by the Football Association to host the match. At that time, Peter Robinson was Chief Executive and Company Secretary of Liverpool Football Club, and in his statement he recalls that day: 'On Monday, 20th March, 1989, I observed on breakfast television that we had drawn Nottingham Forest in the semi-final of the F.A. Cup. We had also drawn them as semi-finalists in the previous year. Upon arrival at the club, I telephoned Steve Clark, the Competitions Secretary of the Football Association, to enquire as to whether a choice of ground had been made. He told me that this would be considered later in the morning and I asked him to take into account our experience in the previous year. I reminded him that there had been much criticism that Nottingham Forest had been given a larger allocation of tickets than us although their average gate and support was much smaller. I informed him that my club felt very strongly that Hillsborough should not be chosen as the venue. We had no complaint about the general facilities at the ground, but firmly believed another venue must be chosen if last year's ticket allocation could not be altered. He promised that he would advise the committee of my club's views when the decision was being made. Later that morning he telephoned me to say that the committee had selected Hillsborough. He said the police would not agree to the allocation being altered and that was the end of the matter. I informed him that I would therefore have to go public with my criticism of the Football Association. There were press present at the club at the time and I invited them in and made a statement, which was widely reported. I criticised the FA over their Cup semi-final ticket plans, saying, "They appear to be living in an ivory tower showing complete disregard for the fans who are the life blood of the game. Their decision is unjust and it means that many of our loyal supporters are going to miss out." I pointed out that our average attendance at Anfield was almost 38,000. This was more than 17,000 higher than Nottingham Forest. For the second consecutive year the allocation provided for Nottingham to receive approximately 4,500 more tickets than Liverpool. I also checked that the Manchester United ground was available and stated that, in the circumstances, it would have been fairer to use that ground for the semi-final. The press contacted Steve Clark about my comments and he said that Manchester United was the wrong location geographically. This was ludicrous, particularly as that ground was selected as the replay ground at the same time as Hillsborough was chosen.'

South Yorkshire Police again refused to allow Liverpool to have the larger Spion Kop end of the ground, for the same reasons as they had previously given regarding travel. Around this time, Chief Superintendent Brian Mole, who had been in overall command of both the 1987 and 1988 semi-finals at the Hillsborough Stadium, was transferred and replaced by Chief Superintendent David Duckenfield, just a few weeks before the semi-final at Hillsborough, which was arranged for Saturday 15 April 1989. Controversy surrounded the departing Mole, and his replacement had little experience of policing a match of this magnitude and only a few short weeks to prepare.

2

Journey to Sheffield

History seldom remembers beaten semi-finalists of any cup competition, which is why for many players and supporters it is one of the biggest games of the season. Over 700 teams enter at the beginning of the FA Cup competition, and by the semi-final stage there are just four clubs remaining, battling for the chance to play on the hallowed turf at Wembley. So many professional players used to grow up dreaming of scoring the winning goal in a Wembley FA Cup Final, and no doubt many still do. FA Cup Final day felt more special and treasured in the eighties than it does today, which is probably at least in part because the money in the game today seems to put more emphasis on Champions League and Premier League football. A famous trip to Wembley is on the cards for the victors, and desperate anonymity awaits the losers. Only the most committed football anorak remembers the beaten semi-finalists through history, so it is a very disappointing game to lose.

Waking up on semi-final day is a great feeling for a football supporter if your team is playing. Joy and expectations run high as you get dressed and prepare for the big day out. On 15 April 1989, Liverpool FC were once again to face Nottingham Forest in the semi-final of the FA Cup. It was a complete rerun of the previous year's fixture, as Damian Kavanagh recalls: 'Same teams, in the same round of the same cup competition. We even had the same kit ... almost. Liverpool had been drawn to play in all red again, so we were made up with that.'

Liverpool fans all over Merseyside and beyond were getting ready for a great day out, and the weather could not have been better as Tony Evans and his brother set off for Sheffield, literally full of the joys of spring: 'It was just a lovely day. Me and my brother were getting a lift so we walked up to Scotland Road to catch the bus. I remember my brother saying to me what a lovely day it was, and I said, "Yeah, well, let's hope we don't get beat". He replied, "What could possibly go wrong on a day like this?"'

It wasn't only Liverpool and Nottingham Forest fans looking forward to the big match, as Nick Braley recalls: 'April 14th 1989, Mike comes round to my student digs with a big grin on his face. "We've got tickets, we've got tickets mate, our kid is bringing them over in the morning, first train like, it's going to be sound!" Mike's Scouse accent, as ever, took some deciphering, but the gist of it was clear – I was going to an FA Cup semi-final, not something that happens too often to an Ipswich fan, but it's a big match and I'm not going to turn my nose up at this. Next morning, I head down to the Halls where Mike is meeting with his brother, and I am one happy bunny to see Neil, as promised, waving the tickets in his hand. I ask him how much he wants and he says eight quid, six for the ticket and a couple of quid to buy a drink for the lad who got them – can't argue with that, can we? Turns out Neil's mate Churchy knows Johnny Aldridge and "Aldo" has come up trumps last minute. Top lad! We get brekkie sorted and head off to the local pub for twelve. No point heading to the ground too early, as the pubs will be rammed and the Old Bill will no doubt be hassling anyone wanting a beer. We opt to go to our local and knock back a couple of quick pints before jumping on the bus and heading off to Hillsborough. The Penistone Road is bound to be busy, but who cares? Liverpool v. Forest. Clough's last chance to reach a proper Wembley final? Liverpool are going for the double again, after messing it up against Wimbledon last year. This is going to be magic and I just can't wait. Watching Ipswich is the dogs, but an FA Cup semi? Bring it on! On the bus I try and wind up the Scouse lads as best I can – 1978 and 1981 are repeatedly mentioned, as well as my favourite quiz question: which team has the longest undefeated home record in Europe? With a droll face I announce it is of course the mighty Ipswich, as a smirk the size of the Mersey comes across my face. You lot are not bad for a bunch of northerners, but the real footballing hotbed, East Anglia, has only one team! The Scousers are laughing and enjoying the banter, happy that we are no longer a real threat to them. Johnny Wark and David Johnson are also discussed with a mutual affection.'

Val Yates was really excited at the prospect of watching Liverpool reach a Wembley cup final and got to the ground very early as a result: 'I was twenty at the time and had a good job working in a bank in my home town of Retford, which is about 30 miles away from Sheffield. I was educated to A-level standard, choosing to get a job in a bank rather than continue on to university, which I could have done. I had been working in the bank since 1987. At that time, it was quite a prestigious job for a youngster, but it was not what I really wanted to do. It was just a job to me. I actually lived (and still live) in a small village about 3 miles north of Retford, and it was from there I set out to Sheffield that day. I got my ticket from someone I knew vaguely as I had seen him before and knew he was a tout. No idea of his name. You did not ask questions in them days and tickets were like gold dust. I paid £20 for it. Think the going face value was £6 but I was happy to pay £20. I knew others would end up paying more. I drove my car from my village and parked it up at Retford train station, then went by train to Sheffield and took a taxi from the station up to Hillsborough. I was outside the ground by about 9.30 a.m. as I was so excited and wanted to savour every last scrap of what I knew would be a great atmosphere. It was the first time I had been to a semi. My dad had not wanted me to go before, young female and all that, but this was close to home, I was twenty and I was going to do as I liked!

'I was up and out the house before he had even got in from his night shift. When I had been outside for a while, I realised I needed more cash, having given the tout £20, so I walked back through a park to a small shopping area where a woman was pushing a little tot in a pushchair. We had a conversation about how I was supporting Liverpool with an accent like mine instead of supporting Forest, the more local team. I went to a cash machine, which was like a brand new invention then, and I had a card because I worked in a bank. She showed me the way as I was not sure, then I left her at the shops and walked back myself. I was back at the ground before 11 a.m., then I just mooched around in the sun and sat on the wall at Leppings Lane, where there is a little bridge over a stream. I was just people watching, taking in every last scrap of the build-up and atmosphere as much as I could because I was so excited.'

'As soon as the gates opened, which I think was about 11.30, I went in through the turnstiles. I must have been about the sixth person in the whole of the ground that day. The turnstiles were very narrow and it was even a squeeze for me at 5 foot 4 inches and 7 stone to get through. I experienced nothing out of the ordinary outside. There were a few people milling about, but nothing out of the ordinary was going on at all. When I went into the ground through the turnstiles it was into a courtyard area and I had no clue about where to go next. I saw the tunnel and just a slight view of the glorious green of the pitch, and automatically went down it, as it seemed to me to be the way in. There were no signposts or instructions about anything different and I went down the tunnel and headed left into what I now know is pen 4. I probably went left because I am left-handed, and always veer left given a choice, or if I am unsure of anything. The only thing I can add to it was that the tunnel was deceptively sloping. From the outside, until you went down the tunnel, you can't really see that it has quite a slope to it onto the terraces, which themselves were quite steep. There was a dividing line fence that separated pens 3 and 4 that ran straight down the middle, from the tunnel to behind the centre of the goal. I went to the very front as I wanted a good view and because I am quite small, but then I moved a few steps back so I could lean on a barrier. There was next to no one in the pens then, so I sat on the terraces in the sun reading my programme from cover to cover while drinking a coffee.'

Paul Dunderdale and his friends set off early, full of expectation and looking forward to a great day out: 'On the day, eight of us met at Graham's house early in the morning to travel to Sheffield in two cars. I drove one of them with Graham, Rod and Gary in my car. It was a beautiful day, not a cloud in the sky, and spirits were high. In our minds, this game was a formality and there is something special about FA Cup semi-final day. We were laughing because Radio City were playing the same song they always played when we were in the car – "I'd Rather Jack" by The Reynolds Girls. A truly awful song, but we considered it to be our lucky song because we had never lost when they played it! The drive over was uneventful but we did hit some slight delays around Glossop before the Snake Pass. We had been to the same ground in 1988 so we knew the timings and roads and had time to stop for a drink at the same pub as the year before, a nice little one on the outskirts of Sheffield called the Holly Bush. We had a couple in there, a game of darts and we were basically the only ones in there.'

Steve Hart remembers that he and his mates planned the day out in 1989 in exactly the same way as they had done for the semi-final at Hillsborough the year before: 'I used to drink in a social club in Kirby, there were a whole group of us who were Liverpool fans, and in 1988 we'd organised a coach. Before the match, a couple of lads drove over into the Pennines, I think it was. They found a pub, and asked the manager if he'd be OK with a coach stopping for a meal on match day, and he was happy. So in 1988 that's exactly what we did. In 1989, we did the same thing. We got in touch with the landlord again, and he was more than happy as we'd been the year before. I got my ticket because I had a season ticket, and I know everyone on our coach had a ticket as well. The way we ran our coach was that lads with a ticket got a seat first, and everybody did. We stopped for a meal, and I had a pint or two, and then set off on the final forty-five minute to an hour journey to Sheffield. The traffic was heavier in 1989 than it was in '88 coming into Sheffield.'

Meanwhile, in Sheffield, Chief Superintendent David Duckenfield was planning to take charge of policing his first football match of this stature, having been promoted to replace Chief Superintendent Brian Mole a few weeks earlier. At around 10 a.m. on the morning of Saturday 15 April 1989, according to his briefing notes, which were reviewed by the Hillsborough Independent Panel, Duckenfield addressed officers sat in the North Stand of the Hillsborough Stadium about the order of the day.

Duckenfield told his officers: 'I cannot stress too highly the word "safety". This ground will be full to capacity today and some of you may never have experienced a football match of this nature. Our job is to ensure the safety of spectators and you must make sure you know the escape routes, the problem areas, and that you are fully conversant with your responsibilities should a crisis arise. There will be a tremendous atmosphere within the ground but you must not be caught up in this by the events that are taking place on the field. You must remain detached and clear-headed at all times to respond to events. The control room, which is in the far corner to my left and is the blue box attached to the South Stand, will be commanded by Superintendent Murray. Superintendent Marshall will have responsibility on the north side of the ground, and Superintendent Chapman will have responsibility for the Nottingham Forest fans, who are approaching from the south of the ground. Let me just say this: firm but fair policing with the correct attitude. Safety of supporters in this game is paramount. Nobody gets in without a ticket. Nobody takes drink or banners into the ground and nobody goes in who is drunk.'

In Duckenfield's briefing there had been no mention of a possible build-up of supporters in the cramped concourse outside the Leppings Lane turnstiles, as had happened in far smaller games than an FA Cup semi-final during the 1980s. There was no mention of how to prevent such a build-up, how to manage the flow of fans towards the turnstiles, or indeed what officers should do if such a build-up occurred.

The problem with the Leppings Lane end of the ground, especially on big match days, was that it allowed more people to arrive in the cramped area outside the turnstiles, and at a faster pace, than the turnstiles could admit to the ground. So it had a high risk of failing if that factor was not managed, according to Professor Keith Still, one of the world's foremost experts in crowd dynamics: 'Let's say the crowd flow on Leppings Lane is "A" and the turnstiles throughput is "B" – both measured in people per minute. When the flow rate of "A" is greater than throughput of "B" a queue will form. If "A" is very much greater than "B" the queue will develop pressure, which is a risk. So the analysis of risk for any system is first to understand the approach flow rate "A" and the limits of throughput at "B". If "A" can exceed

"B" then you need to either regulate the crowd flow at "A" or improve the throughput at "B". In effect, you need to balance the system so that "A" and "B" are the same. It's not complex mathematics, but failing to realise that "A" is much greater than "B" will result in problems such as crowd crushing.'

As stated already, the liaison officer between Sheffield Wednesday Football Club and South Yorkshire Police, Inspector Calvert, had already raised concerns at matches that would require the Leppings Lane end to admit far fewer supporters than necessary on semi-final day. The Green Guide at that time accepted that a variety of factors could affect the rate at which people could pass through turnstiles, but it stated that 'in general based on observation and experience, it is unlikely that the maximum notional rate per turnstile would exceed 750 per hour'. At Hillsborough there were only twenty-three turnstiles to admit 24,256 spectators. For the 10,100 that had tickets for the Leppings Lane standing terraces, there were just seven turnstiles available: turnstiles A–G. Using the Green Guide maximum recommendations of 750 people per turnstile per hour, it would have taken a steady stream of fans with standing tickets around two hours to enter the ground through the seven allocated turnstiles. As Lord Justice Taylor was to later say in his report into the disaster: 'The mathematics are elementary. Both the police and the club should have realised that the Leppings Lane turnstiles and the waiting area outside them would be under strain to admit all the Liverpool supporters in time. Success depended on the spectators arriving at a steady rate from an early hour and upon the maximum turnstile rate being maintained. In fact neither of these requirements, which are inter-linked, was fulfilled. That they might not be so was in my view foreseeable.'

According to his briefing notes, which can be viewed on the Hillsborough Independent Panel's website, no mention of this potential issue was made by Duckenfield in his 10 a.m. briefing on the day. In the witness statement of Superintendent Roger Marshall, the officer in charge of policing outside the Leppings Lane turnstiles, he also made no reference to this potential issue in the subsequent briefing he gave to Chief Inspectors Waring and Purdy – the officers under his command who were in charge of policing areas 2A and 2B outside the Leppings Lane end of the ground.

Around 12 p.m., a decision was taken that was to have significance later this day. As written in Lord Justice Taylor's interim report, 'At about 12 noon Chief Inspector Creaser asked Superintendent Murray whether the pens on the West Terrace were to be filled one by one successively, but was told that they should all be available from the start and the fans should 'find their own level.'

Liverpool supporter Brian Johnson was a regular at Liverpool matches home and away, and he recalls setting off early for Sheffield: 'I'd been watching Liverpool at every home game and some aways since I was ten. My dad was originally from Kirkdale in Liverpool, and we became season ticket holders in 1975, and that is how we got our tickets for the semi-final at Hillsborough. My father was club secretary of the Southport branch of the Liverpool Supporters' Club, which ran a coach to all home games and some away. He was always on the phone to the ticket office and would get tickets for the other members, sometimes managing to get one or two extras for people who were struggling to get them. The supporters' club ran a coach to Sheffield as they had done the previous year. It was the usual crew and faces with a couple of unknowns, but all looking forward to a great day out, another victory and hopefully Everton in the final. If I remember correctly, I think we set off earlier this time. Can't recall why, but Colin our regular driver called the shots on timings and I'm pretty certain we left around 8.30 a.m. The coach would collect from two or three meeting points, ours being the first usually. I think we arrived in Sheffield at around 12.30 p.m.'

Scunthorpe-based Liverpool fan Paul Jarvill was getting ready to make the journey to Sheffield with friends, as he recalls: 'I was driving that day, so I got the short straw on semi-final day, but you take it on the chin. We set off at around 11 a.m. from Scunthorpe, five of us in the car. Run-of-the-mill journey, no problems as far as the roads were concerned. We'd been there the year before so we knew where we were going. We got there in time, and went to the pub. The lads would have had a drink, and the rules are that driver doesn't buy, so I would have been bought my Coke, or whatever I was drinking.'

Ed Critchley had even more reason than most supporters to be looking forward to the day: 'It was my twenty-first birthday, so I do remember the day as being quite special. Twenty-first birthday, FA Cup semi-final ... I was buzzing. I was going with my best mate Carl, and my father was driving us to Sheffield.'

Coaches, cars and trains were all setting off on a beautiful spring day and all full of excited, happy supporters. Richie Greaves remembers the coach travelling a different way because of roadworks: 'We got a coach at half ten in the morning. There were only two of us that went on the coach that day, but usually there were six or seven of us that went together. We were the two with tickets to the Leppings Lane terraces. There were roadworks over the Snake Pass, so we went up the M62 and down the M1.'

Kevin Morland was back at Hillsborough, having been for the previous year's semi-final: 'In 1989, I think the coach left the Fiveways at 11.30 a.m. There were loads of coaches because Everton fans were getting on their coaches to go to Villa Park; there was a great atmosphere, with loads of mates, both red and blue, having banter. I travelled to Sheffield with my dad and my brother Chris. We were season-ticket holders, and they qualified for a semi-final ticket, as we had travelled to many away games between '87 and '89. We got to Hillsborough really early – think it was around 1.15–1.30 – we just went straight in the ground. The year before was definitely more organised, as there was checkpoints before the ground where people were directed to their areas and in '89 we just walked straight up to turnstiles. We entered the turnstiles from the Leppings Lane at around 1.30 p.m. We were searched by a police officer outside the turnstiles, then again by an officer inside the gate. Bear in mind I was fourteen, my brother eighteen and we were with our dad, we all got searched thoroughly – so much so, that our bag with sandwiches in was searched. When the officer asked my dad what was in it he replied "crisps and butties", the officer said to my dad, "Are you being funny?" This was typical of the police attitude towards Liverpool fans that day.'

Mike Wilson had been held up in traffic, and remembers arriving in Sheffield later than planned: 'My father, Dave Wilson, a school headmaster (fifty-seven at the time), also a season ticket holder, had managed to get a semi-final ticket. Jonathan and I (both twenty-four) also had tickets. All these tickets were obtained through LFC via our entitlement as season ticket holders. As dad was going, he volunteered to drive Jonathan and me to the match. He picked us up at our house in West Didsbury, South Manchester at 11.40 to begin the 25-mile journey across the Woodhead Pass to Sheffield. This was before the days of the M60, so our journey was to take us off the end of the old M63 through Bredbury up to Tintwistle and Mottram before heading over the pass. The Stockport area was busy and our route was blocked at regular intervals. It took over two hours just to get through Stockport. We finally headed down the hill through Grenoside towards Hillsborough at about 2.30. We found a parking space in an estate about half a mile above Hillsborough and jogged down the hill towards the Leppings Lane end. Again, Jonathan had stand tickets while dad and I were on the Leppings Lane end enclosure.'

Traffic, roadworks and a slow journey to Sheffield was what many fans experienced that day, which meant that they arrived later than they had planned. Pete Carney describes the lengths they went to in order to avoid the traffic: 'It took about two hours to get over to Sheffield that day. We got stuck in traffic in Stockport, so went through the back streets making like Starsky and Hutch, up and down the backstreets trying to avoid the traffic jams. We arrived in Sheffield and ended up parking in Penistone Road at about 1.45 to 2.00.'

The Snake Pass was not only the most direct route; it was also the most scenic route for supporters travelling from Liverpool to Sheffield. Mottram, a village between the M67 motorway and the Snake Pass, is a village that most Liverpool supporters taking this route would have passed through. The traffic on this route was heavy on 15 April, and that slowed down many Liverpool fans, causing them to arrive in Sheffield much later than they had planned. In his witness statement, a Greater Manchester Police officer on duty in Mottram that day recalls the heavy traffic: 'At approximately 12.30 p.m. (12.30 hrs) I was informed that the traffic was heavily built up from Mottram traffic lights to the Eastern terminal roundabout and down the M67 motorway ... on my arrival at the junction, I took over the traffic lights switchbox and manually changed the lights in favour of through traffic to Sheffield. I continued the procedure until about 2.10 p.m. (14.10 hrs) when the congestion subsided.'

Birthday boy Ed Critchley remembers those roadworks only too well: 'In those days, the way to get to Sheffield was through the Snake Pass. The overriding memory was of being excited, setting off, and then suddenly hitting traffic. This was about three hours before kick-off, but there were terrible roadworks and we sat there for an hour. We were hardly moving. I remember that we started to get a bit worried that we might not get there in time.'

Tony O'Keefe, a firefighter and Liverpool fan, also experienced a slow journey to Sheffield: 'I was living in London at the time, so I travelled back to Liverpool on the Friday to see my family. We got up quite early on the Saturday morning and set off for Sheffield. It was a fairly slow journey, getting through Manchester, and we reckoned we might have crossed over with traffic heading to Villa Park for the other semi-final.'

Despite the traffic problems for many, fans were still arriving in Sheffield in large numbers. Damian Kavanagh recalls the carnival atmosphere as they arrived: 'We arrived in Sheffield and went to the Horse and Jockey pub where we had been the year before for a few pints, and soaked up the atmosphere. It was a beautiful day with glorious sunshine and the Liverpool supporters were all in great spirits, singing our songs and getting really excited about the match.'

Mick Bowers, a Liverpool fan living in Sheffield, remembers arriving at the stadium very early: 'Living in Sheffield, I attended the games alone other than on the odd occasion when I would take my younger brother if I could get him a ticket. But for this game I was alone, thank God. I arrived at the Kop end of the ground at 12.00. The side streets were blocked off by police. I knew the area around the ground well through previous visits and could not understand why they blocked off the streets. However, I was directed down Penistone Road to the Leppings Lane junction, arriving there just after midday. I bought fish and chips and sat on a wall to eat them. There were a few Liverpool fans around, all behaving and no alcohol consumption witnessed. Why the police later asked that question is beyond me, as every football game around the country has an element of fans that have a drink as part of the day. I bought a flag outside the ground. The turnstiles were now open and there was a large police presence around the entrances. There were no queues at the turnstile when I entered at 12.30. I entered through turnstile B. I handed my ticket to the steward and he handed back the stub. Upon entering the ground, a police man stopped me and took the cane from the flag and threw it on a pile of others they had already confiscated. I was searched then allowed to continue. This was a little heavy handed, I thought, for 12.30 and towards an eighteen-year-old alone. I then bought a programme and entered the central pen through the tunnel to get the best spot to get amongst the atmosphere. I knew Leppings Lane well, and knew there were entrances around the side, but I wanted to be central, hence why I headed for the tunnel. If you did not know this part of the ground, you would not know there are entrances round the sides. You come through the turnstiles and into a courtyard. All you can see is the pitch through the tunnel, so most head for that area.'

Eileen McBride was a nurse at the time, but that day she was off duty and looking forward to watching Liverpool try and reach another FA Cup final: 'I got into the ground really early, about one o'clock, and I was seated in the West Stand, which is above the two central pens. I was looking down from the balcony, and at around half past one or a quarter to two there seemed to be a lot of people in the central pens right below me, but not in the side pens either side of them.'

Kevin Morland explains the scene as he entered the turnstiles very early, and headed for the central pens: 'We entered down the tunnel, which was the only obvious entrance to the Leppings Lane terrace, and because it was so early we were one of the first on the terraces. I spotted my "spec" right away, in the middle right pen as you look toward the pitch, first bar up from the front fence and near the side fence. Straight away, my dad wasn't happy at all. Being a kid, I got my own way and we stood there getting into the pre-match build up. By 2 p.m. my dad started saying he wanted to move to the side pen – I can still picture him saying, "Something's going happen here." He knew we were caged in, with seemingly the only entrance to the terraces right behind us, plus the fact the crush barriers were only up to his thighs and miles thinner than the ones we were used to at Anfield. I then got into an argument with him about how I wanted to stay there because the atmosphere was always better behind the goal, I always remember looking round at all the lads around the same age as me in that spec and thinking, "Why can't I stand here?"'

Brian Johnson, his father and friends arrived at the Leppings Lane end of the ground early: 'I don't know if it was because of us getting there slightly earlier, but it seemed a lot quieter walking to the ground compared to 1988. There was also a ring of police checking your tickets as you approached the ground in 1988, but I never saw this – again it could have been because we were early. I remember going into a chippy near the ground and being served pretty quickly, and then we continued walking to the ground. As we approached Leppings Lane, our group broke up, as some were in other parts of the ground. My friends were in the standing area below, but I was in the seats in the stand above with my dad. We all went in through a main gate, pretty easily really – it was busy, but no crushing or jostling. My mates went into the turnstiles and I recalled how different it was from when we had played Sheffield Wednesday in the winter at my previous visit to Hillsborough for a League game – how cold and dark that day was compared to this day.'

Grant Walker and his friends arrived in Sheffield and remember the fantastic atmosphere and glorious weather: 'My memories from that year are turning up on a lovely spring day, all excited about the match. Everyone was in good spirits. I went with three of the lads and our kid, and we had a couple of pints in the pub, you know, nothing mad. Everyone was singing and it was a great atmosphere.'

As well as just over 24,000 Liverpool fans, Nottingham Forest fans were also arriving in Sheffield for the big match, of course.

Danny Rhodes, a Nottingham Forest supporter, remembers arriving at the train station in Sheffield and being met by South Yorkshire Police: 'I took the Football Special train from Notts on the day of the game. Forest were in the form of their lives. We were going to win this one. We arrived in Sheffield at around 1 p.m. and were greeted by the South Yorkshire Police. We were ushered onto double-decker buses heading for Hillsborough. A few of the lads tried to have a bit of banter with the police, but they didn't laugh. South Yorkshire Police never seemed to laugh on match day, but we knew that of course. We had been to Hillsborough before. Some lads went off to the pub for a drink but myself and a mate went into the ground. It must have been about 1.30 p.m. We made our way to the same place we'd been the year before and I sat on the terraces and flicked through the match programme. Nothing for us to do but wait.'

Steve Warner, a Liverpool supporter who travelled on a supporters' coach from Northampton, recalls arriving in Sheffield full of expectation: 'We arrived in Sheffield sometime around 1.00 or 1.30, relaxed, really looking forward to the game and thinking that we could all be going to Wembley in a few weeks' time.'

As time was ticking on, more and more fans started to descend on Hillsborough's Leppings Lane. Paul Jarvill and his friends were also on their way: 'We left the pub for a five-minute walk to the ground at around 2 p.m. We grabbed a sandwich on the walk down Leppings Lane. The previous year, there had been South Yorkshire Police barriers down the road, checking tickets. In '89 that didn't happen; there were no barriers. It was remarked upon, but you don't think that much of it at the time. You've always got a comparison when you've been there the year before. As we got towards the ground, the road bears round to the right and the turnstiles are to your left-hand side. I just remember there being a lot of people. I remember thinking there's a lot more than you would expect for that time of day, but again, you don't think much of it at the time. FA Cup semi-final day, everyone's in a good mood. It's sunny, and everyone is excited.'

Damian Kavanagh and his mates were by now on their way to the ground: 'I can't remember exactly what time I left the pub because I wasn't looking at a stopwatch, but I know that I always made sure I was in the Kop for 2.30 so I could get the spec I wanted. So me and my mates had to decide if we should get another pint or set off for the ground, and because of the time we decided to leave. We strolled down from the Horse & Jockey towards the ground, full of expectation. I went to the semi-final at Hillsborough in 1988 and one of the most noticeable differences between 1989 and the year before was that in the walk down the road towards the ground there were police roadblocks in 1988. It was a staggered journey towards the turnstiles. It was to slow the flow of people towards the turnstiles and to check that you had tickets, I think. That makes logical sense. You'd get searched and ask for your tickets, and if you had a ticket then you could move on. Then a few hundred yards later there was another barricade, as if to reassure themselves that the first check worked. So we walked straight down to the Leppings Lane turnstiles.'

The coach that Richie Greaves was travelling on from Liverpool was nearing the end of what had transpired to be a three-hour journey: 'We stopped at services for about twenty minutes, and then on the final part of the trip as we came off the motorway, the South Yorkshire Police came onto the coach and searched it for alcohol and made sure that everyone had match tickets, and everyone did. That delayed us for about twenty minutes, and we finally got there at about half past one. We parked by the train station and as we got off the coach there was a train just pulling in; a Football Special with all our boys, singing our songs. It was boiling hot and a fantastic atmosphere. We walked down towards the ground and tried to get to a pub for a drink. There were police officers outside one and they told us that all pubs within a mile of the ground were shut. So we walked on and we knew there was a bookie on the corner of the Leppings Lane by a garage, and we just went in there and had a bet. I can even remember it was the 2.15 p.m. at Thirsk. You remember everything about that day.'

At this stage, many fans remember a carnival atmosphere, with excitement building as the big match kick-off drew ever closer, and supporters were enjoying a beautiful sunny day in Sheffield. Pete Carney's recollection perhaps illustrates the glorious weather best: 'We were walking around the ground and it was a beautiful, spring sunny day. I always remember this lad with a canvas holdall selling sunglasses and he was shouting, "A pound a pair to keep out the glare." That shows you how lovely the day was really.'

Damian Kavanagh remembers that those in his group who had been in the centre pens last year didn't want to go in there again this year: 'My mates decided that they didn't want to go right behind the goal because they said that the previous year it had been really congested in there. In 1988, I had been on the wing section and they had been in the middle pens, but this year we swapped positions. So I walked down through the tunnel, which at the end is split in the middle by a fence. You can either go left into pen four or right into pen three. They weren't signposted as such – that is something that I learnt in the aftermath. When I was in the ground, I looked up at the very prominent clock they have at Sheffield Wednesday and it said 2.15, so that is how I know what time I got in the ground.'

Superintendent Marshall was on duty outside the ground that day, and according to his official witness statement he appeared to have concerns about the sheer number of supporters in Leppings Lane a considerable time before kick-off: 'By 2.15 p.m. Leppings Lane was full of fans moving in both directions, I estimate the numbers at about 6,000–8,000. They were spilling off footpaths into the roadway and making the movements of vehicles difficult.' Two minutes later, Superintendent Marshall radioed through to Superintendent Murray in the police control box inside the ground, asking for traffic to be stopped in Leppings Lane.

Steve Hart, having been dropped off by the coach, started to make his way towards the Leppings Lane turnstiles: 'The coach dropped us off outside a pub, which was closed. We were walking up to the ground and the first thing you noticed was that there was no crowd control like there had been the year before. There were crowd control barriers the year before, but nothing in 1989. As you got closer to the turnstiles you could see it was chocka, and there were police horses in the crowd.'

Kevin Morland's dad had been worried about the central pen enclosures as soon as they entered at about 1.30 p.m., but Kevin had wanted to stay. By about 2.15 p.m. his dad took action: 'Eventually, at around 2.15 p.m., my dad grabbed me by the collar and moved me up to the top of the side fencing and through a small gap into the empty pen at the side, to the right of the goal as you are looking at the pitch. We were not far from the police control box at this time, where the police had a bird's-eye view of the terraces. In the build up to 3 p.m., it was obvious what was happening in the pens that we had not long moved away from: singing and raised hands had been replaced by screams and people trying to escape in the very same spot that we had been stood less than an hour earlier.'

Around 2.30 p.m. inside the ground, Match Commander David Duckenfield noticed that the Leppings Lane end was filling up. This was written in his witness statement: 'The North Stand for Liverpool supporters was possibly half full at this time, the West Stand was filling, but there was space at the front and sides of the Leppings Lane terrace. I asked for a tannoy message to be relayed for fans to move forward and spread along the terrace.' This begs the question, how were supporters supposed to 'spread along the terrace' when lateral fences blocked their sideways movement? Eyewitness and photographic evidence shows that only the central pens were full at that time, such was the prominence of the entrance that fed them, but it is unclear how Duckenfield expected people to move along the terraces.

Paul Dunderdale and his friends arrived at the area outside the turnstiles around 2.40 p.m. and assumed the kick-off would be delayed because of the huge crowd of people still outside: 'As we approached the ground, we did notice that there were no police filters like there had been in 1988, so the effect was that everyone was milling around the same place and it was busy. It was about 2.40 at that time and it appeared obvious that the kick-off would be delayed. We had arranged to meet my twin brother, Andy, outside the ground, which we did, and then kept together as a group. I remember being next to a police horse, which is a scary thing close-up, and the crowd was in good spirits with the usual songs.'

Tony O'Keefe remembers arriving in Sheffield: 'We got into Sheffield and stopped at a pub about half a mile from the ground. I knew I could be safe and had a couple of shandies. We walked down to the ground from there. We got towards the top of Leppings Lane and the first thing my brother-in-law said was, "There are no barriers – there were barriers here last year." I didn't think anything of it because I hadn't been there before. When we got nearer to the ground there were a lot of people, and as we got closer there was a lot of commotion. There was a policeman on horseback pulling some guy down off the fence, and the guy was shouting that he had a ticket and that the police needed to open the gates. Most of the people seemed to be queuing for the terrace area, and we had tickets for the West Stand above, so we managed to get into the ground without too much difficulty.'

As time ticked closer to kick-off, the number of Liverpool fans arriving at the stadium increased. The entrance was on the bend of Leppings Lane, and the outer gates followed the bend of the road around outside the turnstiles. The Leppings Lane end of the Hillsborough Stadium was ordinarily used to house away supporters, which meant that it often only had to admit a few thousand spectators at each of Sheffield Wednesday's home matches.

Leeds fans in 1987 and Liverpool fans in 1988 remember a filtering system. This filtering system, in the shape of police barriers or cordons in the approach to the turnstiles, slowed the pace at which spectators arrived in the cramped area outside the turnstiles and gave the crowd a chance to enter without too big a queue forming behind them. The '87 and '88 semi-finals were managed by the experienced Chief Superintendent Brian Mole, and in 1989 he had been replaced just a few weeks previously by the then newly promoted and less experienced Chief Superintendent David Duckenfield. It is not clear if this is the reason why the police cordons were not in operation in 1989, but the Liverpool fans who have contributed to the writing of this book and attended both the 1988 and 1989 semi-finals all agree that the absence of these barriers in 1989 was 'one of the biggest contributory factors to the disorganised build-up', as Damian Kavanagh said. Having allowed a large flow of people to enter the back of a small area faster than the fans at the front could enter the turnstiles, Duckenfield and his officers had caused themselves a problem. As Professor Keith Still explains, 'By the time the crowd reaches crush loading, it is often too late to avoid injury. Understanding the relationship between "A" and "B" leads to appropriate crowd management (or improved design) and is essential for safe operations.' So was it known by Duckenfield and his officers in advance that the turnstiles at that end of the ground would struggle to cope with the number of fans?

The Hillsborough Independent Panel's report included an eighteen minute video compiled from footage shot by the BBC, Sheffield Wednesday Football Club and South Yorkshire Police. It shows the scenes recorded outside the Leppings Lane turnstiles from about 2.37 p.m., with occasional switches inside the stadium to view the central pens at that time. At around 2.38 p.m., a young lad can be seen on a BBC camera climbing up the wall to the side of the turnstiles building, looking over the top, and then coming back down outside the ground. A cheer goes up when he reaches the top, although it is not clear if that is related to his climb or not. At around 2.40 p.m., the same BBC camera shows that the small, cramped concourse outside the turnstiles is absolutely packed, and that the fans who can't even get that close are waiting in Leppings Lane road itself, waiting for the congestion to ease. Two mounted police officers can be seen within the crowd, and they are completely surrounded by supporters. From their mannerisms and actions, the mounted officers do not seem too concerned at this stage. They are simply looking around and sat on their horses, both of which are virtually still.

Around 2.40 p.m., a policeman, who is on foot, clean-shaven and wearing a flat cap, appears to be looking at a supporter's ticket and then pointing as if to direct the fan. The shot is a close-up, but it would appear that the officer has pointed the supporter in the direction of turnstiles A–G, which are for the use of those with standing tickets. This officer is completely surrounded by the crowd, but he looks calm. Just thirteen seconds later, a mounted officer with a moustache and wearing a helmet is seen gesticulating to the crowd in a very animated manner. This officer is on horseback outside the perimeter gates, and is furiously stabbing his fingers in a variety of directions and shouting. It is not possible to hear what he is shouting, nor at whom he is pointing. This officer has featured in many news clips since the disaster, and is by far the most animated and concerned-looking officer that has been shown. Around thirty seconds later, five or six Liverpool fans are seen jumping up and down on the spot together, apparently singing. They are inside the gates, but still a way away from the turnstiles. The crush against the turnstile building wall was caused by a gradual compression of the crowd. Those at the back are edging slowly forward which, over time, compresses the crowd more and more. Around 2.40 p.m., the camera sees a young Liverpool fan at the front being lifted over the crowd from left to right, and handed to a police officer, who is situated next to turnstile G – the furthest right of the seven turnstiles used by those with standing tickets. The officer sets the boy down outside gate C. The video now switches to the view inside the stadium at 2.40 p.m., where the two central pens are very full indeed. A beach ball is being passed around the crowd, despite the cramped conditions. Outside the ground, an officer on horseback, wearing a helmet, turns to face a fan before bending down and trying to strike him. The supporters around remonstrate with the officer for his heavy-handed response, before an officer on foot gets hold of the fan and pushes him towards a fence. The officer had a moustache, but it is not possible to say from the video if he is the same officer that was pointing and shouting a little earlier. An officer on foot is seen surrounded by supporters, and appears to be between the outer gates and the turnstiles. He has one hand in the air and appears to be on tiptoes and acting as if he is trying to attract the attention of somebody outside the outer gates. When he appears to be unsuccessful, he turns away from the camera and faces the turnstiles.

Around 2.47 p.m., exit gate C is opened in order to eject a young supporter from the ground. As the gate opens, it does so onto a mass of supporters outside, who it would appear are there because there simply isn't any room in front of the turnstiles. As the gate opens, around 150 supporters take the opportunity to enter before the police close it again. The camera now switches back to the inside of the ground at 2.49 p.m. and the centre pens are completely rammed. Fans are already trying to climb out of the centre pens into the side pens, which are sparsely populated by comparison.

Peter Carney recalls walking towards the Leppings Lane end: 'We walked from the Pennistone Road end up to the Leppings Lane end, and what was noticeable from the year before is that we had to walk through barriers the year before. You'd show your ticket to go through one barrier and then further down the street you'd show your ticket again to be allowed through the next barrier. There were no barriers in '89 and we noticed that. Anyway we got something to eat in the corner shop, a Mars bar and a pint of milk I think, and we got into the ground at about twenty to three or a quarter to three ... it was obviously packed.'

Liverpool supporter John Joynt remembers arriving later than he had planned in Sheffield because of the traffic: 'My dad's friend drove us to Sheffield in 1989 and because of the traffic we arrived at about 2.20 p.m. We didn't have time for a drink, so we walked straight to the ground. When we got to the top of the Leppings Lane we noticed that there were no barriers like there had been the year before. The police had the ground well boxed off the year before, but we didn't think too much of it at the time. The turnstiles didn't seem to be letting people through very quickly, and the crowd was really building up. The crush wasn't as bad as it was to be inside, but the police had lost control of it, basically. When we got towards the turnstiles, the crowd was building up outside. We made our way into the little pen in front of the turnstiles and probably got through the turnstiles at about 2.45 p.m.'

Ipswich fan Nick Braley had also arrived outside the ground around 2.20 p.m.: 'With the bus stuck and making little progress about half a mile from Hillsborough, we jump off and decide it would be quicker to walk the last stretch. We arrive about 2.20 p.m. and it's not moving, a swathe of fans queuing patiently but not seeming to move much. The pressure steadily builds and the police and their horses decide to wade in. The crush outside gets worse as more and more fans arrive but little progress is made towards the turnstiles.'

Inside the ground, Danny Rhodes, a Nottingham Forest supporter at the Kop end of the ground, was eagerly anticipating the kick-off, but could see that all was not right with the Liverpool end: 'As time ticked on towards 2.30 p.m. the Forest end started filling up. There was the usual semi-final mix of regular supporters and big game glory hunters. We noticed very early that something was wrong with the Leppings Lane end. From where I was you could see the individual people in each of the wing pens, but the central pens were far, far busier and just one big mass of heads. One lad near me joked that the Liverpool fans hadn't sold all of their tickets. We laughed. The difference between the density of the wing pens and central pens was stark, and seemed more pronounced as kick-off drew closer. A regular on matchdays for five years, it was clear to me that something wasn't right. I've often wondered who else might have noticed the obvious uneven distribution of supporters in Leppings Lane. Surely the authorities noticed? It didn't take a trained eye.'

At the other end of the ground, Mick Bowers was starting to get concerned about the pressure of the crowd in the packed pens behind the goal: 'From 2 p.m., I noticed myself getting pushed further down the terrace and over to the left. At the time I was not concerned, as I was used to standing behind the goal and it is part of why I loved to go the game: the atmosphere, the hustle and bustle. However, I was finding that when I was pushed forward there was no going back. This started to alarm me, as normally if you go forward then you can jostle back to your position, but not today. By 2.30 I was becoming concerned, as I had never witnessed a crush like this before. The pressure was now so great that I had my arm in front of me at head height so that it was more comfortable and I could hold myself off the person in front of me. My shoelace was undone, but I couldn't bend down to tie it. There was no way I could get out of pen 4 – it was impossible – and I was now very anxious. The pressure just kept building. It was relentless. The players had not come out for the match so it must have been prior to 2.55. I was concerned for my safety. There was a barrier to my left, so I tried traversing across, thinking that if I get behind that then I can't go further forward as it would offer protection.'

Meanwhile, outside the Leppings Lane turnstiles at around 2.30 p.m., the crowd had swelled considerably and the turnstiles that were too few, malfunctioning, and could not admit fans fast enough. The crowd was building up. Paul Jarvill saw the turnstiles and entered the crowd, along with many others: 'As you got towards the turnstiles, there was no queuing system. It's an open concourse outside the turnstiles, and everyone was allowed onto it. At this stage, you've got the thought in the back of your mind that there's too many out here. Trying to get towards the turnstiles was like swimming in mud. You were totally sucked into it, and you had to move forwards, you couldn't go back because of the people behind you. I looked over my shoulder, to see if I could see my mate Phil. We'd already lost the other three, but Phil and I had managed to stay together. As I looked around there was just a sea of people behind me, and you could see people's eyes getting wider. There was a fear starting to build. There was a mounted officer with a bullhorn shouting, "Get back, step back", but you couldn't. It wasn't possible. Eventually, Phil and I were side by side, and we got towards the turnstile and there was a police officer on a horse. We couldn't go back, we couldn't move sideways and there was this police horse in front of us so we had to take the decision to crawl under the police horse and at that time I was scared and starting to panic. I got under the police horse and went through the turnstile. Immediately inside the turnstile there was a police officer guarding a programme seller. My exact words I don't remember, but I more or less said that he needed to be outside sorting that lot out, or else somebody was going to get hurt. He just laughed in my face and said, 'Well in that case I am better off in here then.'

At around this time, Richie Greaves and his friends arrived outside the Leppings Lane end turnstiles and noticed a difference in policing from last year's semi-final: 'As we walked down the Leppings Lane from the bookie's, which was about a five-minute walk, there wasn't a sign of anything different than any other visit to Hillsborough. We got to the bend in the Leppings Lane where we went into our section, and the police were checking your tickets in 1988. What that did, is it filtered the crowd slowly into the bottlenecked area outside the turnstiles. But in '89, there was no ticket check, so the crowd congregated right outside the turnstiles, which caused bedlam. Outside the turnstiles it was absolutely chocka. We must have got there at about twenty-five past two. There were police on horses; the horses were trying to move about. There was a Liverpool copper on horseback and one minute he was joking that he'd arrived late because it had taken him that long to ride his horse from Liverpool and then the next minute he was shouting at everyone. The crowd was shouting at him to get a grip of the situation. No queues, just a mass of people. In 1988, the police filtered fans slowly towards the turnstiles but in 1989 there was no such filter.'

As the situation outside the ground worsened, Inspector Bernard Murray, who was in the police control box, inside the ground, overlooking the Leppings Lane terraces, started to feel that the turnstiles were not operating correctly and tried to contact Mr Lock, who was Sheffield Wednesday's security officer. In Inspector Murray's witness statement, he said, 'As far as I was concerned, there was something wrong with the turnstiles, or there was something wrong with the flow through the turnstiles. We had a large crowd and the crowd seemed to be getting larger, but it wasn't dissipating. The people were not coming into the stadium at the rate that I would have expected them to and I wanted to get hold of Mr Lock and draw his attention to it for whatever action he could take.'

Inside the ground, the central pens were already becoming too full. People were struggling to keep their footing, and being squashed tightly against each other. Eileen McBride, an off-duty nurse, was standing at the front of the West Stand, looking down on the central pens, and remembers sensing that something wasn't right: 'I looked down a bit later and there were even more people in the central pens, fenced into the central area and yet the side pens were virtually empty. Even this early people looked tense, and as time got closer to kick-off it was getting more and more tense. I kept saying to my partner that something was wrong, but I couldn't put my finger on exactly what was wrong. Normally when you are in a big crowd like in the Kop, you get a surge forward when there is a goal or a corner or whatever, and then the crowd slowly moves back as the action passes. But it wasn't like that on that day – you could see the crowd moving forward, but you couldn't see anyone moving back again.'

The constant flow of people coming down the long, dark tunnel behind was immediately filling any space that a forward motion created, and leaving the crowd that bit more compressed as a result. Nick Braley decided that the compressed crowd outside was getting to be too much: 'As the pressure mounts, I say to the lads I've had enough, I don't care if I miss the kick-off, don't care if I miss the match, this is dangerous and I want out. I love my footie but someone is going to die here, make no bones. I head off to the side, pushing myself out of the crush and towards the edge of the fans. Sorry lads, I just can't cope with that. Then someone shouts, the gate is open and I find myself looking at an open gate, a couple of coppers and a few fans jumping through. I go for it but as I arrive the copper is trying to pull it shut. I stuck my foot on the bottom and jump through, the last one in as the copper pulls it shut behind me. Half expecting to get nicked, I go to show my ticket but the copper isn't bothered. I'm in, but what the hell is going on outside?'

Brian Johnson was by this time safely inside the ground in the far right of the West Stand seated section above the Leppings Lane terraces: 'We were in the far right block looking onto the pitch, about eight rows up. We went and got a drink in the bar area and went back to our seats. A bit later, probably about 2.40ish, we decided to go to the toilets. It was an antiquated place, and while having a pee I noticed that, instead of windows, they had left alternate bricks out on a couple of courses on the outer walls, probably for ventilation. Being a nosy sod I went over to have a look outside. I couldn't believe what I saw. The crowd was just one mass of people being crushed, swaying one way, and then another. There were a couple of police on horseback, but they were just stuck within this mass of people, and they had no control of the situation. People were climbing up walls, gates, anything to get out of the crush. When I got back to my seat, I said to my dad, "There is no way that lot are getting in before kick-off; you wanna see it out there!" In the terracing below, everything seemed fine. It was full in the middle as always, but plenty of room to the right-hand side under the control box.

I remember it being a good atmosphere and everyone looking forward to a good game.'

The crowd in the cramped courtyard outside the turnstiles had become compacted, as the number of fans arriving at the back outnumbered the number that the turnstiles could admit. The people arriving at the back were in a dense crowd, which only grew denser as they got closer to the turnstiles. Professor Keith Still, a crowd expert, explains: 'It is important to note that fans will not know about the crowding ahead, whether approaching Leppings Lane or moving towards or through the tunnel. The pressure builds up at the front of the system as the back of the crowd continues to move forward. Which is why this is such an important safety consideration for design, planning and crowd safety management and operations.'

Closer to the turnstiles, Steve Hart remembers his terrifying experiences pinned up against the wall by the weight of the crowd: 'We got into the crowd and slowly but surely we were edging towards the turnstiles and the crowd was building up behind me bit by bit. Where the turnstiles are there is a wall, and everyone was being crushed into that corner against the wall. I managed to get across the wall a bit towards the turnstile, but then when I got to the corner of the wall and the turnstile's entrance, my ribs got pinned against the corner. I couldn't breathe. People were shouting, "push back," and starting to get panicky. I remember this fella putting both feet against the wall and pushing backwards and trying to drag me back off the wall and that is when I fell into the turnstile entrance. There were people climbing up onto the top of the turnstiles wall, and lifting others out of the crush. This wasn't, as the police later claimed, people trying to get in without tickets; they were trying to help people in the crush outside. They didn't climb up and go into the ground – they stayed on the top and helped other people up. I was shouting at the turnstile operator that it was chaos outside and he needed to do something, and he didn't even take my ticket … he was just clicking people through. I could hear the clicks of the turnstiles going fast behind me, which was people coming through. He didn't even take my ticket; he was just letting people through. I was screaming then at the police inside the ground that it was carnage outside and if they didn't do something it was going to be bad. They weren't interested, and just told us to get in the ground.'

Mike Wilson entered the crowd outside the turnstiles, before deciding that it was better to step away: 'The first observation was that, whereas in the previous year, tickets were checked regularly as we closed in on the ground, in 1989, there were no such cordons. Our path was clear straight to the turnstiles. We arranged a rendezvous point outside the newsagent's on Leppings Lane. Just to confirm, none of us had been drinking in any way. Jonathan left us and dad and I headed for entrance B as instructed on our ticket. The turnstiles were in a quadrant shape with a narrow entrance. The signing over the turnstiles was essentially very confusing and entrance B was rather difficult to identify. This area was already very crowded. Dad and I queued in there for a while. It was approximately 2.45 at this point. It became clear very quickly that it was going to become unbearably uncomfortable in that area, so we decided discretion was the better part of valour and stepped out to a point adjacent to the river that ran along the side of the ground.'

John Joynt got through a turnstile around 2.45 p.m. after being in the crowd outside for a while. Once inside the turnstile, he remembers seeing only one way to go: 'There was nobody inside the compound between the turnstiles and the tunnel directing people where to go. Everyone just headed for the tunnel. There were no signs telling you anything different. We went to the toilet as we'd done the year before, and then went down the tunnel into pen three and stood at the back, where we were hoping to stay.'

Val Yates had been one of the very first people into the stadium, such was her excitement, but by 2.30 p.m. the central pens were rammed and getting worse: 'The central pens were rammed full from about 2.30 onwards, and it was very hot and uncomfortable. Some lads I know joined me and we noticed that the Forest end was starting to fill. One lad actually said that it was rammed in our end but they had so much room they could have a party. We were singing, "We've got more fans than you Nottingham," and knocking a beach ball around between the pens. Everything was good-humoured, but I was already getting jostled about as people were singing and dancing. "Jocky is back, Jocky is back, woa woa" and "Brucie, Brucie Grobbelaar, Brucie Grobbelaar in our goal". All I thought to myself was to try and keep my spot because I still wanted to get a good view and am only about armpit level to everyone else! To my mind, the crush started at 2.47 and I thought that because I had just looked at the clock eager now for it to just get underway. The sways and surges were getting more and more violent, and I was just thinking that I was going to get shoved about for ninety minutes. I was starting to get a little concerned, but the surges always went back a second or two later.

Grant Walker remembers the scenes outside the stadium as the crowd continued to swell: 'We made our way down to the ground at about a quarter past two. We'd been there the year before, so we knew how long it would take. As we got nearer the ground, there was just a mass of people. It reminded me of a Glastonbury concert or something like that, just a mass of people. I remember seeing one policeman on a horse, but very little else. I couldn't see any stewards, and everyone was just congregating around the ground.'

Inside the central pens, Damian Kavanagh recalls the crowd getting tighter and tighter: 'Slowly but surely, more and more people were coming in, and getting busier and busier. There was a lot more singing before the games in those days. You'd get people together, and if you wanted a good spec you had to get in early, and if you got in early there wasn't much else to do, so the singing tended to start earlier. Timings are difficult to recall, but I can remember everything that happened. It's very much etched on my mind, of course. Timings are difficult, though, other than to say that I was in the ground at 2.15 and slowly but surely things built towards the events that happened. There's an element of a false sense of security here. Because I've been in so many big crowds before, you kind of expect it. No harm had ever come to us before. The nature of crush barriers is to stop the pressure of having one big crowd all leaning on each other from the back of the terrace to the front. They were there to stem the flow of people. It was very much my practice to try and stand in front of a barrier, with my back on it. As a crowd gets busier and busier, though, people are coming in all around you and you're slowly but surely getting moved forward, so you'd be a bit further down with another crush barrier in front of you. And that is uncomfortable, with the weight of people behind you and an iron bar in your chest. So we moved down further still to try and get a barrier behind us again, because experience told us that was the best place to be. As more and more people are coming in, you end up working your way closer and closer towards the front.'

Nick Braley moved to the side as gate C opened briefly and he took advantage of the opportunity: 'My mates are still there and that is dangerous out there, really dangerous. Fans are getting agitated so there's lots of shouting. 'Open the f***ing gates, people are going to die outside,' is heard by a number of people and the coppers are standing taking it, looking scared and out of their depth. I decide to hang on and wait for my mates and am stood for a couple of minutes until the call to open the gate is made – thank God for that. As the gate is opened I dodge the first few fans coming in as I try to wait around, but the numbers coming in becomes a flood and I am swept away, up the tunnel onto the entrance to the terraces. I recall a small dividing fence that sends me into one of two pens. I opt to go right [pen three]...'

Those who had been delayed in traffic over the Snake Pass were still arriving in Sheffield, as Ed Critchley remembers: 'We finally arrived in Sheffield and then we were struggling to find parking. My father was driving us around and around looking for somewhere. We finally found somewhere to park, and walked towards the ground. There was a feeling of needing to rush because of the delays and time was getting on. We were about an hour and a half later than we had intended to be because of the roadworks. We wanted to get there early and soak up the atmosphere, but now it wasn't long to go until kick off time. The time now would have been something like 2.30 or 2.45. I remember it being particularly busy, particularly crowded, and people asking the policeman on horseback if the kick-off was being delayed. It must have been asked six or seven times, and the policeman said, "No, you need to get yourselves into the ground." Carl and myself had tickets in Leppings Lane and my father had tickets to one of the side stands. So my father left us there and went off to his stand, and we arranged where to meet after the game.'

The police roadblocks that fans recall from the match in 1988 had the desired effect of slowing the flow of supporters as they approached the stadium, even if that was perhaps not their primary role. Many fans talk about their experience before the 1988 match of walking up to a police roadblock, waiting to show their ticket, and then being allowed further down the road. Without those barriers in place, fans were left to congregate in the small, cramped courtyard outside the turnstiles and as the crowd swelled in size behind, once you were in there it wasn't possible to get out.

Richie Greaves recalls getting into the ground and then making a critical decision that he has reflected on many times since: 'We got into the ground at about twenty to three. We went to the toilet, then down the tunnel into the back of the Leppings Lane standing terrace. At the end of that tunnel you could go right into pen three or left into pen four. We had always stood in the same sort of place, so we naturally went into pen three. We took up a position about half way up the terrace, in line with the right hand goal post. There was still movement in the crowd at that point, but it was uncomfortable. The lad I was with, Ian, wanted to move away towards the right because it was a bit worse than normal. I said that it would be all right once the game kicked off, but he insisted and I went with him. I think that was decisive really. If I hadn't moved when the police opened the gate, we would have been in trouble.' After being crushed against the wall outside the ground for what felt like an eternity, Steve Hart fell through a turnstile, with his ticket still intact, and was struggling to get his breath back in the concourse area between the turnstiles, exit gate C and the tunnel: 'By the time I got into the ground I had lost my mates. I was in agony, I could hardly breathe, and I was gasping for air. I decided I'd wait by the tunnel for a bit to see if my mates came through the turnstiles, so we could go in together.'

The situation outside was now dangerous, and clearly wasn't going to be resolved without urgent action. Match Commander

Chief Superintendent David Duckenfield was watching the crowd on CCTV from his position in the police control box overlooking the Leppings Lane terraces. Duckenfield explains the moment that he gave the order to open the gates in his witness statement: 'A further message came over the radio from Superintendent Marshall to open the gates and he used words to the effect that if the gates were not opened someone was going to be killed. This was an urgent message, conveyed to me by the tone of his voice that this was a serious situation, and was a demand rather than a request. The previous thoughts crossed my mind once again about monitoring and control of supporters entering the ground. It was a serious step to take. I looked at the CCTV monitor – there was crushing outside, supporters were climbing over the turnstile walls, officers were under pressure. On the inside of the ground, there was space in the terrace, there was space on the inside of the turnstiles in the concourse, and room to ease the situation. If the gates were opened there may be crushing and injury on the inside but the message I was receiving from the outside was that unless I opened the gates and eased the pressure people would have been seriously injured or killed. Superintendent Marshall is a very experienced police officer and if he wanted the gates opened, which is not normally a consideration, then the situation must be very serious indeed. While I am considering the position and considering the options, Superintendent Murray said to me, "Mr Duckenfield, are you going to open the gates?" I remember standing there and saying my thoughts aloud so that others, if they heard it, would realise that it was a considered decision. I said, "If there is likely to be serious injury or death, I've no option but to open the gates – open the gates."'

In Duckenfield's own words, opening an exit gate to allow entry is not normal practice, but many people could understand the decision, given the situation faced by the police. The opportunity to better manage the flow of supporters towards the cramped waiting area outside the turnstiles had passed. The opportunity to deploy the police cordons in the approach to the ground recalled by fans of Leeds at the 1987 semifinal, and fans of Liverpool from 1988, was also gone. It was too late now, in Duckenfield's estimation, to delay the kick-off and reduce the anxiety in the throng outside. Worse than missing some of the match, people could be killed in the compressed throng of bodies outside. It was 2.52 p.m., and there was no way that the thousands outside were going to get in by kick-off unless something was done. This was policing in the moment, and something had to be done about the situation that faced Duckenfield and his colleagues immediately.

While waiting in the concourse area, recovering from his ordeal, in the hope that he would be reunited with the mates he'd been separated from outside the ground, Steve Hart saw Duckenfield's order being executed: 'I saw a policeman with a couple of stewards, and they had keys. The policeman had a flat cap, so he was obviously not an everyday bobby. They walked over to the gate and I could see they were opening the gate. At that point I thought there was no point hanging around any longer, so I went down the tunnel.'

Phil Thomas had also been caught in the crush outside the ground, and was struggling to compose himself once inside the ground. 'On entering the ground, I was covered in sweat and had to take several puffs on my Bricanyl spray ... I started to walk down the tunnel with my cousins when one shouted, "Don't go down there, remember last year we got crushed?" and so we exited the tunnel and made our way round to the side pen by the police control box. As we did, the gates opened and supporters poured in. I have never forgotten that moment. Only for the foresight of my cousin, I don't think I would be here today.'

Ed Critchley was outside the stadium and on the other side of the gate when Duckenfield's order to 'open the gates' was carried out, but he remembers the moment just as vividly: 'There were so many people outside the turnstiles, and then I remember hearing someone saying that the police were opening the exit gates. I've never been back to Hillsborough since, so the details are a bit foggy, but I clearly remember that Carl and myself had to jump over a small wall and then we walked through the exit gates.'

Tony Evans and his brother walked through that gate: 'It was busy, but in the particular place outside the turnstiles where we were it didn't seem that bad. The police looked a bit panicky on their horses, and we could hear some shouting going on, but there were no alarm bells ringing at that point. I've seen films since, and the other side looked worse, but we weren't too bad. So we got towards the front and we were waiting to go in, and then this big gate next to us just flew open. So the pair of us walked in through the gate. People didn't charge, they just walked in and there was still no problem for us at that point. My brother and I had tickets to separate parts of the ground. I had a ticket in the South Stand and my brother had a Leppings Lane ticket. I said to him, before we went our separate ways, "Don't go down the tunnel. Go up and around the corner where it goes up high. It's a better view from there."'

As Ed Critchley walked through the open gate, he recalls how he and Carl found their way onto the terraces: 'Straight in front of us was this dark tunnel, which we walked down, and we popped out in the light at the back of the Leppings Lane terrace in what I later came to know as pen three. At that point, it was a relief to get into the ground before kick-off. There was no concern for safety at this point, but Carl said that a lot of people were going to miss a large chunk of this game. There were so many people still outside, and we just couldn't believe that they hadn't put the kick-off back.'

Peter Dalling remembers walking through the gate into the tightly packed tunnel: 'We went in through the gate. It was chocka outside; there were coppers on horseback hurling abuse at us. We were outside the ground for a long time – there were thousands still outside as time got on towards kick-off, and all of a sudden a gate opened. We were three turnstiles away from the gate, and the coppers just said go in there [the gate], so we walked through. Once you were through the gate, access to the terrace was through the tunnel. You tend to follow the crowd, don't you? That was my first ever visit to Hillsborough and I thought if everyone is headed for the tunnel then that must be the right way. It's like if you were walking towards a stadium you didn't know, and everyone in front of you suddenly turned right, you'd think that must be the way to go, so you'd follow them. The tunnel was a squeeze, but we made it down, probably more by luck than judgement. There were a number of people seriously hurt in the tunnel, but I think we must have missed that. There were no exits left and right, so you could only go forwards or backwards, and there were that many coming in from behind that you could only go forward, really. We got into the pens and the crowd had stopped moving by then. I said to Paul and Norman, "We can't stay in here, we've got to get out." We went left at the end of the tunnel into pen four. I looked around and there were people being dragged up into the stands behind us and I said to the lads let's try and get back towards the wall, because at least if there was a wall behind us we're not going to get hurt.'

Grant Walker also recalls the moment that the gate opened: 'Everyone was worried that we were going to miss the kick-off, and we were in the crowd by now and getting swayed side to side by the movement of the crowd. Next minute there's a cheer, and the exit gate opened up, so we all filed through the gates. In front of you was a tunnel and when you looked through the tunnel you could see the top of the goal. There were no signs showing anywhere else to go, no stewards or nothing. So we all walked down that tunnel. Once you got into that dark tunnel … horrendous … the nightmares I've had over it since. Straight away you knew there was something drastically wrong here. You realised it was too busy, too full, but you couldn't go back because of the weight of those coming in behind you so the crowd compressed further as it inched further and further forward down the tunnel.'

Opening the gates was no doubt a serious undertaking and a decision not taken lightly. The very name, 'exit gate', tells you that they were not designed to allow fans to enter. However, despite taking this drastic measure, effective management of the crowd from this point onwards could still have averted disaster. In 1987 and 1988, the police closed off access to the central tunnel and directed fans to the less obviously marked wing pen entrances when they thought capacity had been reached in pens three and four. The various officers that recall this happening in '88 have varying ideas on if that was a directive from above or 'common sense' taken by officers on the ground, as Sergeant Howard Cable alluded to in his statement, but there seems little doubt that access to the tunnel was blocked off by police officers in previous semi-finals.

Bearing in mind that the tunnel leading to the central pens was directly in front of exit gate C, the simple act of blocking access to the tunnel and directing fans to the side pens would have stopped thousands more supporters using the only obvious entrance to enter the already packed pens. Only 20 per cent of the total crowd with standing tickets were supposed to be in pens three and four, yet a far, far higher percentage of people entering the ground were likely to use that tunnel in the absence of any direction, which was bound to cause overcrowding in the pens behind the goal. Police Constable Jim Warpole noticed the uneven fill of the pens roughly one minute after exit gate C was opened. His witness statement read, 'At 2.55 p.m. the central pen for standing at the Leppings Lane end seemed to be absolutely packed solid, whilst the pen towards the police control box [one and two] was about half full and the pen towards the north stand [five and six] was only one sixth full.'

The tunnel, being the only obvious entrance to the terraces, had to be managed to avoid overcrowding in the central pens. There was another problem with it, though, in that it was dark inside, and it initially sloped slightly upwards in the dimming light of the entrance before falling away downwards to a one in six gradient slope and into the dark. That rise and fall, in a densely packed crowd, caused many people to lose their footing, as Peter Carney recalled: 'We went into the ground and went to go for the tunnel. We met a lad that we knew in the concourse between the turnstiles and the tunnel, and his wife had just had a baby a couple of weeks before, so we spoke to him and gave our congratulations and what-have-you. In 1988, we were in the North Stand. We had really good seats overlooking the penalty box at the Leppings Lane end of the North Stand, about twenty rows back, I think. We knew that it was chocka behind the goal that year, but we never realised, even from all the people that said it was chocka, just what it would be like in '89. As we walked into the tunnel we heard the roar of the crowd as the teams came out onto the pitch. And we strained our necks upwards to see if we could see. As you looked down the tunnel, you could see a little bit of the pitch, and there was only a small gap that you could actually see down. The next thing we knew we went tumbling forward down the tunnel. There was actually a slope halfway down the tunnel, you see, and so what happened is that people were shuffling forwards in the crowd and when you got to the slope you'd lose your footing, and the crowd and the slope together carried you dead quick. As I went down the slope, I went into the terraces in one movement and by the time I got myself together and regained my sense of direction and what-have-you, I realised that I was looking back at the way I had come in. I had lost me mate, I couldn't see him anywhere, I think what happened is I was carried to the right with the crowd of people trying to find their footing into the terrace.'

Dr Glyn Phillips realised straight away that the central pens were abnormally full: 'As soon as we got in through the tunnel, we knew it was a very packed crowd. We made our way towards the right, although through the closely packed fans. We got split up from our mates and Ian and I found ourselves near the front, on the pitch side of a steel crowd barrier. I've been on the Kop many, many times and I've never been in a crush like that before. It was on a completely different scale to my previous experiences. I'd been going on the Kop since the age of twelve, for very big games, derby games, Leeds and Man United games, European games. We always used to go right in the middle behind the goal and I'd enjoy the movement, the surges, the swaying of the crowd. It was part of the fun. But this was abnormal, quite sinister. We had to get away from there. I knew this was not a good place to be and we decided to move higher up the terrace. By then, people couldn't stand aside, so we went down on hands and knees and crawled through legs. Higher up, it was still so tight that standing up was difficult but we did it and even managed to meet up with our two friends. Then we were looking at each other with faces of incredulity. What's going on? There wasn't much you could do, though, because you were stuck, penned in by the side against railings. Imagine having your elbows down by your side and your hands up in front of your chest. You just couldn't move your arms because you were so crammed together.'

What followed was hell on earth for those trapped in the central pens. If you watch the CCTV footage after gate C was opened, the viewer can observe that a steady stream of supporters entered at walking pace, and the majority made for the central tunnel for reasons already explained. As that steady press of bodies edged downhill, through the tunnel and into the back of already dangerously over capacity pens, the slight space that existed was soon filled. As people realised halfway down the tunnel that it was already packed solid, there was nothing they could do to go back, because of the weight of the crowd behind them. In '87 and '88, the crowd going down that tunnel had only been as dense as seven turnstiles could admit, and the police sealed access to the tunnel before things became fatal. In 1989, on a bright sunny day in Sheffield, an exit gate had increased the density of the crowd considerably and, with no direction and no attempt to seal access, the lives of thousands were about to change forever.

3

Hell

In the 1980s, crowd surges were part and parcel of going to the match. As the action on the pitch ebbed and flowed, so did the supporters on the terraces. Goal celebrations or near-miss action would get people excited and a ripple of movement would take huge sections of the crowd forward as one, before slowly moving back again. Crowd surges are one thing in terraces that are filled with the correct number of people, but as eyewitness evidence tells us, the central tunnel entrance was the only obvious route to the terracing, so the central pens had often become over capacity. In a properly filled pen, the crowd has the chance to move back after a surge, but when a steady flow of fans are allowed to pour down a dark tunnel into the back of an already overcapacity pen, the little spaces that people leave when the forward surge occurs are immediately filled, and as a result the entire crowd is more compacted.

As the exit gate at the back opened, allowing over 2,000 fans to walk into the stadium with no direction, many headed straight for the tunnel. CCTV footage shows that fans were walking, but the density of the crowd, coupled with the darkness in the tunnel and slope at a 1 in 6 gradient, led to fans losing their footing.

Nick Braley remembers the tightness, and the surge, and then the panic: 'I hit the back of the terrace and it is full. Like properly full. I have no idea of the terrace layout, size, etc., but recall my trips to Wembley to watch England and how the entrances onto the terrace were always more crowded. Push away 10 feet or so and the density was much less, so I knew standing here was silly. I pushed my way through the crowd, something that took every bit of strength I had. I was constantly apologising and I eventually made it to a crash barrier. Decision time: go under or stand behind it. I knew at Ipswich the best place was in front, as behind it you get crushed when the goals are scored, but in front you are protected. I decided to go for it and squeezed underneath before popping up. The people around me weren't happy, but then neither was I. This was a nightmare and I still could not see the pitch, rather just a few spots of green. After a couple of minutes, the teams came out and a cheer went up. The match started and I had no idea what was going on – rather I was starting to get scared, really scared. Something's not right here. This is no way to watch a game, but I am stuck, and could go nowhere. After a couple of minutes, Beardsley hit the bar. I know this only because I have been told that was the cause of the surge that sent things into another dimension; this is close to what hell is like. Bang, a surge (a collapsed barrier?) and I am suddenly thrown forward and bang, I stop as suddenly as I started, as I hit a fence. Only this surge doesn't retract, no one moves back, this is just a surge that stops.'

Fans were reaching the end of the tunnel and describe it as being like hitting a wall. The pressure of bodies compressed and squeezed the crowd inside ever closer to the fences at the front, but a steady stream of people were still walking down the tunnel behind, and then, when they got to the slope, their pace quickened as some people fell. Every time anybody on the terraces found even the slightest bit of space to move into, the space they had just left was filled by another person, and so the crowd was compacted that little bit more. Grant Walker was in the tunnel when movement in any direction was impossible: 'The crowd was so tightly packed into that tunnel and I remember there being a sway, and a couple of hundred people fell on the floor, myself included. Our kid helped me up, but you knew there were people under your feet but you couldn't help. I remember feeling something under my foot, and it was somebody's arm. It was literally every man for himself at that stage, because if you bent down too much you'd go down amongst it all yourself. You could see people's faces turning purple in the tunnel and there is nothing you could do.'

Mike Wilson also remembers the tightness in the tunnel: 'A few yards into the tunnel and it was a wholly different story to 1988. The lighting was damaged in places, causing my dad to liken the experience to being in the Black Hole of Calcutta. As we moved forward we hit a wall of people, a wall that was virtually stationary. The problem was that more people were arriving behind us. We became part of that wall. It took five minutes for us to progress out into daylight and this was essentially down to the force from behind. As we came out in the pen, the one on the left when exiting the tunnel (Pen 4 I believe), the extent of the crush was starting to become apparent. Whereas I edged left, dad was carried in a current of people straight down the terracing. At that point, alarmingly, we lost sight of each other. It became somewhat about self-preservation but there didn't seem to be any major panic around. People were being pretty careful, ensuring that those around them weren't pushed down. I remember seeing younger children being lifted overhead and passed forward, though I didn't see where they ended up. There was another who started to faint next to me and while another guy and I tried to make space, another chap lifted the struggling guy up. Again, I didn't see where he ended up. Movement was steady and sideways for me. On two or three occasions, I was inadvertently smashed against the end of crash barriers. I remember this left a scar on my hip for three or four months after that. The game had started but had become an irrelevance very quickly. I don't really have much recollection of the game being stopped. It took all our effort to stay upright. Eventually, I found myself up against the side fence in the pen. There was nowhere else to move. The other side of the fence was a further internal fence with a narrow walkway in between. This is largely used for stewarding, though there were no stewards in there at this time. The fence wasn't moving and I was getting crushed against it more and more. So I started to give people a "bunk-up", allowing them to vault the fence into the walkway. At the front of the walkway was an opening in the perimeter fence onto the playing surface. The pitch, by now, had fans on it who had escaped from the pens. I must have been there for ten minutes lifting people over. My own leg felt trapped through the fence.

Eventually there was enough room for me to vault over the fence myself. I remember all my coins dropping out from my pocket onto the floor as a lad much smaller than me tried to catch me. We fell in a heap; I thanked him and headed out onto the pitch.'

Barry Devonside had taken his seat in the North Stand before kick-off, and his son, Chris, had a ticket for the Leppings Lane standing terrace, so they had gone their separate ways outside the ground. Barry remembers the scene: 'Those central pens became fuller and looked overcrowded as the time reached ten to three, then five to three and then all hell let loose. At first I couldn't make out what was wrong, and then I could see people trying to climb out of the central pens and I immediately thought of Chris. It went through my mind that Jackie, my wife, had said to me years before that if I ever brought Chris home hurt from a football match, then me and her have got a problem.'

Paul Jarvill recalls thinking the central pens looked full but not thinking much about it until Beardsley hit the bar: 'I remember thinking that the central pens looked crowded, but you don't think too much of it at the time. The game kicked off and, after a few minutes, Beardsley hit the bar and after that everything seemed to change. Fans started coming over the fences onto the side of the pitch. You could see it wasn't a pitch invasion as some people first thought, because they were on the side of the pitch. I knew there was something wrong and I think I knew it was serious when I saw people being hoisted up by their arms into the stands above.'

Tony Evans was sat in the stand, and remembers when he first realised that something was wrong: 'I think the first time I realised that something was wrong is when I came up into the stands. I was around the 18-yard line, and actually about eighteen rows back. I looked out across the pitch, and it was as green as any pitch has ever been. The teams were coming out, Liverpool all in red and I thought, yes, this is why the game is great, you know? Then I looked over to the Leppings Lane and thought Christ, those middle sections are crowded. You could see how empty it was on the side, you could have swung your arm on the sides. The game kicked off and you could see there was a bit of commotion behind the goal, and as Liverpool fans you're thinking, what's going on there? When Beardsley hit the bar it seemed to escalate. It's hard to articulate really, it wasn't like a shrieking, it was more like, more like a groan and people started coming over the fences and on to the pitch. All of sudden I saw this lad coming onto the pitch and he had his elbow in his hand, and his forearm was broken at a right angle. I thought Christ, people are injured, you know? Then there was a big lad, really big, and they pulled his shirt over his head. I said out loud Jesus Christ, there are people dead. The fella next to me shouted there's no one dead, there's no one dead!'

Tony O'Keefe was in the stands above the terraces and remembers looking down at the central pens: 'We got into the ground and went above the Leppings Lane area. The players were out warming up and I just glanced down to the terracing below, and thought it looks really heavy down there, there was a lot of commotion. The game kicked off and a couple of minutes in I remember a lad in a white shirt being pulled out behind the goal. Bruce Grobbelaar, the Liverpool goalkeeper, kept glancing around to see what was going on.'

Having watched the police open the exit gates, Steve Hart had decided to head down the tunnel before the crowd came through the gate. He had hoped to hang around in the concourse area between the tunnel and the turnstiles to wait for the mates that he'd been separated from in the crush outside the ground, but as the police started to open the gates there seemed little point in waiting with the subsequent number of people that were likely to flow through: 'You can see the pitch and the top of the goal as you go down the tunnel, and when you got to the end there were people there in front of you – solid at the end of the tunnel. I went right into pen three and being a little lad I tried to wiggle my way forward a bit. Within minutes, though, you could feel the pressure building and it was a bit uncomfortable at first. I thought it would be OK and it would sort itself out, but it gradually got tighter and tighter, and it was literally like somebody was turning a vice. People were starting to get panicky around me and people were starting to get agitated. Normally a crowd would sway, but this was different, it didn't move – it was solid.'

Steve Hart walked down the tunnel just before Duckenfield had given the order to open exit gate C, yet before that he had already found it incredibly difficult to get any space at all on the central pens.

Paul Dunderdale remembers the moment when he realised that the pens were overcrowded, but being unable to do anything about it: 'We were by the gate that was suddenly opened – it wasn't forced, you could hear the big bolts, or perhaps chains, being drawn back. It was a metal-on-metal noise, in any case. At that stage, we all went through the gate onto the concourse, where it opened up and was a lot less congested. We had time to look around and get together so that we all went in at the same time. In 1988, we had tried to go down the tunnel, but there were two policemen and a steward at the entrance telling us those pens were full and directing us to the outer pens. This year [1989], as there was no police presence, we assumed that those pens were not full and so headed down the tunnel. Halfway down, we realised this wasn't right. It felt like hitting a wall, and once in the daylight, you went in the direction the crowd took you. I was carried to the right and hung onto my brother and lost sight of Graham and my other friends. The crush was unbelievable and just breathing was an effort, and I knew in my heart that someone was going to be hurt that day. My brother was really struggling, I held on to him but he was turning grey and blue and I was very worried about him and knew we had to get out somehow. We were about 10 feet from the open gate in the pen and at first I thought we should try and make it to that, but it was impossible to go forward and a lot of people were crying and screaming.'

Inside the pens, Damian Kavanagh remembers trying in vain to help a fellow supporter who was suffering behind him. 'As the crowd congestion had built up, there are a couple of things that stand out in my mind. There were a couple of lads behind us and I don't know what happened to them to this day. Over one shoulder, one of them was behind us pressed against the crush barrier and he was saying, "Come on, help us out here lads, help us out." It sounds a bit weird this, but he was asking us to back heel the toes of his feet as if it would help spring him over the bar he was in that much pain. He couldn't move at all from there and we were trying our best. Over the other shoulder, there was a fella that was pinned against the barrier, and all he could say was "please". Begging and pleading, "Please!" A few feet further forward, there was a young girl, who I think was up against the next crush barrier, I'm guessing. She was in a lot of pain, and there were two men there who said, "Let's get this young girl out." I'd say that if she was in her teens then she would have only been in her early teens, and again I don't know what happened to any of those people to this day.'

Ed Critchley was getting worried about how packed the crowd was: 'We tried to make our way down the terrace a bit, and I remember saying to Carl that we were going to really struggle. We were stuck at the back and it was really packed. We tried to move down the terrace, and we could only make it about a third of the way down, and literally couldn't get any further. At this point, we thought that this wasn't right. We're too squashed, it's not right. The first signal that something was wrong came next. I was pushed up against an elderly gentleman, and he had fainted. He was standing up, but he'd fainted. I said to Carl this isn't right, and we tried to help this guy and he had thankfully just fainted. People around us were starting to comment that it was too busy and something wasn't right. It was really uncomfortable and we couldn't move any further. We looked back towards the tunnel, and noticed that people were starting to be lifted up by fans in the stand above the Leppings Lane terraces. Carl made a comment that we should go and do the same, and we tried to make our way back towards the back. Movement was even harder at this point, as it was even busier, but with a lot of effort we managed to get back. By this point it was jammed at the back, jammed back into the tunnel.'

After tumbling down the steep tunnel and arriving in the pen facing the way he came, Pete Carney remembers how hard he had to concentrate on a simple thing like breathing: 'I got myself together and tried to face the pitch, and as I was doing that I could see people down. People who were in real trouble. I shuffled left and tried to work out where the barriers were, because I'd always thought that it was safer to be in front of a barrier, so that is what I was looking for. All the time you're trying to get your breathing together and keep your head about you. You could hear people screaming at the police at the front. I know for a fact that policeman were pushing people back into the pens when they were trying to escape the crush. There is no way they were letting anyone come out of the pens and onto the pitch. The game had kicked off in the meantime and I remember seeing a Forest player called Parker. I think his name was Gary Parker, and I was just trying to focus my attention on him to try and keep myself together and to distract myself from the pain of the crush. I was screaming as well and asking for help, but I just thought if I could try and focus on that player I could keep calm. There was a copper right in front of me at one point on the track the other side of the fence, and he just wasn't listening to people. All the time I was trying to concentrate on my breathing, and trying to distract myself from the crush because it was really painful. So as it's going on, I was struggling to get any air, and I kept changing my focus to try and focus on different things and Gary Parker was one of them. I basically just watched him run in a straight line. I was trying to distract myself from the crush. This went on and I was really struggling to breathe, and I kept looking at the clouds, and then Gary Parker and then into the distance beyond the South Stand to try and keep my focus. Then I was just seeing the clouds, and in my mind they became like a pipe, like a tube made from clouds and I was floating down this cloud tunnel. My last conscious thought was what about Tina and the baby, because my wife was pregnant at the time – we'd only found out ten days before. I then found myself looking back on myself in the crowd in a perfect circle of people going down. I think that was actually the reality of what was happening to me at the time. I've since spoken to another survivor who was on a psychology course, and he showed me what a near death experience was and I am sure that it what I was having. I don't know for sure what happened next, but I think I went to the floor, and I fell between the legs of the crush barrier and there was a pocket of air down there, and as I'd gone down I was able to get air again.'

Having just felt a surge pushing him forward with no movement back afterwards, Nick Braley started to panic as the simple act of breathing became difficult: 'What the hell just happened? Jesus, this is mental, this isn't right, I got to get out of here, I can't breathe, what's going on? Some of this my brain has partially blocked out, probably for the best. When I think about the fans in front of me, where did they go? Underfoot? Did I trample people to death? Dark thoughts that would reoccur many times in the dark moments that would follow over many years. Somehow I landed within feet of a gate. I have my left shoulder on the fence and I am facing sideways away from the pitch, but I can see the gate. The cries are simple ones. "Open the gate, people are dying." "Open the gate, people are dying." How the copper turns his back on us is beyond belief, but he does. Ignoring the pleas of dying people, he turns his back on us. The fight for life takes over and I locked my elbows, determined to protect my space, to allow myself to breathe. Again, years later you go over this, every breath I took, I stole from someone else, every breath could have kept another alive, just by living you are killing someone else … a trauma like no other, but one you go through no matter. "Open the bloody gate, at least let some of the kids out…" Finally, the copper shows some humanity and allows some of them out before, bang, he shuts it again. There's more kids in here, I lie, as I plead to him, beg him to reopen it, and he does. This time I am not denied as I scramble up a step and onto the pitch, where I fall to my knees and collapse. The match is still going on and I am one of the first to escape. My luck in going right at the top, in fighting my way through, landing so near the gate, this means I spent barely a few minutes on the terrace compared to many, and I know I am very lucky to be alive, and lucky not to have suffered the worst of it.'

Paul Dunderdale decided that the best chance of escape for him was up and into the West Stand above: 'I looked around and saw people being pulled up into the Upper Stand from the back of Leppings Lane. I thought this was the only chance we would have. We managed to turn around and head back. It was surreal. We were in the middle of a huge crush where breathing was an effort but it was almost like a parting of the waves – for some reason, people were able to step aside for us to get to the back. I am not a religious person, but I do believe we were able to make it back from a section that so many people didn't for a reason.'

A while after the gate had been opened, Eileen McBride's initial concern about the crowd in the central pens was sadly proving to be well founded. The sheer number of fans coming in through the open exit gate at the back of the West Stand and down the tunnel into pens three and four were immediately filling any space that was created by forward movement in the crowd. The crowd coming down the tunnel at the back had no way of seeing that the crowd at the front were compacted and in distress. The tunnel was packed solid with supporters because the pens in front of them were in the same state. On a terrace that isn't grossly overpopulated, there would be space to move back after a forward crowd movement, but any space that was created that day by a forward surge was immediately filled by the fans coming in behind, making it impossible to move back, and leaving the overall crowd even more densely packed together. Eileen recalls her thoughts and feelings as she looked down on the Leppings Lane that day: 'The more I looked, the more I could see fear on people's faces. They weren't happy, it was fear. I couldn't work out exactly what was happening, but I just knew that something was wrong, and that people didn't have enough room. I could see a man being resuscitated on the side of the pitch. I said to my boyfriend that we have to go. Initially, he thought I meant leave the stadium, but I said no, we have to go down and help. So we went down the nearest exit, down the stairs, and leading towards the outside when we came across a young policeman. I stopped him and told him that I was a nurse, that there were problems on the side of the pitch, and that I thought I could help. As I was saying this he got a message over his radio saying can all officers report to the pitch, there's a pitch invasion. I told him that it wasn't a pitch invasion, and that I could see people getting crushed. I told him people were frightened, in distress and people were dying. The officer tried to radio this through, but as he started he got the same message come over, but the same message came again that all officers were to report to the pitch as there had been a pitch invasion. The officer kept trying to radio through, and eventually he got through and told control that he had met a nurse and told them what I had seen. They acknowledged the message, but nothing else came back.'

Richie Greaves and his mate Ian had moved to the side of pen three, but despite later thinking that the decision to move there could possibly have saved their lives, the situation was still dire: 'Within minutes of us moving there was less and less movement, to the point where you couldn't move at all. We started hearing shouts that people were getting crushed at the front. People were trying to climb over the front fence, and people were being pulled up to the West Stand seating area above. Gradually, we ended up behind a crush barrier, but you always felt safer in front so we were trying to get under so we could be in front. Ian managed to get under, and I managed to get one leg over, but I had my other leg stuck behind me, crushed on the barrier by the crowd. Eventually, someone managed to breathe in enough so that I could get my other leg over and we were both in front of the barrier now. There was a gate at the front that led onto the perimeter track, and I don't know if it was the pressure from the crowd but the gate kept springing open and the police kept pushing people back in and closing the gate. Inch by inch, we ended up next to the lateral fence that led to pen two, and lads in pen two put their hands through so you could get a foot up and climb over into the relatively empty pen two. You could have run around doing cartwheels in pen two, and inches way you could barely breathe. While we were in pen three, we were in front of this barrier and the pressure was intense. It was difficult to breath for a couple of minutes with the pressure on our chest, and then we were able to get over the fence. Such was the distress around us that we didn't even know the game had kicked off.'

John Joynt and his mate were forced into each other from the pressure of the crowd, and his mate was screaming at John to get his elbow out of his side: 'We were about halfway down and there were fans shouting to the police that there are people being crushed here. To my left was the gate that opened onto the pitch and the police let this one lad out, who said there are people dying in there. They just shut the gate back up. That was it then, and it seemed like the whole crowd was shouting to say there was a real problem. At that time, I was getting more and more crushed. I was with my mate Steve, and I had my elbow in his side. He was screaming and saying he was in pain, but I couldn't move my arm. My little finger had got caught in his coat pocket, and so I had to push my arm further into him before I could release my finger to get him free. I put my arm over his shoulder to try and get us a bit more room, but his throat was moving closer and closer to my arm, and I thought that this is every man for himself here. I was moved a bit further forward, and I was just behind the barrier that eventually snapped. There were two or three bodies under my feet and then you realised that there was a really bad situation going on. I tried getting people to push back but there wasn't a hope in hell; everyone was in the same boat. There was so little space, and had I tried to go down to help those underneath us I'd have been pushed down there myself. I passed out at that stage for a few seconds, and then a bloke said in my ear, "Are you all right, lad?" I said I was and got myself together then, and then I thought I really need to get out of here now. I counted that I was ten heads from the front, and by this time there were people climbing over the fence at the front. There was someone with a scarf trying to pull the fence down. I noticed that people were being lifted up into the stand behind, and I somehow managed to push backwards and two lads lifted me up into the stand above.'

So many Liverpool fans in the central pens remember the seemingly endless period of time that they were screaming and pleading with the police on the outside of the perimeter fence to open the gates to relieve the pressure. Steve Hart picks up the story: 'The police must have thought that it was a crowd disorder situation even though it was blatantly obvious that it wasn't. It didn't take a rocket scientist. These coppers had been to football matches and they knew the score. I mean, you're not going to get your own fans fighting among themselves in the first few minutes of the match, are you? It's not going to happen. I was aware that the game had kicked off, but I was concentrating so much on the pressure of the crowd that I didn't pay much attention to it. People were trying to get over the fence, but they were designed to keep you in, not to help you get out. So I don't know exactly how, but the pressure of the crowd sort of pushed me up in the air so my feet were off the ground. I was convinced, at first outside the ground when I was crushed against the wall, and then again inside the pen, that I wasn't going to make it.'

Having been carried into pen three by a 'quicksand tidal wave', Steve Warner was already in serious trouble: 'I realised that I was quite literally fighting for my life. I looked around me and there was a man on my left shoulder who was quite clearly dead. His head was against my shoulder, and there was vomit down my arm from this chap who had been suffocated against me. His eyes were staring and his face was blue. The same the other side. The screams for help were so loud, and the smell was horrendous. The smell of death, which I hope I never have to experience again for as long as I live.'

Ed Critchley and his best mate Carl were rescued from the crush by those supporters who were in the West Stand above, which was overlooking terraces. These fans in the upper tier were stretching their arms down as far as they could and then grabbing people's hands to lift them up out of the bedlam below and into the safety of the stand above. Ed recalls: 'Eventually, Carl was lifted out to the stand above, and then he made sure that I was lifted out about three or four people later. We then stood and watched a surreal experience in front of us. The game had kicked off by this point, and I think we hit the bar, which is when we noticed people starting to climb over the fence at the front onto the pitch. It took a while to realise that this wasn't just people fainting, because it was a warm day and it was so busy down there, but then you started to realise. I can only describe it as surreal. You don't expect to go to a football match and watch people literally dying in front of your eyes.'

Grant Walker was also pulled out of the crush by those in the West Stand above: 'The year before was bad enough, but you knew this was going badly wrong. When I got into the terrace, luckily enough I managed to push backwards so I was right at the back of the terrace and some kind-hearted soul put his arms down and pulled me out to the seating area above the Leppings Lane terraces. As I looked down from there, I was thinking to myself what's going on here? This is crazy. At this point, everyone was trying to climb up the fences to try and escape the crush onto the pitch.'

Dr Glyn Phillips remembers the moment when he realised that the crush had taken some people's lives: 'I became aware of people climbing the fence, trying to get out, and police paying increasing attention. To the side of us, on the right, down towards the pitch, alongside the fence running perpendicular to the terrace, people were becoming very agitated. That was an area with loads of space to move around, in contrast to where we were. Lads were yelling, "Get back, get back. There's fans crushed at the front." They were becoming very upset because people didn't realise what was going on. And you see very limp bodies getting hauled out and you think, "Something really bad is happening." Then someone ran on the pitch, yelling at Liverpool's goalkeeper Bruce Grobbelaar to stop the game. Minutes later, we'd climbed over the railing into the next pen, which was relatively empty. I was looking down at the pitch and could see the state of some people and I thought, "God, they're dead. I'm going to have to go and try to help."'

Superintendent Greenwood was stationed at the players' tunnel as the match kicked off, and explains in his witness statement the scene once Brian Clough had taken his seat, and the photographers hoping to snap the Nottingham Forest manager before the game had dispersed: 'The match having kicked off and the press photographers gone from the front of the tunnel, I then surveyed the scene in the ground. I looked to my left and saw one or two spectators climbing over the perimeter fence at the Leppings Lane end behind the goal. Two or three police officers were with them. I immediately realised that there must be a crowd problem, not fighting because that would not happen so early in a match, so I immediately went to the Leppings Lane terracing, where I saw two or three police officers by the track gate, which I believe was open.'

Steve Warner was in a desperate situation, and the pressure of the crowd had him slowly but surely moving closer and closer to a crush barrier near the front. Despite there clearly being no room, the 'vice-like' compression was moving people forward and into ever more desperate situations: 'There were people screaming for the police to open the gates, and they wouldn't do it. I think they thought we were hooligans. Football fans weren't treated very well in those days, and the only reason I can think that they didn't help at first was because they thought we were hooligans. There were police officers at the top of the fence at the front pushing people back into the crowd. People who were desperately trying to climb out of the crush were pushed back off the fence and back into the terrace. At this stage, the pressure of the crowd had moved me further down the terrace towards a crush barrier, and I can't emphasise enough just how much my height saved me. I am 6 foot 4 inches, and my feet were still off the ground, so rather than my vital organs being forced into that crush barrier it was against the tops of my legs. Anybody smaller than me might have had their stomach or chest crushed against that barrier.'

Steve Hart, having been crushed against the wall outside the turnstiles, was now being crushed in pen three. 'Everyone knew something was wrong. I ended up being moved down to be quite close to the gate at the front, and the voices around were all shouting at the police and asking them to open the gates. That it was chocka in here and they had to do something. The voices were getting louder and it was getting tighter and tighter – this copper next to the gate was taking no notice of us. They were literally ignoring us and we're screaming at him by now because it was unbearable.'

Nick Braley, by pure luck, ended up near the small exit gate at the front of pen three. Having escaped on one of the occasions, he remembers a police officer opening it, and also remembers being approached by a police officer. 'A copper picks me up off my knees and takes me back towards the gate from where I escaped. "No, no, I ain't going back in there … people are dying in there, dying – nick me, I don't care, I ain't going back in there," I scream, and he realises it isn't going to happen. I get taken to a side gate, where I am put into what is a half-full terrace towards the side of the stand. I walk high up and realise I am okay, but faces all around me are scared. That's mental in there, people are going to die in there, I tell those around me, before sitting down and taking some much needed deep breaths.'

As more and more Liverpool fans managed to escape the crush over the tall, overhanging perimeter fence, the Nottingham Forest fans at the far end of the ground had started to notice, as Danny Rhodes recalls: 'The game kicked off and Forest started well, forcing a few early corners and snapping into challenges. Liverpool also forced a corner of their own and Peter Beardsley slammed a shot against the bar. Forest broke clear and took the ball down to the Liverpool end. It was then that I first noticed Liverpool fans climbing over the fences separating the terrace and the pitch, and other fans clambering over the fences that separated the central pens from the sparsely populated wing pens. Fans were being pulled up by other fans to the seated tier above the central pens too. I didn't have time to think why it was happening. It was just something that was happening in front of my eyes. The Forest fans started giving it to the Liverpool end, singing songs, taking the piss because we didn't know what was going on.'

Superintendent Roger Greenwood, now on the perimeter track looking into the terraces, could see that a serious situation was taking place, as he said in his witness statement: 'From ground level I looked at the crowd in the pen (pen 3) behind the goal and I saw quite clearly that supporters were being squashed against the fencing. The area behind the gate was heavily congested, preventing persons from exiting. I should mention that the perimeter fence is not wide enough to allow mass exit of persons being in the order of a normal door's width. The actual terracing is at a lower level than the perimeter track and one has to mount one or more steps so as to exit from the terracing through the gate onto the pitch.'

Around 3.06 p.m., Greenwood radioed control to tell them that the crushing was serious, and that the match would have to be stopped. After waving his arms to the control box to indicate this, he ran onto the pitch to tell match referee, Ray Lewis, to stop the match and to take the players off the field.

BBC's *Grandstand* were broadcasting live from Hillsborough, and so as things started to go wrong, concerned families and friends at home could see the live pictures of fans on the pitch. Margaret Aspinall was at home making a cup of tea when she first heard the word Hillsborough: 'The first thing I knew about what had happened is when we put the television on. My sister-in-law was sitting in the living room while I was making a cup of tea. She said, "There's something going on, Margaret, at Hillsborough." I didn't know where Hillsborough was. I only knew that James had gone to Sheffield Wednesday; I hadn't heard it called Hillsborough before. So I said to my sister-in-law, "What do you mean, where's Hillsborough?" She said, "Isn't it where James is with his dad?" I said, "No, he's at Sheffield Wednesday" and she said, "Margaret, that's Hillsborough." She said she thought it might be a pitch invasion, and I went out of the kitchen into the living room and looked at the television. I could see people being laid down on the pitch and said, "That's not a pitch invasion, Rose, that's definitely not a pitch invasion. People are dying there by the look of it, something's going on." Rose said, "No, no, no they've probably just fainted." The longer we watched the television the more the numbers kept going up. They thought that there might be seven injured, maybe seven dead, and numbers kept going up and up and up. I knew my husband was there, but Jimmy went by car and James went by coach and the reason for that was James's friend would have been on his own on the coach, so James decided to go with his friend rather than leave him on his own. There wouldn't have been room in the car for James and his friend, because five people were already in the car. So Jimmy got to the ground and went into one of the side pens. He'd warned James the night before not to go behind the goal, because Jimmy had been to that game in 1988 and that was James's first away game. So Jimmy said to James the night before, "Don't go behind the goal tomorrow, go on the side." Unfortunately, James and his friend went behind the goal into pen three.'

Brenda Fox was also back on Merseyside, watching the chaos live on television: 'It is very hard to put into words what came next, the match was on television and suddenly the most horrific images were in front of your eyes, and the match was abandoned. There was a phone number to contact for concerned people, and after what we had witnessed, and news flash fatalities at the ground, we were concerned and tried to phone the emergency number but all of Liverpool must have been concerned too as it was constantly engaged.'

At Hillsborough, Liverpool fan Tony Evans decided that he couldn't stay in his seat any longer and went down onto the pitch to see if he could help: 'I went down onto the pitch at this stage. I'd done a little bit of CPR training so I thought I might be able to help. So I went down towards the Leppings Lane end, and when I got there I saw people milling around. There was a line of bizzies just standing there looking on. Just standing there … There were people on the floor and I thought to myself, Jesus Christ, this is no time to be sunbathing. But as I got closer I realised. I went up to this bizzie and said how many? And he sobbed. He just tried to take a deep breath but couldn't, you know? I looked around and thought, I can't help. And I ran away, out of the stadium and back up the hill. It probably took me fifteen years to stop running."

Having been pulled up to safety in the stand above, Ed Critchley and his friend, Carl, had a bird's-eye view of the desperation in the central pens below: 'I remember seeing bodies on the pitch seemingly being revived, and people applauding from the sides, only to see them die straight afterwards. Awful. Carl was crying at this point; he was really upset. They were just awful, awful scenes. Everyone was trying to help which is one of the overriding memories of the day – fans doing everything they could to help.'

Val Yates was in trouble, and fell unconscious as she watched a man die in front of her face, powerless to help: 'I don't remember any of the game to this day. I remember going unconscious in the crush for the first time, the weight of the crush pushing me to the floor. I had already seen one person die by then. He was a big, big lad. His mate was a lot smaller than him and he had his arm hooked under his mates chin trying to hold him up so he could get air into him, and actually trying to push the crowd back with his other while screaming at people to help. I was watching him die literally a foot away from me, powerless to move myself as I was fighting for every breath. I somehow managed to cross my arms to try and get a little extra space for my lungs but they felt like they were going to explode and I knew I was going down. To this day I do not know who he was. I just have pictures of some of the victims who it possibly could be. The man with the moustache. His face has haunted me.'

Mick Bowers was now in agony: 'I progressively got to the barrier. We were shouting to the police at the front to let us out but they ignored our pleas. People at the front were trying to scale the fence but the police were pushing them back. How could they do that? They could see the terror in our faces and hear the pleas for help but they just stood there or pushed supporters back into the pen. I got my whole body behind the barrier but that was a big mistake. The pressure was now grinding my hips into the metal. I was in tremendous pain. To my left was a fence with a gap, which had a gate to the pitch. We were screaming at the police to open the gate but to no avail. I could see the section beyond the fence had lots of room but there was no way of getting to this area due to the fence. The top half of my body was getting pushed over but due to the waist high barrier my legs were stuck. My head was forced into the person in front of me and my arm was trapped behind someone else. I could now only see to my left. There were a few people alongside me who tried to go under the barrier to come up the other side but when they went down they just got buried. The space they created was immediately filled, leaving them no way back. They were now trapped and people were standing on them but no one could help it, as you had no control over your movement. As you breathed in, that space was taken. My arm was trapped around a boy's neck. He was screaming at me to move it but I had no control over it. The only part of my body that could move was my eyes. I thought I was about to die. There was another surge, which pushed me bent double over the barrier. I was in immense pain. The lad on my back was limp and lifeless. I remember another surge and huge cheering, and at this point I think I passed out. I had a hat signed by Kenny Dalglish and I was clutching hold of it. The last thing I remember was letting go of it.'

Steve Warner was being pushed ever closer to a crush barrier and had his legs rammed against it before the barrier, made out of wrought iron, snapped under the pressure of the crowd now crushed into the two central pens behind the goal: 'There were two lads near me, I don't know if they were brothers or mates.

The lad higher up the terrace had hold of the other lad by the hand and he was holding on for dear life to try and stop his mate lower down being swallowed by the crowd. It was like he was stuck in quicksand, slowly sinking. He was slowly but surely losing his grip on his mate's hand, though, and then he lost it completely and his mate was gone. The guy who lost his grip was just hysterical as he watched his mate disappear under the crowd and he could do nothing to stop it. When the gate at the back was opened, I could feel the pressure worsen – the crush multiplied. Even though I couldn't see it happen, I could feel when the exit gate at the back had been opened by the increased intensity of the crush. I was about two crush barriers away from the front, and bent over, in midair, with the pressure of the crowd crushing my legs against the crush barrier.'

Peter Dalling tried to move himself backwards towards the wall of the West Stand. The wall led up to the West Stand above, and its width was broken only by the mouth of the tunnel. He was in pen four, which is the central pen to the right as you look at the terraces from the pitch. His thinking was that, if there was a wall behind him, at least he wouldn't get hurt. He was near the lateral fence on the outside edge of pen four, and on the other side was a thin, sterile area, often used to segregate supporters. At the very back of the lateral fence was a small gate, but it was locked: 'At this time, a copper came up the walkway and people were screaming at him to get the gate open, but he didn't have a key.' The only two gates that allowed sideways movement were at the very back corner of pen four, which led into a sterile area, and the very back of pen three, which led into pen two. Peter Dalling was at the back of pen four, and the gate was locked.

Before the match even kicked off, the central pens were already dangerously overcrowded, and fans were screaming at the police to open the gates at the front to relieve the pressure. Fans in the central pens recall that people were already dead at this stage, and the pressure from the steady flow of people coming down the tunnel, from the open exit gate at the back, was increasing the vice-like grip in the pens by the second. Every time somebody struggling in the pens managed to move into an inch of space, the inch of space they had just left was filled by another body as the flow of people from the tunnel was constant. People were being pushed into metal barriers. Pushed against the perimeter fence at the front. Pushed into the lateral fences. Pushed into each other.

Towards the front of pen three, a crush barrier snapped. One unnamed Liverpool supporter describes that moment, in his witness statement, which is available on the HIP website: 'My hips were against the barrier, my hands were pinned against my chest. Initially I had been able to move my arms and I had tried to push against the barrier to relieve the pressure on my hips. The crush continued to intensify and got worse and worse. As the crush worsened my movements became more restricted until I couldn't move my arms at all and I can't remember if my feet were on the ground. I think they were. The pain in my hips was so bad that it was hard to concentrate on anything else. People all around me were shouting at the police to open the gates. I remember seeing a policeman opening the gate on the left, which was in pen 4. I wasn't even aware that there was a centre fence separating pens 3 and 4. The policeman let one child out through the gate before he shut it again. There was a constant increase in pressure against my hips and it got so bad that I really thought my hips would break under the pressure. After this point everything seemed to happen in slow motion. The barrier in front of me broke. It seemed to snap under the pressure. I could hear the sound of metal twisting, it was really loud, it was like the sound of a ship leaving dock. As the barrier broke, the main part twisted away to the front and to the left. There was a small stub on the right which stayed in place. I was twisted against the broken stub by the force of the people around me and I was pushed across it. The lower part of my abdomen seemed to run across the stub and I felt it cut into me. I was totally pinned down and unable to move. My arm was pinned across my mouth and my neck and I couldn't breathe. I really thought I was going to die.'

Barrier 124A was at the front left-hand corner of pen three as you looked at the terraces from the pitch. The Health & Safety Executive examined the barrier two days after the disaster and found that, 'A relatively large amount of metal had been lost by corrosion' and that the barrier was 'approximately sixty years old'. The old, rusting barrier had been placed under constant pressure from the extreme overcrowding that had been allowed to build, and at around the time that Liverpool's Peter Beardsley hit the crossbar at the other end of the ground, the pressure became too much. That was around 3.04 p.m. When the crush barrier snapped, people had been pushed hard against it, and they fell forwards with those behind following. A wave of humanity fell forward, one on top of the other, and a pile of bodies formed immediately. Steve Warner had his legs pinned against the barrier when it broke: 'I was still fighting for my life here, and then the crush barrier that my legs were pinned against snapped. A steel bar just snapped under the pressure of the crowd. The people who had been pushed into the crush barrier all fell forward now that it was no longer holding the pressure, and there were piles and piles of bodies in front and underneath me. I saw the opportunity to live. Had I not been 6 foot 4 inches, I wouldn't be here today, I can't emphasise that enough. As the crowd fell forwards after the crush barrier snapped, I managed to raise myself above the falling bodies, and reached out with my arm and managed to grab a hold of the fence. My other arm and the lower half of my body was still pinned in the crush and I couldn't move my legs at all, but I managed to reach the fence with one hand and grip a hold of it for dear life. I saw my opportunity to live and I took it, but sadly that meant my feet were now on top of the bodies on the floor in front of me. There was nothing I could do for them. I was hanging onto that fence for dear life, and somehow I found the strength to stop the crowd taking me down over that buckled crush barrier with them. I'll never be able to fully describe the guilt I feel that I trampled over dead bodies to get myself out. That will stay with me until the day I die.'

Mick Bower's last memory before becoming unconscious was his hand letting go of one of his prized possessions. As he regained consciousness, he remembers being on the pitch: 'The next thing I remember was coming round in the 18-yard box and Bruce Grobbelaar was looking over his shoulder with a look of horror on his face. How I got on the pitch I do not know, but I was one of the first. I was in the 18-yard box and Bruce Grobbelaar was just a few yards away. As I came round I tried to get to my feet, but was very unsteady. There were other fans around me, but not that many. Everyone appeared in a state of urgency. A young police officer came to me and tried to push me back into the crowd. Another joined him, stating, "He's drunk." They had their hand on my head pushing me back. He said, "Piss off back to where you come from. If you've walked this far you can walk back." I was eighteen years old and not into drinking. I had not touched a drop of alcohol. It was a total assumption on behalf of the police officers.'

Damian Kavanagh explains it was a scary time for those fans just a few feet from the police officers on the track: 'All the time the police were very visibly there, and people were shouting at them, open the gates, open the gates. I remember that very much being the case. You can imagine that at a time like this in that crowd you're getting crushed and your head is being forced forward through the sheer weight at times, but there was one clarion moment that told me we were in a lot of trouble. I made eye contact with a police officer on the other side of the fence at the front of the terrace. It felt like I was no more than 6 feet away from him at the time, and he looked right at me through the fence, and I mouthed to him while staring straight at him to open the gates. He looked straight back into my eyes at me and pointed back towards the tunnel and mouthed to me to get back. Nobody could move an inch now, and he told us to get back. I already knew that we were in a lot of danger by now, but at that point I thought this fella either didn't care or couldn't grasp what was very clearly happening in front of his eyes, and that man there with that uniform on was not going to help me get out of this, so I had to think of something else.'

Val Yates, having fallen down under the crowd, unconscious, remembers being pulled up: 'My next memory is of being dragged up by my hair. Someone hauled me up to my feet by my hair. I was like a rag doll. My eyes opened only briefly and then closed again. When I woke up again, I was trapped right at the end of a crash barrier. My left arm was on the corner, my elbow digging into my ribs. A lad had got his shirt hooked on the end of it and it was choking him. He asked me to help him unhook his shirt. I tried but I could not move and I was telling him to rip it – a white T-shirt.

There was a man nearby and he was the wrong way round over this barrier. My eyes closed again.'

Having scarcely believed that an officer on the other side of the fence had mouthed and pointed to Damian to 'get back', his mind turned to his parents: 'The other thing that went through my head at that time was that I hope my mum hadn't heard about this. I knew my dad would be listening to the radio at home, and I'd seen people being dragged out and pushed back in by the police. The game had stopped by now, and I was mindful that this would have been reported on the radio. My mum was such a fretter that I was hoping my dad hadn't said too much. The other thing was, "Oh God, please get me out." Is God going to let me get out of this? People started to crawl over our heads to try and get to the fence at the front. There was a gate in the front fence that led from the terraces to the pitch, and it sprang open under the pressure of the crowd and the police forced it shut it again. I couldn't believe it. I was incredulous. It was clear that we were in a lot of distress and that people were dying.'

PC Illingworth was on duty on the other side of the perimeter fence to the fans in the central pens. In his witness statement, it is unclear at what time he reacted to the crushing in front of him. He states that he had gone for a meal break and returned to the outside of the Leppings Lane perimeter fences at about 2.45–2.50 p.m. 'We were served and I returned to the track around 2.45–2.50 p.m. PC Smith went to the toilet and I walked on to the Leppings Lane End where I found PC 700 Helliwell was standing behind the goal. I saw the centre pen (CN & CS) was very full but the two outer pens were only about half full. This surprised me as I'd never seen the fans so badly distributed. At first there didn't appear to be a serious problem, the fans were swaying back and forth and some were climbing from the pen marked N on the map into the stand above. This is a common occurrence at large matches. The swaying and pushing became much worse at the extent that the females were screaming and fans were beginning to panic. I put over a radio message to the effect, "There is a serious crush down here, it is serious." I don't know if it was received or not as I was unable to hear my radio due to the noise. At this time I was near gate 4 and it was obvious that people against the fence were in serious trouble. There was only PC Smith and me at this section and I think he was near to gate 3. I opened gate 4 and assisted the first injured man who I saw onto the track.'

Damian Kavanagh decided that he had to go forwards: 'Me and my mate made a decision that if we wanted to get out we'd have to follow these people over the top of the crowd. I always had my hands up in front of my chest in a crowd, which was a bit of luck on my part, because my hands weren't pinned to my side. I don't know how he did it, because I didn't think it was possible, but my mate was slowly pushing himself upwards off the crowd and inch by inch levering himself against the crowd to get himself in the air. He got one of his feet up near my hand, and I put my hand out to help him up and he was suddenly on top of the crowd. He made his way towards the front by balancing on top of the crowd on his hands and knees. I knew what I had to do now if I wanted to survive this, so I very slowly started to edge myself up bit by bit. A fella that was next to me said, "'ere are mate," and he grabbed my foot, and he helped me push myself up on top of the crowd. It was a really weird experience. I had no leverage up there, but I tried to crawl to the front. As I made my way forward, there was a fella that shouted "there's people dying here!" I didn't say anything to him, but I already knew. As I got to the front there was a small gate and a policeman in front of me. I remember exactly what he looked like. He had a completely bald head, which was unusual for that time. I grabbed hold of the top of the gate and this copper grabbed hold of me by the lapels and pushed me to go back into the crowd. I thought no chance! If I am going to get in trouble I'll do it out there. I couldn't believe that this fella wanted to push me back, and the swear words he called me. Quite clearly, everyone's life is in danger here. I wasn't the first on the pitch by any stretch of the imagination, and there were people dying behind me, yet he wanted to push me back in! I managed to get past him and he sort of threw me down on the pitch side. To give this copper his due, I later found out that he helped a lot of people individually later that day. The inquiry had reports about this guy who helped to save their lives. So I don't know if it dawned on him later that his reaction to the situation was wrong. I don't know, but I found it incredible that he wanted to push me back in.'

Val Yates was in and out of consciousness. The pressure of the crowd, and the lack of oxygen, was proving too much to bear: 'The next time I woke up, I was upright but in a different place in the pen, right by the fence. I was the wrong way round and a man's arm was across my throat. My feet were not even touching the floor and the weight of the crush was keeping this arm across my throat. I could not breathe and it felt like my eyeballs were bulging out my sockets. I was pleading with this man to move his arm, tears streaming down my face. Then I saw him. His tongue was lolled out of his mouth and he had vomit and dribble coming out. He was surely dead and I was hanging off his arm. I gave up at that point. I resigned myself to the fact that I was going to die and I was so calm and, strangely enough, I was not scared. I just let the last of the air out my body and closed my eyes. I suppose you can describe it as a near-death experience. I was moving down this tunnel-like thing, it was grey and it had yellow criss-cross almost like whale bone has hoops in it, like arches. I was not walking or floating, I was just moving down this tunnel and there was music. I could hear music. It was a bit like when someone puts a seashell to your ear. One minute I could hear, and the next I couldn't. I could hear a man screaming that there was a girl. He was screaming there was a girl dying and they had to take the girl. I didn't realise the girl he was screaming for help for was me. Next minute, I could feel warm air on my face but I knew I was not breathing. I also knew I was not going down the tunnel anymore. I woke up on the pitch flat on my back, arms outstretched, desperately trying to suck air into my lungs. Gasping. I couldn't move. I couldn't speak. I was just gasping for air and could not get it in quick enough.'

Having escaped the crush, a barely conscious Mick Bowers staggered onto the pitch: 'I fell to the floor and two different police officers came over to me and shouted to an ambulance man with a stretcher. It was a proper stretcher on wheels. They put me on the stretcher and took me to an area under the North Stand. I was placed on the floor with two blankets over me. I remained with some St John's ambulance cadets. I was among a few people at first, but the area filled up very quickly. I was falling asleep briefly then coming round. I lay there for thirty to forty-five minutes. To my left there was a supporter lying down – he had injured his ribs – and to my right a supporter was sat on a chair with stomach pains. While laying there, a police officer with pips on his shoulders came between me and the lad on my left, who was crying. He put his arms around us and he told us everything would be okay, and then went off to help others. I remember seeing a lad come round to us. His arm was totally disfigured. It was like it had been moulded around the crush barrier. I was then taken via ambulance to the Royal Hallamshire hospital.'

At the opposite Kop end of the ground, Nottingham Forest fans initially thought that the activity at the Leppings Lane end was misbehaviour. Nottingham Forest fan Danny Rhodes remembers how events escalated: 'The number of Liverpool fans on the pitch grew. The game was stopped and the players trudged off. I saw people being laid down on the pitch. Two, three, ten … just lying there. Gradually, the pitch filled with injured fans and fans trying to help the injured. Even then, I don't think people in our end truly understood what was happening. Fans were being treated at our end of the ground by this point. There was only one ambulance at the Leppings Lane end (as far as I recall) but there seemed to be a few overwhelmed stewards and possibly St John's Ambulance staff trying to deal with increasing numbers of injured fans at our end. Then things completely changed. There was this bloke lying on the grass by the Forest goal and the guys around him covered his face with a jacket. That's when it really hit me. People were dying. By this time the singing had stopped, and the Forest end was hushed. People were staring ahead, unable to comprehend the enormity of the horror unfolding in front of our eyes. At a football match, for God's sake. Others were arguing amongst themselves, as if that was all they could think to do. I don't even know what they were arguing about. They were just arguing. Liverpool fans were ferrying the dead and injured on advertising hoardings, which had been ripped down to make temporary stretchers, running the length of the pitch from the Leppings Lane to the Kop where the Forest fans were.'

Peter Dalling, having escaped the crush, was now looking to help others, which was typical of the Liverpool supporters' attitude that day: 'I said to Norman then that we couldn't just stand around and that we needed to help, so we went down through the pen and onto the pitch. I climbed up onto the fence at the front and started to pull people up over the fence – I don't know how long that went on for, but it was a good while.'

Steve Hart had managed to get out of the gate at the front of pen three, and he was now on the pitch looking back at the central pens: 'I stood up and looked back at the pens, and I couldn't believe what I was seeing. People being dragged up at the back into the stands, there were people screaming everywhere. You could see that something was desperately wrong. I remembered jumping up onto the fence and trying to pull people up but I just couldn't do it. I just couldn't get them over; I couldn't lift anyone up over the fence.'

Damian had got out. He had climbed over the heads of those in front, and been challenged by a police officer as he tried to escape the pen when he got to the perimeter fence, but now he was out of that hell and to this day he is thankful that he didn't look back: 'I'm glad to say that I didn't look too closely at the central pens, because I'd have had a few more pictures in my head now. I remember kneeling down on the pitch and I started to cry. Two things stick in my mind about that. Firstly, it must have only been for a second or so, because I snapped myself out of it. The second thing was that when I got up the knees on my jeans were wet. It had been a beautiful sunny day [no rain] and so it occurred to me that they must have watered the pitch to help the slick, passing football that Liverpool and Nottingham Forest were famous for at the time. It's funny what goes through your mind at a time like that. At this point, you do what anyone else would do, and so I got stuck in and tried to help. I walked back towards the goal, and there was a fella unconscious on his back with people over him trying to give him mouth to mouth. I'd seen people rip the advertising hoardings down to use as stretchers, and I'd seen them taking casualties to the other end of the pitch, where presumably the medical people would administer the treatment these people needed. I remember shouting, "Come on, let's get this lad on a board." This fella was over him, a bit older than me, and he just very calmly turned around to me and said let's get him breathing first. He was obviously in control of that situation, and I didn't really have a clue about what to do about anything. So I ripped an advertising board off the side, and I got a little cut on one of my fingers, and I thought that was the only physical injury I got that day, although a few days later my mum saw a bruise on my back, which was in the shape of a hand. Nobody whacked me. It was obviously the pressure of someone leaning into me when I was in the crush.'

John Joynt, having been pulled up into the West Stand above, was now looking for his mate: 'My first thought then was to try and find my mate Steve. He'd actually been taken out onto the pitch and passed out. I was looking for him for about twenty minutes. I went back to the other end of the stand and eventually spotted him on the pitch. The side pens were virtually empty, so I said to him come through here Steve and I'll lift you up. I'll never forget the look of horror in his face, as if to say, "I'm not going back in there." I said again, look this pen is virtually empty, and eventually he came through and we lifted him up. You could see people getting over the fence. You could see Liverpool fans with the hoardings, taking people up the pitch. By this time, a load of police officers were up on the front fence and shouting for people to get back, but it was impossible to move in there. The Liverpool fans were the ones that were offering the majority of the assistance. There were people trying to give mouth to mouth, certainly some of them with no experience. I know it made me go and take a first aid course as soon as I could after, because I wouldn't have known what to do in that situation.'

Eileen McBride had identified herself to a policeman and offered nursing assistance. She remembers getting onto the pitch: 'In the end, this policeman walked us out and around the ground, and back into the ground at the Notts Forest end, and onto the pitch. I hadn't gone 50 yards up the pitch before I came across a young lady lying on the floor, unconscious, and her friends were standing around her and they didn't know what to do, so I stopped. It's then that I realised that I had nothing with me in terms of equipment. I didn't have anything to put in her mouth to make sure her tongue was depressed so she wouldn't choke. In the end I had to wipe down a comb, and use that to make sure her tongue was away from her airway. I always regret doing that. As a nurse it's awful to use a comb, but it's all we had so we had to use it. We put her in the recovery position, and it turned out that she was breathing and I thought she'd be OK. At this time there were two ambulance men on the pitch and I told them that they had to put this young lady in the next ambulance, because she was having breathing difficulties and needed a mask with oxygen and medical attention. Next, there was this young boy lying on the pitch and he had obviously had a neck injury, because he was saying that he couldn't feel anything from the neck down. His mates were all around him, trying to make him laugh to keep his spirits up. There was me and this doctor with him, but we didn't have a neck brace or anything, so we got some sandbags and we used them either side of his lad's neck to make sure he didn't move. The doctor said that he needed to get his sweater off, because he couldn't examine him like he was. We couldn't find any scissors, so I went outside and asked someone where the first aid room was. I was told that it was three quarters of the way around the ground. When I asked if it was open, she said, "I don't know, we don't always open it on matchdays." So I told her that she needed to find out now, and get me a pair of scissors. After a lot of fuss, they couldn't find a simple pair of scissors. The copper told me he had a penknife but it wasn't very good, though it might help. So I started to saw down this boy's sweater with the knife, and I remember this boy saying that his mum bought this sweater and she hasn't long bought it. "She's gonna kill me when I get home!" The ridiculousness of that statement now hits you, with the enormity of what was going on all around, and he was worried about his sweater. His mates were telling him that his mum won't care as long as he comes home safe. Anyway, the knife couldn't cut through his sweater ... we had him stretchered to the Forest end and asked that he was made a priority for the next ambulance.'

The desperation around the stadium was palpable. Richie Greaves remembers a heart-breaking moment when the crowd, desperately looking on, thought that a young boy had been saved:

'After the game was stopped, we saw a very young lad lying there on the edge of the penalty area in front of the South Stand. He was having heart massage and the next minute he was sick, and it looked as if he was breathing again, and everyone cheered. Those watching from the South Stand cheered, and then the next minute he was gone again. Just a little lad. There were lads ripping the advertising hoardings off the wall in front of the South Stand, so we went and helped with that. We put a lad on the advertising hoarding and there were people shouting, "Get them down the other end and the first aiders will sort them out." There were about eight of us carrying him, and we starting running towards the other end. This lad's face was covered in sick, and his skin was a terrible colour. I don't know if he was alive or dead. We were just trying to get him down to the other end and that haunted me for ages. That he could have still been alive and we left him there on the edge of the penalty area at the Kop end.'

Sat in his seat in the North Stand, Barry Devonside was desperately trying to spot his son, Christopher. The time ticked on and the situation seemed to get ever more serious: 'As it got to ten past three, it was obvious that there was a very, very serious problem. There was a fella next to me with a portable radio and I remember him saying there were nine dead, then it went to ten, eleven … and you couldn't comprehend what was being said on the radio and how it corresponded with what you were seeing in front of you.'

Grant Walker remembers the sense of panic when he realised he had no idea where his brother was: 'A bit later, when many people had managed to get out of the terrace, you could see the railing was all twisted, and you couldn't believe that human pressure could do that. There were supporters all over the pitch, some just lying there and others trying to help the injured and the dying. I then realised that I couldn't see my brother. A mate of mine who we'd come to the match with was down in the terrace and he shouted up to ask where my brother was. I got the lads to lift me back down into it all, which was horrendous. I literally had to climb over hordes of people just lying there to get to the pitch. On the pitch I was running around trying to find our kid, and was lifting coats off people's faces to check if it was my brother.

The guilt of being content that the poor soul lying there wasn't your brother was horrendous as well. I was walking around in a daze, desperately trying to spot my brother. There were people attending to the bodies, people ripping advertising hoardings off the wall to use as stretchers ... it was just horrendous, like something out of a disaster movie.'

Val Yates was lying on the pitch, after a horrifying ordeal in the pens: 'I wandered round in a daze, trying to work out where the players were and why I was on the pitch. I looked at the clock and thought, "Oh, it's half-time, that's alright then," and carried on staggering around in a daze. I could just see carnage on the pitch and hear chants of "shitty ground, shitty ground, shitty ground" ringing out, but could not take it in. I started to stagger towards what I thought in my confusion was the way out near the Forest end. I could see a line of police and went towards it. I kept stumbling; I was so tired, so weak. I just wanted to sink to the floor and sleep. My chest hurt so much. I told myself to keep walking. I must not go down again. I might not get up. The police stood in a line across the middle of the pitch. As I got nearer to it, even though I tried not to, I collapsed in front of it. At that time, I didn't know or care if I would ever move again. I just lay there face down on the pitch, semi-conscious. I was thinking they must be able to see me, someone just help me. Surely one of them would? I was taught when I was brought up to respect the law and if ever I was in trouble, a policeman would help me. They had not done so, so far. Eventually, one came. He put his hand on my shoulder. I opened my eyes. He said something, but I can't remember what. He probably asked me if I was ok. I told him to leave me alone and go to the pens. Eventually I got up again and carried on making my way to the Forest end. Behind me, all I could hear were the screams of the dying.'

Tony O'Keefe went down from his seat in the West Stand to see if he could help: 'Obviously, I was a trained first-aider. I had only been in the fire brigade about three years but I was confident enough to identify myself. I carry my ID with me wherever I go. It took a long time to make my way down; it seemed like forever to get to the downstairs area. I identified myself to a policeman and I actually walked through one of the pens to get to the pitch.

The players were off the pitch by then, and I can't remember the actual time. I came across an ambulance, and was given a first aid band. I automatically thought, right, let's see what I can do, and I started to run around, pretty helpless at first, wondering which way to go. Coming across groups of friends, or they could have been brothers, I attempted two or three times to do mouth-to-mouth on some people. This one lad in particular ... it's hard to say this, but I was trying to give mouth to mouth and I got stomach contents come back up. I knew in that case it was probably too late. I came across a firefighter and I identified myself to him. He had an oxygen cylinder that we used to use; it was a type of resuscitator that would pump oxygen in at a certain rate. I said to him that I could use that. I asked him where all the others were, and he said words to the effect that there were loads outside but they were asked to hold back because there was some sort of disturbance.'

Dr Glyn Philips also identified himself to police officers in the hope that he could help the injured and the dying on the pitch: 'So I made my way down to the front where there was a gate in the fence, on top of a low wall. I shouted to a policeman, "I'm a doctor. Let me on the pitch." I put my hand out to him and he pulled me up the wall, but we didn't realise there was a cross bar in the gateway. As I leapt up, I cracked my head on this bar. It nearly knocked me out. I was seeing stars. A hell of a blow, causing a scalp laceration. Blood was streaming down my face. I shook the blow off and walked onto the pitch, which was full of people milling around. Chaos, chaos. I'm thinking what to do and literally the first body I came to was this young lad, a teenager. He wasn't breathing: no pulse, ashen, grey, clinically a cardiac arrest, and I knelt beside him and started doing CPR (cardio-pulmonary resuscitation). There was a guy next to me – he said he was a male nurse – so while I did mouth-to-mouth, he did chest compressions. As we worked away, I was aware of a lot of people suffering in the pens. I thought if this lad is this bad and he's on the pitch, then the ones still in the pens have no chance. I thought, I've got to give him a decent chance, so I stayed with him. I asked some policemen for oxygen and an oxygen cylinder arrived. This is a big bone of contention in the statement I made afterwards and the subsequent inquiry into the disaster. To my best knowledge, the oxygen cylinder was empty. The gauge was reading empty. But this was part of the inquiry when at least one QC wanted to discredit my evidence. It was eventually deemed that, on the balance of probabilities, I was wrong because I admitted I was angry and I'd had a heavy blow to the head. Anyway, we carried on working on the boy, as he didn't have a pulse. We must've been there five to ten minutes and I was on the point of giving up when I felt a femoral pulse. He had developed a healthy, bounding pulse. Against the odds, his heart had spontaneously started again. He was completely unconscious, but he started making some efforts at breathing. So we got a stretcher and carried him into an ambulance behind the goal. There were two others on the floor inside but they were dead. We put the lad on his side in the recovery position and I decided there wasn't a lot more I could do. I don't know if that was the correct decision, if I should've stayed with him, but his heart was going, he was breathing. I remember saying to the ambulance man, "Keep an eye on him. If there are any problems, give me a shout." The daftest thing to say, with all this chaos going on, but you didn't think that at the time. As we had carried the lad to the ambulance, I'd been aware of eight to ten bodies in the goal area. Inside, you're struck with this desire to be professional and do what you can, but at the same time I was incredulous this has happened in the space of half an hour, at a semi-final, on a sunny day. There are all these young lads lying dead.'

Chief Superintendent David Duckenfield was in overall command of the policing that day, despite limited experience of policing football matches at the stadium, and having only been promoted to that position a few weeks earlier. Chief Superintendent Brian Mole had been in charge for the semi-finals held at Hillsborough in 1987 and 1988, and the policing outside the ground in 1989 was as different as the match commander. There were no police cordons in 1989, which fans remember from the previous two years, and had the effect of slowing down the arrival of fans into the cramped concourse area outside the turnstiles. The failure to manage the arrival of fans into that small area had led to a crush outside the ground and as that crush worsened and became a risk to fans, Duckenfield gave the order to open the exit gate to relieve the crush outside. As he stood in the police control box, overlooking the Leppings Lane terraces, he gave the order to open an exit gate that allowed over 2,000 additional fans to enter, and it didn't seem to occur to him that, with all fans entering at that end of the ground, the tunnel would be the obvious route for most fans if not directed away. In 1987 and 1988, fans remember the police closing access to the tunnel once it was estimated that the central pens had reached their capacity, but on 15 April 1989, no such measure was taken. As officers' own witness statements had mentioned, the central pens were far, far more populated than the wing pens. PC Illingworth, on duty pitch-side, and in front of the perimeter fence, was moved to say, 'I saw the centre pen (CN & CS) was very full but the two outer pens were only about half full. This surprised me as I'd never seen the fans so badly distributed.' PC Jim Warpole also recognised the uneven distribution of fans, as he said in his witness statement: 'At 2.55 p.m., the central pen for standing at the Leppings Lane end seemed to be absolutely packed solid, while the pen towards the police control box [one and two] was about half full and the pen towards the north stand [five and six] was only one sixth full.' Around 3.15 p.m., as Duckenfield stood in the police control box overlooking the Leppings Lane terraces, watching Liverpool fans carry the dead and injured towards the other end of the ground, Graham Kelly and Glen Kirton from the Football Association visited the control box to find out what had happened. He told them what Lord Justice Taylor was later to label 'a disgraceful lie', which set in place media reports around the world.

Graham Kelly recalls that moment in his witness statement: 'After about fifteen minutes, I went to the police control box with Graham Mackrell and Glen Kirton, which is situated between the South Stand and the West Stand and affords a good view of the terraces in question, looking directly along the goal-line from the corner of the stadium. Closed circuit television cameras placed at various places around the ground scan the terraces and areas just outside the grounds. The police in the control box were apparently under the impression that a gate or gates had been forced. They told me so and showed me a picture which purported to represent this. They said that the match would have to be abandoned because there had been fatalities. They did not know how many. The Police Commander was present in the control box, together with the Assistant Chief Constable, Mr Jackson. The Police Commander was Chief Superintendent David Duckenfield. We were told that when the gate had been forced there had been an in-rush of Liverpool supporters.'

Glen Kirton has a similar recollection in his witness statement: 'It was at about 3.15 p.m. that it became apparent to us for the first time that there might well be fatalities. Graham Kelly and I then went immediately with Graham Mackrell to the police control room and spoke to the officer in charge, Chief Superintendent David Duckenfield. Chief Superintendent Duckenfield told us that a gate had been forced and there had been an in-rush of Liverpool supporters that had caused casualties. He pointed to one of the TV monitors to show the gate.'

Graham Kelly was interviewed soon after by the media, and in good faith he told that story, which within minutes was flashed around the world. The rescue effort was still in full swing in front of Duckenfield's eyes. Duckenfield later admitted to this falsehood, but the mud had already been thrown and some of it stuck.

We may never know what was racing through the Match Commander's mind as he stood transfixed, watching his junior officers desperately trying to free people from the crush, while Liverpool supporters, many of whom had only just escaped the crush themselves, were heroically trying to save lives. Was he scared for his job? Was he horrified at the scale of the disaster unfolding? To blame the disaster that was still unfolding on the Liverpool fans, when it was he who had given the order to open the gate, was unforgivable to most people. Lord Justice Taylor's assertion that it was a 'disgraceful lie' doesn't seem to do it justice in many ways.

After being crushed against the barrier that snapped, Steve Warner finally managed to get out onto the pitch: 'Eventually, I managed to pull myself free, climb the fence and clamber head first over the fence at the front. I had lost my trainers and my trousers were half off but I didn't care in the slightest, as I had got out what I can only describe as hell. And it was hell. From the moment I was swept down that tunnel to the moment I managed to get out of that pen, I don't think my feet touched the ground once. When I got onto the pitch the scenes were pure chaos. There were people everywhere, and I would say that the police had lost control, but I can't, because to lose control you would have to have had control in the first place and they didn't. I was walking around on the pitch in a daze. I didn't know what to do. I felt like I'd been battered by Mike Tyson. It was pure chaos. I asked a few people if they were OK and whatever, and saw fans ferrying the dead and the injured on advertising hoardings. The fans seemed to be more organised than the authorities. To be fair I don't blame the foot soldiers in the police because they had their orders, and many tried to help eventually. It's the management that I blame.'

Damian Kavanagh had ripped down an advertising hoarding to use as a makeshift stretcher, and went in search of somebody who needed help: 'I grabbed that advertising board and went looking for someone who needed help. The board was dead flimsy. I saw someone on the pitch spread out, and I could describe him. He was out of it, and in my heart I knew he was dead at the time, but you also hear of things when you're watching the telly about people surviving, and what-have-you, so you don't give up. As I put the board down, there was a young lad there, and a policeman nearby. It was a split second in slow motion that seemed to last forever, and I was thinking, well, who's going to drag him onto the board then? And between me, the young lad, and the policeman it was me. So I just basically got down on the floor and got my arms around him and dragged him onto the board. His trousers came down to show his underpants. It was unimportant, of course, but it's funny what sticks in your mind. So we got this lad up and started to ferry him towards the other end of the pitch where the Nottingham Forest fans were. There was chaos in front of the Liverpool goal, and people that needed help and needed taking away from that chaos so we headed up the pitch, sort of following where other people had been taken. We thought hopefully that is where the medical staff will sort them out. There was a severe lack of any direction from police or medical staff, so we just assumed that was the best thing to do.'

Steve Hart, having escaped a terrifying crush both outside and inside the ground, remembers carrying a lad to the other end of the pitch: 'I remember seeing that the advertising hoardings were being taken down, so I shot over there and helped them with that for a bit. I looked around and saw this lad on his own, just lying there. He was just a kid, so I shouted for somebody to give me a hand, and the next thing I know we've put him on a board and we're running across the pitch with him. As we were running across the pitch, we came across a line of police standing there, and I remember screaming at them because they were just doing nothing. They let us through because we had the lad on the board, but to be honest we weren't stopping anyway – we were running full tilt. We got down to the other end of the pitch to the north-east corner, where the Forest fans were, and we put the lad down next to this copper. I remember vividly saying to this copper that this kid needs help, and his exact words to me were, "F*** off back down the other end of the ground." And we did. That's the hardest bit, because I'll never forgive myself for leaving that kid there. Nothing anyone can ever say will change that because I should have stayed with him. I had kids of my own. If somebody had told me they had left one of my kids there, would I have thought that they had done their best? I honestly don't know. It eats me up.'

One of the other fans who helped carry that advertising hoarding with Steve was Tony O'Keefe, who was a stranger to Steve on the day, yet they came together to carry who they later learned was Kevin Williams across the pitch. Tony recalls the officer telling them to leave and recalls carrying Kevin Williams: 'I started noticing that people were taking the injured across the pitch. I saw one group in particular carrying a young lad, who I now know to be Kevin Williams, and I remember when we put him down at the other end of the pitch. I thought, he's in a good place here. There are obviously medical people around and we thought he'd get help there. I looked down at him and his chest was pushed in like a lot of the others, but he had colour and he seemed like he was still there or thereabouts. This was just before 4 p.m. A lady, some kind of medical person, came and took over from us. In my opinion, he was still alive when the lady started to look after him.'

Steve Hart and Tony O'Keefe did as the officer told them, and made their way back down to the Leppings Lane end of the ground. Steve Hart recalls the scene: 'We went back down the other end and there was a lad in the goalmouth, he was sitting leaning against the goalpost. He'd done something to his leg, I don't know if it was broken, but I was trying to pacify him because he was a bit upset. It was horrendous, it was like a war zone. Grown men crying – trying to talk to someone and they didn't know you were there, just walking around in a daze. Somebody put a hand on my shoulder, and it was one of my mates who were in the stand. They took me in there and I remember getting upset and telling them that it was really bad. In those days, people used to carry little radios to the match, especially that day, because Everton were playing in the other semi-final. I was standing there, and it was coming over the radio that the fans had put the gate in. I knew that didn't happen, because I had seen the police open it with my own eyes, so I wanted to take my mates around to the gate to show them. Had the gate been put in, there would be foot marks all over it, there would be dents and what-have-you and there was none of that. I was dead upset.'

Peter Dalling had also seen the police open the exit gate, and was furious when he started to hear the stories that were being told on the radio: 'When I heard them say we charged the gates I was fuming, because I knew we didn't. I saw the gate being opened, and when we got to the gate there were stewards and coppers inside. There was no damage to the gates. Had they been kicked in, they would have been damaged, and the coppers would have made a point of leaving them like that, because it would have backed up their argument. We know now, of course, that it was opened on the orders of Duckenfield.'

Back on Merseyside, Margaret Aspinall was getting increasingly worried. Emergency numbers were being displayed on the television, but with so many families and friends trying to call at the same time, getting through to an operator was proving very difficult: 'They were giving emergency numbers on the television but I couldn't get through. At that time, I had heard that there were maybe thirteen deaths. So you start panicking; you just want to know that your child is all right and that your husband's all right. Eventually, we got through to the emergency number, and gave a description. I told them that James would have a bus pass on him as well – I knew he'd have that on him. They said that at that time they didn't have any details, but when they did they'd get back in touch.'

Having had a near-death experience, Peter Carney remembers slowly regaining consciousness and the sensations along the way: 'The next thing I remember was a sensation of thumping on my chest. I don't know if that is somebody was giving me heart massage, but what I think is going on is that people have lifted me above their heads and they are passing me back towards the tunnel, and I think the sensation I can feel is pairs of hands into my chest as they are passing me from person to person. Then I remember feeling stretched, as if my arms and legs were being pulled from different angles and the sound was all like a confused echo. I couldn't see anything at this time, and it was all black. I've since rationalised that as people carrying me by my arms and legs back out of the tunnel. When I woke up, I think I was in the recovery position because I was on my side, and I saw a big lad next to me with a denim jacket over his head who was obviously dead. My first conscious thought was, "I'm here – I'm alive!" My mate had come out by this point and he was shaking me by the shoulder, and he said that my first words were, "Don't touch me because I'm hurting all over," and I was. I was battered and bruised. That's when the recovery started, and they moved me from there to the wall at the back of the Leppings Lane. I couldn't feel any sensation in my legs at first, which is funny because I had previously had the sensation before regaining consciousness of being stretched by my arms and legs.'

Eileen McBride, the off-duty nurse who had been trying to help people on the pitch, went to the gym: 'I walked from the pitch back to where the gym was. As I got to the door where the gym was, there was a young boy on an advertising hoarding, and I mean a young boy. I remember his face so clearly, he had a little strip of freckles across his nose and he was so young. He was breathing but barely conscious, and I wondered why he had been left there. He seemed to be on his own outside the gym. There was an ambulance nearby, so I went and asked him what was happening with him and they said they were waiting and I said no, he's got to go now, he's unconscious! Anyway, they came and looked at him for a bit and I just stayed with this boy. He was like a little angel, gorgeous little face and such lovely little freckles and he was on his own. So young. Eventually, they came and took him off to hospital. I went inside the gym.

'As you walked inside the door there were rows and rows and rows of dead bodies. They weren't covered up; they weren't screened off at this point. They were just on display. If you walked on a bit there were rows of the walking wounded. So they were being brought into the gymnasium, and being forced to look at scores of dead bodies while they were waiting to be treated. I couldn't believe the insensitivity of it. I introduced myself to another girl, who was also a nurse, and there were two boys there who we were working with. They were both doctors. So I asked them for the plan, and they said, "We don't have one." I asked who was in charge, and they said that they didn't know. So I went towards these two officers in the flat caps rather than a bobby's helmet, and I introduced myself and asked them what was happening. I asked them what they had set up to deal with casualties and they just looked at me blankly, as if I had asked some really stupid question. One of the officers said, "Well, people are just doing whatever."

'So I went back the other nurse and said this is silly, we need to sort some sort of plan, some sort of triage here. So I suggested that we started at different ends and worked towards the middle. Setting up triage to see who needed to be seen to immediately, who was in danger, and who could wait, and that is what we did. I couldn't believe that these two officers were just standing there chatting, and they still hadn't thought to get some kind of system in place to deal with the casualties. They didn't think to screen off the dead from the injured … they hadn't thought to get some screens or something to cover the dead. These were people's loved ones … just lying there like pieces of meat, like they were not important. The walking wounded were just sitting, waiting to be seen to, and looking at that; it was just awful. At the back left-hand corner there was a table, and there were people sitting at it counting money. I assumed that money had come from the café ... they were sitting there counting the takings in front of all these poor dead people, and I just lost it. My mind couldn't take in what I was seeing. I mean, how could you be sitting there counting money when you're looking at all these dead bodies? I lost the plot and went over and knocked the table over, sending the coins everywhere and I shouted insults at them, I was so angry.'

Val Yates was trying to help others, despite being in a really bad way herself, and remembers kicking down an advertising hoarding to use as a stretcher: 'I got right to the Forest end and then my legs gave way again and I sank to the floor. I just lay there right in front of the Forest fans. I could see them, trapped in their pens. Another fan, I have no idea who, hauled me to my feet. There was this young Forest lad – can't have been more than ten – his fingers wrapped around the gaps in the fences. Snarling, his face full of hatred. "I hope you all die, you Scouse b******s," he said. I was too dazed and stunned to react. I just looked at him. The lad who had dragged me up was crying and was trying to get to him. He swung his arm at the fence and swore at him. I pushed him away and he said to me, "Come on," and started kicking at the hoardings right in front of this kid. On autopilot, I just joined in. I didn't really know what I was doing. I was dizzy and could not breathe properly, but I kicked with him. This copper came over and told us if we didn't stop he would have us both arrested. I told him to sod off and just carried on kicking the hoarding with the other lad until we got it off.'

Val was by no means the first to rip down an advertising hoarding to use as a makeshift stretcher, yet she still encountered a threat of arrest. Surely by now the police officer who challenged her must have realised why they were doing what they were doing? Val Yates remembers taking the advertising hoarding and heading back to where the injured were lying: 'We then ran back down to the Leppings Lane end. I don't know why, but I stuffed my programme in my mouth as we ran down. I didn't know where else to put it. I have seen that clip on television occasionally. It is not as famous as the one of a load of us running back is. They always play that clip on the news. The photo of us was in the *Daily Mirror*. I never knew it existed for twenty years until a neighbour fetched it round when the *Mirror* did its tribute. There was one from a different angle in the Today newspaper I was aware of a few days later, though. Running back, I kept turning round to look at this man on the board. He was unconscious – could have been dead already. I don't know. His head was bouncing on the board as we were running and I was worried we would hurt him – silly now, when I think of it. We tried, but there was nothing that could be done, or was there? I don't know. Was he one of the 41?'

The '41' that Val is referring to is the number of those who died that had the potential to be saved. When the Hillsborough Independent Panel published its report in September 2012, it revealed that 41 of the 96 could possibly have been saved, had they received appropriate medical attention more quickly. Val continues: 'I don't know who he was. If I ever did, I would tell his family that we tried to help him and we did our best. Not that that would be any consolation, though. There has been a void in their lives ever since that day, an empty space at the table at Christmas, birthdays and other special occasions. Memories that were never even created. After we had laid the board down, I stepped back as someone, I don't know who, tried to work on this man. I knew he was in a bad way and I could not comprehend it as they covered his face up with his scarf. I just walked away backwards in horror. I saw a gap that I thought was a way out and walked into it. It took me to the gym area. It was carnage. There was body after body just laid on the floor and I was trying to pick my way through and not stand on anyone. What had happened? We were at a football match and all these people were dead. Dead! One body caught my eye and I stopped. I had become separated from the local lads and this guy, just laid there on his own, just abandoned, was identical in build and clothing to one of the lads I had gone with. His jumper was pulled up over his face and I could not see who it was. I recoiled in horror, just staring at the body of this man, wondering if it was Paul, wondering what I was going to tell his mum. I did not dare lift the jumper off, so I just sat on the floor with my knees tucked up to my chest, hugging them. I was too much of a coward to lift the jumper off his face to check. So many thoughts went through my head. I was cursing myself for being too nesh to look. I sat there for what seemed like ages while the chaos was going on around me not knowing what to do. I decided it had to be him and got up; deciding I now had to go home and face the music. To tell his mum he had gone to a football match and was not coming back.'

Brian Johnson remembers filing out of the stadium, and the feeling when one of their party was unaccounted for: 'A couple of my friends turned up – one was hurt and had lost his shoes. Then another two turned up, and then another and we waited and waited. My friend, Phil, who was hurt, had gone in with his brother Gary and his cousin Peter, but Gary was nowhere to be seen. We waited for what seemed an eternity then decided to go back to the coach. We thought that he might have gone onto the pitch and come out the other side. Phil was struggling to walk so we had to carry him – Phil liked his chips and it was a fair distance to the coach. All the way, I prayed Gary would be there, but I had a horrible feeling deep down. On the way back to the coach, people were queuing outside houses. The good people of Sheffield had opened their doors for people to phone home and let their loved ones know they were okay. We got back to the coach; most of the others were already back, but no Gary. Phil was inconsolable as we waited again. My dad decided he would go back to the ground to see if he could find anything out. As we waited, some of the coaches and minibuses had started leaving. They were the lucky ones with no one missing. My dad returned with the address of the hospital and vague directions so we headed off in search of Gary. The mood on the coach was sombre and really silent. We got to the hospital and found that Gary hadn't been admitted, so someone, probably my dad, decided to ring his parents.'

Back home, Lynne Fox was watching the awful scene unfold on BBC's *Grandstand* programme and thinking about her brother, Steven, who was at the match, as she recalls: 'The television was still broadcasting events live from the stadium. I sat down to watch. I couldn't believe my eyes. There were fans everywhere. Advertising boards had been ripped down and fans were carrying injured people across the field. I saw police officers giving mouth-to-mouth resuscitation. Grown men were sitting on the field openly crying. I noticed people laid out with jackets covering their faces. They were obviously dead. I stared at the television in disbelief. How could this be happening? It was a football game, for Christ's sake! I shook my head. I didn't understand it at all. As I made my way into the hallway I could hear dad talking to someone on the phone. "Okay Tommy. Thanks for calling; let us know if you hear anything." Tommy was dad's best friend, and had gone with Steve to the game, along with three other men from the local pub. Calling to see if dad had heard from Steve, he was still at the ground, but wasn't able to find him. I looked back at the television; the death toll was at twenty-three. It hadn't occurred to me that Steve might be one of those dead. The commentator was saying people had been crushed, and I found it hard to believe that anyone could crush our Steve. He was a large bloke. As I passed dad in the hallway, I assured him, "There's no way he could ever be crushed. He's just too big!" Sarah and I had plans for that evening. We were meeting a group of friends who lived further away from town than we did, and had more than likely already left to be on time. So we rushed to get ready. As we were leaving, Sarah said, "Should we stay in, just until we've heard from Steve?" But I didn't want to let our friends down. With a promise to ourselves to call and make sure he got home okay later that night, we left for the evening.'

There were no mobile phones in those days, so cancelling an arrangement was more difficult.

As the Taylor Report and the Hillsborough Independent Panel both reported, there were problems with the emergency response. The initial call to the South Yorkshire Metropolitan Ambulance Service was revealed in the documents which the Hillsborough Independent Panel reviewed and, at 3.06 p.m., when the game had been stopped. That call transcript read, 'We've got um an incident at Leppings Lane um end on the um Sheffield Wednesday Football Ground. We may need a few ambulances it's just to advise you at this stage...'

The report also showed that in those crucial early minutes, the call was one of 'operational support' because the assessment of the situation from the police control box was still one of crowd disorder. As the HIP report explained, 'Ground Control should have asked Force Control to implement the major disaster plan, which would have resulted in the information being cascaded appropriately, including to SYMAS, and acted upon.' According to the Hillsborough Independent Panel report, 'The absence of complete activation of the major incident plan had significant consequences for the emergency response within the stadium. The SYMAS [South Yorkshire Metropolitan Ambulance Service] plan provided for specified senior officers to attend and adopt their designated roles, including Incident Officer, Control Officer, Casualty Clearing Point Officer and Emergency Support Team Officer.' According to the Hillsborough Independent Panel report, and a West Midlands Police report that was compiled for the Taylor Inquiry, it was confirmed that the responsibility to activate the Major Incident Plan 'lay with the SYP Control Box, which had responsibility for crowd safety as well as crowd control'. However, the initial reaction of the control box, according to the West Midlands Report, was that the situation was one of 'crowd disturbance' so the initial request was for 'operational support' and not the 'major incident plan'. The report went on to say that there was a code word 'catastrophe' that should be used by the police control box when implementing the major disaster plan, but it wasn't until approximately 3.07 p.m. that there was a 'move away from operational support' calls, and towards 'a fleet of ambulances.' The major disaster plan was not however implemented until far later.

The first ambulance arrived on the pitch at around 3.15 p.m., but many of the forty-two ambulances that arrived outside didn't make it onto the pitch. Some of the early ambulances arrived, and left their vehicle to head to the Leppings Lane end of the ground on foot, but their abandoned ambulance was causing an obstruction. According to the witness statement of one ambulance driver, the police were also reticent to allow ambulances through onto the pitch.

In his witness statement, which can be found on the HIP site, an ambulance driver speaks of the resistance he at first received from a police officer when trying to get onto the pitch: 'At this stage, there were rows of police with vans and stretchers coming out of the entrance on to the pitch. It was clear that there were dead bodies on at least two of the stretchers. I would say the time was about 15.35 hours. We were stopped by a police officer at the entrance to the corridor to the pitch. The officer at the front of the ambulance said that we could not get through. Spectators were shouting at us about a body on a stretcher. We stopped and Hopkins came up to the ambulance and opened the door. I said that the police officer said that we could not go through and he replied that he wanted us on the pitch immediately. He said that there were casualties at the far end of the ground and he needed us on the pitch and that we were not to stop for anyone until we got to the far end of the ground. He told us to put our two tones on and go through. We did as we were told and went past the policeman.'

The difficulties in getting the ambulances on the pitch meant that around forty ambulances, with trained first aid professionals, were left outside the ground.

Dr Glyn Phillips recalls the last person he tried to help, and his chance interview with the BBC: 'I went back looking for others to help. I tried CPR on a few more people but they were gone. It's horrible trying to resuscitate people who are effectively dead, the taste of vomit and all that kind of thing, but I have to say there was no hint of alcohol on any of the young people I attempted CPR on. And getting into the game we did not observe any misbehaviour. A bit of boisterousness you get with any football crowd but no bad behaviour, nobody inebriated or out of control, in contrast to the allegations made later in some newspapers. By now, I was basically on the pitch scouting for somebody to help. It must have been well after 3.30 and by then people were walking and talking or sitting and talking or they were dead. Nothing much in between. The last person I tried to resuscitate was in his twenties. I think his brother was trying to revive him and I remember this girl wearing a Celtic top saying, "Leave him, he's gone, he's gone." I had a go but he was dead.'

'Now I was down the far end of the pitch, where this mass of Forest fans were just standing, watching in stunned silence. I saw two photographers by the goal and what was growing in my mind, among all this clinical stuff and the incredulity, was that I was very conscious of what the media did to Liverpool after Heysel, where the majority of 10,000 fans did nothing wrong and as a result of the incompetence of stadium officials, UEFA and Belgian police, twenty-six nutters were able to cause mayhem. Juventus had their share of morons, too, but that was conveniently forgotten. I thought they will try to blame this on the fans. I can't let that happen. So I went up to the photographers and said something along the lines of, "I hope you're going to hammer this ground when you write it up." I made a few remarks about the lack of facilities and they asked what I did. I said I was a GP and I've just been trying to resuscitate dead lads. As soon as they heard I was a GP, not just an overgrown scally fan, they thought here's someone worth quoting, so the notepads came out and photographs were taken. Then I thought I've got to speak to someone from Liverpool Football Club, to make sure they don't let the fans get the blame. I boldly went to the players' tunnel. There were police all around. I said I was a GP and had to speak to someone from LFC. They didn't even attempt to stop me. I think they were all stunned. Anyone who sounded as though he had any degree of intellect they let through. I made my way up the players' tunnel and by chance Jimmy Hill from the BBC was there, looking pale and concerned. I forced him to listen to my account, which he did. Unbeknown to me, Alan Green, the BBC football commentator, was standing there listening, and he asked if I minded repeating it on radio. Next thing he was introducing me live. I was saying what I'd witnessed and it came out, almost in one breath:

'"There's no doubt this crowd was too big for this ground. Liverpool just filled the end they were given. The police allowed the fans to fill the middle terracing section to the point they were crammed in like sardines. And yet the two outside portions of the terracing were left virtually empty and I stood and watched police allowing this to happen. It got to a point where they lost control completely. Lads were getting crushed against the fence right down near the pitch and there were so many people in that part of the ground that nobody could even move to get out. I climbed sideways into an emptier section and then made my way on to the pitch to try and help. Now, unfortunately, there are guys who have died down there on that pitch. I've seen about eight to ten, I don't know how many there are. There was one chap I went to; he was clinically dead. He had no heartbeat. Myself and another guy – I think a nurse – we resuscitated him for about ten minutes. We were just about to give up when we got his heart beating but I don't know what the state of his cerebral function is going to be like. We asked for a defibrillator. I've been informed there isn't a defibrillator in the whole ground, which I find appalling for a major event like this. We were given an oxygen tank to help with our resuscitation and it was empty. I think this is an absolute disgrace."'

'After cleaning up in the referee's room, I then chanced upon Liverpool manager Kenny Dalglish, looking ashen-faced because, as I learned later, his son had been in the crowd. I introduced myself and told him very, very quickly what I'd just witnessed, and I said you mustn't let them pin this on the fans. This was not fan trouble. The crowd conditions here were a disgrace. He said something like, "We [Liverpool FC] didn't want to play here but had little say in it." I then walked back on the pitch, returning to the Leppings Lane end. I made my way through the gate I'd used to get on the pitch. I went up the terrace and rejoined my brother and two friends at the top, where they'd stayed while I was on the pitch. They were stunned, disbelieving at what had happened. I'd done what I could. I'd tried to help revive people. I'd also made sure people who needed to know what really happened had somebody with some credibility telling them. Bizarrely, I'd got a chance to speak out on the radio, which had one personal advantage. My wife was at home in Glasgow, very upset and anxiously watching events on telly, knowing we were in that terrace. Thankfully, one or two friends heard me on the radio and phoned her within minutes to say we were OK.'

Mike Wilson remembers the moment that his frantic search for his fifty-seven-year-old dad came to an end: 'I could see bodies stretched out on the pitch, and supporters making the makeshift stretchers from advertising hoardings. My only concern at this point was trying to find dad. At fifty-seven, his fence vaulting days were past him and there were only a few openings in the perimeter fencing. I scrutinised the terracing from a vantage point on the edge of the pitch but I couldn't see him anywhere. After five minutes of this, I feared the worst. I started to walk around the pitch, now littered with bodies and with injured supporters. Dad was a larger chap, so I looked around to see if he was among the fallen. It was not a pleasant exercise. Supporters and policemen were giving first aid to many of the injured. I couldn't see dad anywhere. If he wasn't on the terrace and he wasn't on the pitch, where was he? I decided to have another look at the terracing in the vain hope he was there. It was finally emptying out. To my huge relief, I spotted dad halfway down the pen close to the fence that separated it from Pen 3. It was exactly 3.50 p.m. when this happened, as there was a clock on the Leppings Lane stand. This is where my biggest regret of it all comes in. On seeing dad, I physically collapsed, sobbing on the side of the pitch. It was a relief that was impossible to quantify. My regret is that I was so broken up I couldn't and didn't offer my support to those heroes transporting the injured across the ground to the emergency services.'

One of the only bright spots to be found in the story of the Hillsborough disaster is the fantastic way in which the ordinary people of Sheffield went out of their way to help the distressed Liverpool fans leaving the stadium that day. Many opened their doors to allow people to use the phone, and as Barry Devonside was just about to discover, others came out to see how they could help. 'This lady came up to me and asked if she could help me. I said, "Who are you?" She said, "My name is Betty Thorpe. I'm just a person who lives in Sheffield, and came here to see if I couldn't help someone." I replied that I'd just been told that my son has been taken to the gymnasium and she pointed me in the direction, which was only 20–30 yards away – the entrance. I went there and gave a knock on the door. It seemed like a lifetime before this copper answered the door. He was the biggest copper I have ever seen in my life. I sort of bent my head backwards, because he kept on going and going up, he was that big. My first thought was that he'd been placed here because they think Liverpool supporters are going to cause trouble. He asked me in a very pointed way, "What do you want?" I said that I had just been told that my son had been killed and carried to the gymnasium. Again, in an aggressive manner, he told me to wait there. No empathy for me or my son's situation and then he went away. It seemed like half an hour to me, but it was probably only ten minutes or so. He came back and said that he wasn't there. I said, "He's got to be here, I've just been told by his mates that brought him." The copper, again very aggressively, said, "I've just told you, he's not here." I wanted to swear at him but I didn't. So I went back to speak to Betty and she asked what he said. I said Jason said he carried him here and that he was dead. Nobody with even half a brain cell could make a mistake like that ... he's got to be here. Betty then asked if there was anything else she could do to help, and I said that I've got to call my wife. Does anyone have a telephone? This police sergeant was nearby, and she stopped him and said this man has been given news that his son has been killed and that he's in the gymnasium, but an officer there said he's not in the gymnasium and he wants to call home to his wife. The officer said to come with him and he took me inside a room adjacent to the gymnasium and he said, "What's your number?" And I couldn't remember. I was in freefall, in total shock, and I just couldn't remember my own number. So he [the officer] tried directory enquiries, and spoke to a lady that was saying I was ex-directory. The officer told me this, and I said that I wasn't ex-directory and have never been ex-directory in my life. He relayed this and said have you heard that there has been a disaster at the football stadium in Sheffield, and the lady said that she had heard. The sergeant told her his rank, serial number and asked her again ... she still refused to put the call through. I just couldn't believe it ... it's beyond all comprehension, that one. Anyway, he asked me for another telephone but I could only give the address of my brother-in-law and we eventually got through to him, and he drove up to my house to see Jackie. John and my brother, Roger, drove up to meet me in Sheffield.'

Kevin Moreland remembers hearing that the crush barrier he, his dad and his brother had been standing next to earlier, before his dad insisted they move, was the one that collapsed and where so many had lost their lives. Kevin recalls the mood as people left the ground: 'After the game was abandoned, we waited on the Leppings Lane for a good hour and a half (as advised), so we obviously witnessed everything. On leaving the ground we walked back the coach, our Chris tried to phone me mum from someone's house that were letting fans in, but he couldn't get through. For some reason, I remember kicking a Fanta can in anger. Before I got on the coach, I remember repeating to my dad, "They can't blame us again like Heysel." Everyone was saying it. On the coach, the Everton commentary was on the game v. Norwich. I thought it was weird, as obviously loads of our fans had died. They then cut to the studio and they said five had died. I felt numb. Once the coach started moving, the numbers were going up; I think by the time we had just left Sheffield it was up to eighty dead. There were empty spaces on our coach coming home. I felt sick, numb and shocked. It was horrible. We got off the coach at Fiveways and I ran home the length of Queen's Drive to see me mum and tell her we were okay. My nan and granddad and aunties were all there in tears, the relief on my mum's face when I got through the door will live with me forever; my nan was just shaking out of control. My uncle from Australia had been on the phone. Later on that night I heard a friend in school had died. I had spoken to him in the spec we started off in, and I had had a gut feeling he was dead before I heard.'

Liverpool fans continued to do whatever they could to help the rescue effort. Some, having only narrowly escaped death themselves, were attempting CPR on those laying still on the grass; others were carrying bodies from the Leppings Lane end of the ground to the Kop end, where they hoped that the medical professionals who had arrived outside the ground in a fleet of ambulances would be able to help. As time ticked on, the efforts of those supporters meant that there were less and less people that needed attention at the Leppings Lane end of the pitch. After doing what he could to help the injured, Richie Greaves remembered that his family would be watching on television, and his thoughts turned to them: 'My dad had a triple heart bypass the year before, so I was conscious that I needed to get to the phone to tell him we were alright. I was worried about his heart, so at about a quarter to four or four o'clock we left the ground through the South Stand. As we were going out there were a load of Forest fans arguing with the police and asking when the game was going to kick off. I shouted a load of abuse at them and said there are people dead! We went out onto the road at the Forest end, and there were just ambulances for as far as you could see ... just a massive queue of ambulances. We went to a retail park not far away and asked the people in an electrical store there if we could use the phone. They charged us, but they let us use it. It took a while to get through.'

Paul Dunderdale and his friend, Andy, had been saved from the crush in the central pens earlier by pushing backwards and eventually being hauled out by those fans who were above, in the West Stand. Once there, they were stuck there as spectators, looking out at the chaos below. As time moved on and eventually the game was called off, Paul remembers how they wanted to find their friend Graham: After Andy and I had been hauled up to the upper stand we waited for a while not really knowing what to do, the game was abandoned so we headed outside to regroup. We stood at the top of Leppings Lane and slowly got everyone together – everyone except Graham. At that stage, we couldn't contemplate him not being safe; he was just looking for us somewhere else. I suggested he might be waiting for us at the cars so we headed back. On the way to the cars we passed a park and I remember passing a small hot dog cart with some old guy with a radio. As we passed him, he said, "There's fifty-three dead, lad." This sent a shiver down my spine and it was at that moment I feared the worst.'

'We headed to the nearest hospital, The Hallamshire, and were directed to a large room, a canteen I think where there were loads of people waiting for news. Periodically, someone would come in with a list and stand on a table to give a list of injured people at other hospitals so the crowd numbers got thinner as a result. There were only a few phones and getting messages through was difficult. I rang Stan Roberts a couple of times telling him we were still looking, and I know he was going back and forth to his local police station, Manor Lane, which is five minutes from the Roberts home.'

In 1989, there were no mobile phones, no Internet, Facebook, Twitter or any of the other sources of immediate information available to us today, so football supporters used to rely entirely on the radio for scores from other grounds. It was a part of the matchday ritual. Richie Greaves remembers the haunting sight of the empty seats on his coach on the way home, and the rising death toll on the radio: 'We headed back to the coach, and there were a load of empty seats on our coach on the way back. You don't know what happened to those people. We had the radio on, and all the time the reports were coming through that the death toll was going up and up until a lady ran to the front and asked the driver to turn it off. The rest of the journey was silent. I remember getting back to Liverpool, got off the coach and got a bus home. When I got off the bus near ours, I couldn't face going home, so I went to the nearest pub, bought a pint and sat down, but I was just staring at it. I couldn't drink it. I couldn't believe that life was still going on all around me.'

Mike Wilson met up with his father and left the ground: 'Eventually, as calm was being restored, I left the pitch and headed back onto the terracing in the corner. I could see dad was safe, and returning to that pen to be with him while so many people were still getting out didn't seem to be an option. Stewards/police (can't remember which) had started to lead us into the corner terrace anyway. Everyone was numb, shocked, upset. People tried to talk to me but I couldn't actually get any words out myself. After some time I sat on the floor in the corner pen, they started to encourage us to exit the ground. I arrived at the newsagent to meet dad and Jonathan, still unable to speak.'

Grant Walker remembers leaving the ground with the awful feeling that he hadn't been able to find his brother. They were separated in the crush, and despite spending ages looking around he hadn't been able to locate him: 'I can't remember at what point, but we started to be filed out of the ground. I'd given up hope of finding my brother by now. Everyone was in tears, getting emotional. It was like hell. I remember coming out and somebody said that they had made a makeshift mortuary up the road, but I couldn't handle that. I thought I am going to have to call home and tell them that I can't find my brother.

No mobile phones in those days, but fortunately enough the people of Sheffield were fantastic. This old couple came out of their house and asked me if I wanted to use the phone, so I rang home and I started to tell her, but my wife said, "No, it's okay, your brother's in the hospital!" So we jumped in the car and shot up to the Hallamshire hospital. There were priests and vicars and all kinds of clergy people trying to comfort people. Even then you were still seeing people being carted into the hospital. I remember there were reporters everywhere, winding you up and trying to get you to say something. I'm sure they thought, "Oh, it's Scousers, they've caused all this." I even heard one of those journalists ask if we thought this was some sort of divine retribution for Heysel … disgusting questions designed to make you lose your rag, I'm sure. Anyway, I found my brother at the hospital and you can imagine the relief and emotion of that!'

Tony O'Keefe went to help whoever he could in the gym, before making his way out of the ground: 'A little while later I headed towards the gym. There were rows and rows of bodies, and there were dead bodies in the same place as the living. There was this one lad, Gary Unsworth from Southport, and I remember that because he was asking me to go and ring his mum. I wrote his name and phone number on a programme to call later. I was in the gym until about 6 p.m. The ground was empty, I had seen enough and there was nothing else I could do. On my way, I saw the crush barrier twisted and bent. I thought that these poor people have died a horrible death. Something has gone badly wrong here, and someone's to blame for that. I didn't think for a second that they would blame us. Outside the ground, I remember seeing people outside their houses asking if I needed a drink or if I needed to use the phone. I went in to call this lad's mum. She answered and she told me she was a trained nurse, and she wanted me to tell her what her son was like. I said he's OK, he'll survive, but he's not well. I got back to the car, and my brother-in-law was quite frantic, asking where I had been. It's strange, because I had known they were safe and hadn't thought about it. He said that thirty people had been killed, and I said there's more than that – there are more than a hundred … that was my impression at the time from being in the gymnasium.'

Margaret Aspinall, back on Merseyside, was desperately waiting for news from her husband Jimmy and her son James, who were both at the match: '5 p.m. came, 6 p.m. came … eventually my husband got hold of me and asked if I had heard from James. I said no, and asked Jimmy where he was? He said he didn't see him in the side pens and that he had a feeling that he might have been behind the goal. I said, "Please check every hospital; please don't come home without him." Jimmy went to all the hospitals and couldn't find him. I had been trying to get a hold of the coach company that James had travelled with and eventually I got through to them at about 9.30 p.m. in the evening. They said to me that all passengers were accounted for. Straight away you have a sigh of relief, and thank God for that. I feel awful that some people have died, but thank God my son isn't dead.'

After the game was called off and fans were leaving the ground, Nick Braley remembers setting off to try and find his mates: 'I headed back up Leppings Lane to the place we had agreed to meet up if we got split, but they weren't there. I hung around for a couple of minutes before heading back to college. No point getting a bus, the roads were needed by the ambulances, so I decided to walk back, the 4 miles taking a couple of hours. As I walked, dazed, worried and distant, I popped into shops on the way. "How many mate?" Fifteen, twenty-three, thirty-seven, this was a tickometer that wasn't going to stop. I made it halfway into the town centre and headed through the shopping area. Some shoppers were happily talking about their day's bargain hunting stopping only to give me a dirty look … for the first time of many I snapped. What the hell you staring at? "Had a good day's shopping have you?" They looked at me in disgust before someone else spoke to them, whispering the news that they never knew. They held their hands over their mouths, but I couldn't be arsed to apologise. All I wanted to do is get to the halls and find the lads.'

Barry Devonside set off from Hillsborough's gymnasium in search of his son, Chris: 'Betty suggested that it might be a good idea if we visited a number of hospitals. It's at that point that I had the barmiest of thoughts that he was still alive, but I kept saying to myself that Jason couldn't have made a mistake like that; he's not the type of lad to make a mistake like that. So we went to hospital number one – I think it was the Royal Hallamshire, but I might be wrong – and we were all sent up to the canteen. When we arrived it was absolute bedlam. I saw people in an absolute state. I have never seen people in such a state before and never do I want to see that state again. Horrendous. People screaming and crying. This hospital administrator came in and stood on top of a table and started to call out that they had six people in casualty that are still alive, and another number who were dead. I just shouted above everyone else, "Is there a man with a Welsh international rugby shirt?" I knew there wouldn't have been many people dressed like that at Hillsborough that day. I shouted again, "His name is Christopher Devonside." The administrator said no. We went to the next hospital and it was the same thing. I was living basically on hope, but I also had the wildest thoughts. Why should my son be alive when so many others were dead? I've believed that all my life I'd been a caring individual, so why should I be so selfish towards my own when so many others were dead? We were at the second hospital for an hour or so, and somebody suggested that we go to the mortuary at the hospital, which was a separate building in the grounds. We knocked on the door and a fella with a white coat answered. When we walked in there must have been a dozen police officers, helmets off, and sat around on the floor. There was a pile of clothing that must have been about 3 foot high. Nobody said a word. I asked the guy in the white coat if he had someone by the name of Christopher Devonside here and he said no. I asked if he had a lad in a Welsh international rugby shirt and he said no. This was about 9 p.m. at night. I had been travelling around with Betty, who was providing immense support, just on the hope that Chris was alive. More recently, while speaking with the Bishop of Liverpool, I found that I was not the only family treated in this manner.'

Having finally got through to the coach company with whom her son James had travelled to Hillsborough, and having been told that all passengers on the coaches travelling back were accounted for, Margaret Aspinall recalls the moment that her husband Jimmy called home again from Sheffield. Jimmy had been looking around the hospitals for hours before calling home again: 'When Jimmy got back in touch with me, at about 10.30 p.m., he told me that James wasn't on any of the lists at the hospitals and I told him, "No, Jimmy, thank God. Come home, he's safe." I told him, "All passengers were accounted for and they will be arriving in Liverpool at about midnight. Come home and we'll go and meet him." We waited for every coach, and when the last one came in at about half past twelve I said to the driver, "Where's my son?' He said, 'I'm sorry love, I don't know." People had just jumped on the coaches to get home; they weren't the people that we took, which you could understand, really, under the circumstances.'

Having panicked for so long, and then felt the relief that James was 'accounted for', it was time for panic to return. The coach company had, in good faith, told Margaret that every seat in the coach was full, but they didn't know that some seats were now occupied by traumatised supporters who had not travelled to Sheffield on that coach, thus masking any empty seats. Margaret recalls what they did next: 'We went to the police station and the list hadn't come through yet, and they said that they would get in touch if they hear anything at all. We thought he might be walking around Sheffield in a daze, so I thought we'd have to go back to Sheffield, but Jimmy said that he'd go back and I should stay home. He said that he would keep phoning home and if he comes home in the meantime that he could turn around and come back. I went home and Jimmy went back up to Sheffield.'

Barry Devonside had been searching for his son, Christopher, for about six hours by the time he arrived at Hammerton Road: 'Next stop was Hammerton Road Police Station, and we arrived there at about 9.30 p.m., or so. Again, there was a phenomenal amount of people there searching for loved ones. Total chaos. I asked a few people but got no clear response as to where Chris was. About thirty minutes later, we got a message to board a bus outside the police station, which was going to the gymnasium back at the Hillsborough Stadium. I asked an officer, "Why would we want to go back to the gymnasium?" I was probably in total denial, and he said, "I think it's time that you went to the gym." We got on the bus, but I just couldn't grasp why we were going to the gym, as stupid as that may sound. Maybe I didn't want to go to the gym to face reality, I don't know. Then we were taken to see a board on a wall, which had photographs on, and I was asked to pick out Chris. The first time I didn't pick him out, I probably didn't want to see him. I didn't want to see him as one of the casualties. But then I saw him. The officer who helped carry Chris with his mate was the man who brought Chris to us in a black body bag. He unzipped the bag, and I bent down to kiss Chris and he tried to stop me, so I shoved him away. I felt so angry that he could invade my space at the most upsetting moment of our lives. He just stood back, then said, "Is this your son?" I said yes. He asked me what his name was. I said, "Christopher Devonside."'

Lynne Fox, sister of Steven, was back at home and had gone out for the night with a friend. She'd seen the news break in the afternoon, but was convinced that Steven would be alright because 'he was just too big' to be crushed. Her friend kept calling home for news: 'The first bar wasn't too busy, and everyone was there by the time we arrived. I noticed the absence of a friend. "Where's Cathy tonight?" I asked. A friend told us she had stayed at home as her brother was at the game that afternoon. She hadn't heard from him and was worried. Sarah and I looked at each other. Her eyes held a flicker of guilt. I found a phone and made the first call home – no news. As we moved onto the next bar, I felt warm inside from the alcohol and my memory of the events from the afternoon began to subside. Convinced that Steve was probably sitting at home, having a beer, I set out to have a good time. After a few more drinks, all that was on my mind was fun. I laughed, I danced, and I purposely forgot all about anything that really mattered to me. Sarah had made the last call home at around 10.30 p.m. "Still no news," she said. Had I paid closer attention, I would have noticed her eyes telling me she thought there was something wrong.'

Lynne Fox had been out with friends, and recalls the moment when she found out that her brother wasn't coming home: 'It had gotten chilly when Tony arrived to pick us up. It was 2 a.m. People were milling about on the streets as the clubs were closing. Tony had been at a friend's place all evening. He chatted with us about the night, and I asked if he had heard any news about Steve. He hadn't, but it was only a short ride back to the old Victorian house we both lived in. It had been Sarah, not me, who had been calling home all night for news. Tony had made a move to go home at around 11 p.m. that evening, but his friend's mum, our mum's best friend, had encouraged him to stay a little longer. He ended up coming straight from their house to pick us up. Both of us were oblivious to the news that was about to come. As we walked up the driveway I noticed all the lights in the house were on. I assumed it was because mum and dad were still up, waiting for Steve. I reached for my keys to open the door, but it was already open. Dad was just standing there, unable to look us in the eye. He said, "Come inside, we have something to tell you." Auntie Joan took Sarah to the television room, and dad led Tony and me into the lounge. This room was normally reserved for guests; we very rarely used it as a family. Mum was on the couch. We both sat down. She said quietly, calmly, "Steve is one of the people that was killed today." "How do you know? Did you get through on the helpline?" I asked calmly. "Tommy called," Dad said, "He said he identified him at the ground. He found him." He paused, "In the makeshift morgue." I looked around at Tony. He'd begun to cry softly. Dad had glistening eyes and looked like he had been crying earlier. Mum's face, though, was stony, expressionless … after a brief period I excused myself and went to bed.'

It seems amazing to many people that relatives and friends had to spend so long looking for those who were unaccounted for, when there were only four main places to look: the Royal Hallamshire Hospital, which is a little over 3 miles away from the Hillsborough; the Northern General Hospital, which is a little over 2 miles away from the stadium; the Hammerton Road Police Station, which is just over 1½ miles away, and the Hammerton Road Boy's Club, also around 1½ miles, which was being used as a 'holding area to house relatives' who had visited the police station searching for loved ones. The only other likely location was Barnsley District General Hospital, which was around 12 miles away, and only treated three people with minor injuries.

The clock at Sheffield Wednesday Football Club sits at 3.06 p.m., the time the match was stopped. (John Giles/PA Archive/Press Association Images)

Fans are helped by those in the upper tier as they try to escape the crush. (Ross Kinnaird/EMPICS Sport)

Kenny Dalglish, Liverpool manager, at the scene of the Hillsborough tragedy. (Ross Kinnaird/EMPICS Sport)

Liverpool goalkeeper Bruce Grobbelaar looks around in disbelief as the tragic events unfold around him (Ross Kinnaird/EMPICS Sport).

A fan in despair after the disaster. (Phil O'Brien/EMPICS Sport)

Players and supporters of Liverpool FC attend a memorial service at Anfield to mark the 22nd anniversary of the Hillsborough disaster. (Peter Byrne/PA Archive/Press Association Images)

Wreaths and flowers laid at the Hillsborough Monument in Liverpool.
(Martin Waters/Demotix/Press Association Images)

John Alfred Anderson (62)
Colin Mark Ashcroft (19)
James Gary Aspinall (18)
Kester Roger Marcus Ball (16)
Gerard Bernard Patrick Baron (67)
Simon Bell (17)
Barry Sidney Bennett (26)
David John Benson (22)
David William Birtle (22)
Tony Bland (22)
Paul David Brady (21)
Andrew Mark Brookes (26)
Carl Brown (18)
David Steven Brown (25)
Henry Thomas Burke (47)
Peter Andrew Burkett (24)
Paul William Carlile (19)
Raymond Thomas Chapman (50)
Gary Christopher Church (19)
Joseph Clark (29)
Paul Clark (18)
Gary Collins (22)
Stephen Paul Copoc (20)
Tracey Elizabeth Cox (23)
James Philip Delaney (19)
Christopher Barry Devonside (18)
Christopher Edwards (29)
Vincent Michael Fitzsimmons (34)
Thomas Steven Fox (21)
Jon-Paul Gilhooley (10)
Barry Glover (27)
Ian Thomas Glover (20)
Derrick George Godwin (24)
Roy Harry Hamilton (34)
Philip Hammond (14)
Eric Hankin (33)
Gary Harrison (27)
Stephen Francis Harrison (31)
Peter Andrew Harrison (15)
David Hawley (39)
James Robert Hennessy (29)
Paul Anthony Hewitson (26)
Carl Darren Hewitt (17)
─────── Michael Hewitt (16)
─────── Hicks (19)
─────── e Hicks (15)
─────── dney Horn (20)
─────── Horrocks (41)

The horror of the Hillsborough disaster is too much for a young Liverpool fan. (John Giles/PA Archive/Press Association Images)

The eternal flame and memorial for the 96 at Anfield. (Peter Byrne/PA Archive/Press Association Images)

The Shankly Gates at Anfield. (Peter Byrne/PA Archive/Press Association Images)

Floral tributes are left outside Liverpool's Anfield stadium to mark the 23rd anniversary of the Hillsborough disaster. (Dave Thompson/PA Archive/Press Association Images)

Tributes to the victims at the Hillsborough Memorial outside Anfield. (Tim Hales/AP/Press Association Images)

If they were not in one of those places, they were likely to be in the gymnasium, which was being used as a temporary mortuary. Fans were initially brought into the gymnasium, and if injured, they were then ferried to one of the hospitals for treatment. If dead, they stayed in the gymnasium where police officers wiped their faces, and took a photograph of them that was then pinned on a board, and used for relatives to identify them. If somebody was taken to hospital and later died, they would be transported back to the gymnasium to be photographed and laid down to wait for a family member or friend to identify them. Many people searching for loved ones spent many, many hours travelling between these venues. Paul Dunderdale had been searching for a friend that he had driven to the match, Graham Roberts, from when the game was stopped until midnight, when he was approached by a policeman and asked to go back to the Hillsborough Stadium to identify somebody that he thought could possibly have been Graham. As Paul remembers: 'At about midnight, a policeman came to us and asked if one of us would come for identification at another venue. I said I would, and my friend, Dave Fellows, said he would go with me. We were driven to the gym in a minibus and handed over to another policeman. He knew we were there to identify a twenty-four-year-old male. He told us to walk past two boards with Polaroid pictures of faces. There were men, women and children on that board – I want to know, even today, why they could not group them and spare at least a bit of the horror of that day. I got to the end of the boards and my heart skipped – he wasn't there! It was all a huge mistake; he was in a hospital somewhere with a broken arm or something. The policeman just looked at me and said, "Look again." At the second pass, I found him. His face was battered and it just didn't look like him. I was devastated, totally shocked.

'The same guy then took us to an area where he showed us Graham's body to identify him formally, which I did. He then took a statement and asked questions. He wrote it and got me to sign it. His first four questions were about beer: Where did we drink? How much did we have? Was Graham an alcoholic? I found this totally insensitive and I just wanted to be away from that place. The crying and grief in that gym from other families haunts me still today. If you have ever seen that scene from Jimmy McGovern's film, you will get a feel for what it was like. As I signed my statement, I asked him to get in touch with Graham's family and break the news to them; I couldn't handle being the one to tell them when I got back. They took us back to the hospital to meet up with the others. When I got back to them I just said, "He's gone." They all seemed to slump as one and we just held each other for a few minutes.'

Margaret Aspinall recalls getting regular phone call updates from her husband, who had travelled back to Sheffield to try and find their son, James. She feared the worst when the phone calls stopped: 'He phoned home at 1.30 a.m. to see if I had heard, and more or less every half an hour. I think the last phone call I got from Jim was around about 4.30 a.m. 5 a.m. came and there was no phone call … 5.30 a.m., no phone call. I said to Rose, "There's something wrong." I went out the front at about 6 a.m. – I don't know why, probably to get some fresh air. As I was standing there, I saw the car come around the corner with Jimmy in the passenger seat. I ran away down the street when I saw him, screaming – I just knew when I saw him. I didn't want Jimmy to tell me because as long as he didn't tell me then my son was still alive.'

Around fifteen hours after the match was stopped at Hillsborough, Margaret got the worst news that any mother could ever receive.

Paul Dunderdale and his friends drove back to Merseyside having just identified their friend, Graham, in the gymnasium at Hillsborough. Distraught and exhausted, Paul recalls the journey back to Liverpool in middle of the night: 'We knew we had to head back and get into the cars. The drive back was just a blur. I had Gary in the car, and my brother-in-law, Rod Sheldon. We dropped Gary off and then headed to my mother-in-law's house, where my wife and her two sisters were waiting. We parked the car at about 6 a.m. and then saw Sandra, Graham's fiancée, running out to us screaming, "My Graham, my Graham!" The police had not informed them as they had promised they would, which just added insult to injury as far as I was concerned.'

Families were left to make their own way from hospital to hospital, in an unfamiliar city, and late into the night in a desperate search to find out where their missing loved ones were, and whether they were alive or dead. Many recall a cold, unhelpful and unsympathetic attitude towards them from many South Yorkshire Police officers. Many also recall that minutes after identifying the body of a loved one, they were asked questions about how much the deceased had to drink and if they had a ticket.

At some point on the night of 15 April 1989, or the morning of Sunday 16 April, two CCTV tapes were stolen from the Hillsborough Stadium. These tapes had been in a locked cupboard, in a locked room, and yet they were stolen. Who took them, and for what reason? In whose interest was it that they disappear? Also that night, coroner Dr Stefan Popper gave the unprecedented order to take blood alcohol readings from the deceased, without their families' consent or knowledge, and including a little ten-year-old boy. It seemed as if the victims of Britain's worst sporting disaster were already being investigated as if they were suspects, and the cover up that was uncovered by the Hillsborough Independent Panel in September 2012 was already well underway.

4

Twenty-Five Years

The 'disgraceful lie' told by David Duckenfield, the Match Commander, at around 3.15 p.m. on the day of the disaster, was just the start of the misinformation that was to pile additional pain on the families of the deceased and the survivors of Hillsborough. Stories of drunken, ticketless and violent fans were released to the press by the police, and it was a story that was enthusiastically run by sections of the country's media. Liverpool was a city in mourning. In the days after the disaster, Anfield, Liverpool FC's ground, had become a shrine to the dead, with flowers, teddy bears and scarves covering half of the pitch.

On 17 April 1989, just two days after the disaster, the Home Office appointed Lord Justice Taylor to chair the inquiry into the disaster. Lord Justice Taylor was asked 'to inquire into the events at Sheffield Wednesday football ground on 15 April 1989 and to make recommendations about the needs of crowd control and safety at sports events'. It was interesting that, as with the Popplewell Report published in the aftermath of the Bradford fire disaster, the word 'control' preceded the word 'safety' in the terms of reference given to Lord Justice Taylor. West Midlands Police was tasked with gathering evidence for the inquiry.

While funerals were still being arranged on Merseyside and beyond, the press coverage of the disaster took a very different turn on Wednesday 19 April, when *The Sun* ran a headline 'THE TRUTH' under the editorship of Kelvin Mackenzie. Underneath that headline ran three subheadings, which read, 'Some fans picked pockets of victims', 'Some fans urinated on brave cops', 'Some fans beat up PC giving kiss of life'. The general reaction from Liverpool was shock, and then anger, especially from those who were at Hillsborough; shock that the story was so different to their own experiences, and anger that such lies were being printed, especially as Liverpool hadn't even buried their dead at this point.

Brenda Fox was still coming to terms with the news that her son, Steven, had been killed, and remembers how her son's friends had told her of a completely different experience: 'The radio, television and newspapers were full of reports of Hillsborough – the lies about fans were unbelievable. One paper's headline told of fans robbing the dead and being drunken yobs. Steve's friends, who were at the match, told a very different story. They explained their horrific experiences and said that the police were to blame and that they would never forget the screams of the dying and wounded. They described how fans had torn down the hoardings with their bare hands to carry the injured across the pitch to the ambulances, which had not been allowed to come into the grounds and had been kept outside by the Sheffield police.'

Damian Kavanagh had escaped the pens, and remembers the shock and anger: 'Waking up the next morning and finding out my mate, who I'd got a ticket for, was dead. Finding out the following night a lad I went to school with was killed and another of my mates was in hospital. Tasting the sadness that was in the air, the flags at half-mast, the minute's silence and the impact that it had on the community. I wasn't prepared for what happened the following Wednesday. I'm not even going to mention the name of the paper because I can't without putting swear words in front of it. I never saw that coming – it was like somebody had hit me around the side of the head with a cricket bat. We were wronged, we were on the floor, and it was all over the telly. If we had done anything wrong, it would have been doubly shown all over the telly. It was plainly lies.'

John Joynt, another survivor, also recalls the disbelief at the story in *The Sun*: 'I'd have never bought that paper in the first place, but straight away when you saw that headline you knew it was lies, having been there. I am so glad that the boycott has been so strong for twenty-five years – you very rarely see anyone reading a copy in Liverpool. Scurrilous lies.' Ed Critchley remembers the headlines being completely at odds with his experience at Hillsborough: 'The hurtful stories that ran in the papers afterwards could not have been more opposite to what I experienced that day. Liverpool fans did everything they could, and the people that should have helped didn't. The horrendous lies that they were printing were so damaging because people believed them. I remember people telling me people were drunk and that, and I'm not a violent man but I felt like throttling them. I would never have read *The Sun* anyway so I didn't have to change a habit, but me and my family would never even touch that newspaper again. It was sickening.'

Mike Wilson remembers the anger, and that his dad actually wrote to the papers: 'When the newspapers started to print lies about what happened, dad sent his account to the tabloids. The Daily Star was the only newspaper to print it. It's amazing how, now that we know the truth, dad's account is exactly aligned to it.'

The Sun was not the only newspaper to run with this story, but it was the most vicious, and Mackenzie's refusal to apologise for years afterwards did them no favours. On the day that the story ran, some on Merseyside took copies of the paper into the street and burnt them to show their feelings. In 1989, the media set the agenda. There was a one-to-many system in place before the internet, which meant that newspapers could run a story that would reach millions of people in one day, but those most affected by that story had no right to reply. There were just over 24,000 Liverpool fans at Hillsborough that day, a high percentage of them from the Merseyside area, who had witnessed first-hand what happened that day, but there was no forum for them to tell their stories to the country. Newspapers had millions of readers, and collectively they could influence the thinking of most of the country in just a single day. The stories that *The Sun* and others ran around that time were traced back to White's News Agency in Sheffield, and White's got their stories from unnamed South Yorkshire Police officers and a Conservative MP.

It appeared that the post-disaster investigations by the police hinged firmly against the fans, and their response to the disaster had been to look for evidence of drunk and ticketless fans, rather than to learn lessons. They drove over the Snake Pass, the route many Liverpool fans would have taken, looking for empty beer cans and bottles. They interviewed publicans and off-licences in the area about the level of drinking on the day. However, the assertion that alcohol was to be blamed was made far earlier. Many families of the bereaved remember being questioned, immediately after identifying their loved ones in the gymnasium at Hillsborough on the night of Saturday 15 April 1989 or in the early hours of Sunday 16 April 1989, about how much their family member had drunk prior to the game and if they had a ticket. On the evening of the disaster, the coroner, Dr Stefan Popper, ordered the taking of blood alcohol levels from all of the deceased. The victims of the disaster were being treated as suspects, and the taking of blood alcohol levels from the deceased at a disaster scene was unprecedented.

Barry Devonside was interviewed immediately after identifying his dead son in the gymnasium: 'At that point we were led to a table. There were lots of tables and a massive screen between where the bodies were being kept and where the police were interviewing the relatives. We were taken to a table and asked to confirm who I had just identified. I gave them Chris's full name and his address and confirmed that I was his father. The copper then said, "How did you travel here today?" I asked what that had to do with identification? The officer said that they were trying to get a broad picture of everything. He asked if we stopped anywhere en route. Again I said, "What's that got to do with anything to do with identifying my son?" At that point, my brother whispered in my ear and I took him to one side. He [my brother] was getting very angry about the police questions, and he recognised straight away what was happening. I said to him listen, whatever happens here tonight or on subsequent days no embarrassment can be brought to Chris's name. He never brought any embarrassment onto his mum or dad or his family while he was alive, so just bite your bottom lip. I went back to the table and my brother stayed away. The officer said, "When you stopped did you have any alcohol?" I realised then. Not with the severity we've learnt about over the last twenty-five years, but I realised that these questions had nothing at all to do with identification. This was a slant, pointing the finger at Liverpool supporters, and trying to blame Liverpool supporters for being drunk. I had one can, and Chris had one can. It [the interview] went on like that.'

The West Midlands Police were asked to investigate and gather evidence for the Director of Public Prosecutions and the Taylor Inquiry. Steve Hart was convalescing in bed when the officers came to take his statement: 'The West Midlands Police came out twice to see me. The first time they came out they were there for about half an hour, and my wife chased them out because of their questioning – it was pretty aggressive. I think it was about a week after the disaster, and they turned up unexpectedly at the house. I was in bed because I could barely move; my ribs were wrecked. My wife came upstairs and told me that the police were downstairs, and I said, "The police? That's a bit strange." So I went downstairs and they introduced themselves, it was a lady and a man from the West Midlands Police. We sit down, and talk for a bit and they tell me that they are going to take a statement. Virtually the first question they ask if you were on a coach: How much did you have to drink? Straight away, my hackles went up – it was the first question out of his mouth. I told him that we did exactly the same in 1989 as we did in 1988. We hired a coach; we went to a pub outside of Sheffield and had a meal. It worked well the year before, so we did the same thing in 1989. He carried on asking questions and then he asked, did we have a drink on the coach? I said to him, "You know full well we didn't, as you're not allowed to take ale on the coach." I asked him, "What is it about the ale? You've been here about ten minutes and three or four times you've asked me about ale?" He said, "You lot must have had a drink when you got to the pub?" I said, "I've told you we went for a meal and a drink. I had a pint, but there were fifty people on that coach – do you honestly expect me to remember what everyone had to drink?" He then asked if I saw any unrest on the way towards the ground. I thought you're fishing here, and I started to get upset. Then he asked me how many people got in without tickets. I said to him that I got into the ground with my ticket intact, and he said that I couldn't have done. I said, "Actually, I've got it here." I didn't go through the gate, I went through a turnstile, and it was that bad outside the gateman must have literally thought I've got to let everyone through. I could hear the turnstiles clicking continuously behind me as he was letting everyone through, so I got into the ground with a full ticket in my hand. I gave them my ticket, which was a bad mistake, because I never got it back. The officer then started going on about the fans putting the gate in. So I said to him, I know that's not right because I saw the police open it with my own eyes, and I knew that on the day. As we were coming out of the ground I took my mates around to show them the gate, because it was already getting reported that fans had forced the gate and I knew they hadn't. I showed them, look, there's no footmarks, no damage or nothing. So on the day I went up to this senior copper, and I knew he was senior because he had the flat cap and a cane, and I said to him, "You're a liar, the gates got opened, they weren't kicked in." My mates dragged me away in the end. The questioning kept revolving around ticketless fans, drunken fans and I was arguing back, but I was getting upset so the wife said to them you're going to have to leave – I'm not having it, and that was that.'

'It must have been a week or two later, and they came back. The same policeman and woman, but when they came back they didn't continue the statement. I thought they would continue the statement from their first visit, but they didn't, they started again. There is no trace of that first interview anywhere. They were there a lot longer the second time, and the questioning was along the same lines. All about ticketless fans, and drunk fans – you knew where this was going. It didn't take a genius to work out what was going on. In the meantime, all the stuff had hit the papers with these allegations as well and that had upset me no end. The policeman was asking the questions and the policewoman was writing it down as I was saying it. I went through the events of the day with them – it must have taken well over an hour, and after each piece of paper was full I was given it and asked to sign it. Obviously I did sign them, but I didn't get a chance to read it. After the amount of time they had been there, and the questioning, it was upsetting and you just wanted them out of the house and gone. I asked if I would get a copy of the statement, because I was in no mental state to sit there and read back everything. They assured me that I would get a copy, and if I was required to give evidence at any stage they'd be in touch. That was it. I heard nothing after that.'

Lord Justice Taylor had a huge body of evidence to consider for his inquiry, and he also had the benefit of reviewing all of this while everything was fresh in the memory. As a result, the report is an extremely detailed piece of work, which looks in depth at a number of the issues that caused the disaster, and I would urge anyone who hasn't already done so to read it. To use Lord Justice Taylor's own summary: 'The immediate cause of the gross overcrowding and hence the disaster was the failure, when gate C was opened, to cut off access to the central pens, which were already overfull. They were already over full because no safe maximum capacities had been laid down, no attempt was made to control entry to individual pens numerically and there was no effective visual monitoring of crowd density. When the influx from gate C entered pen 3, the layout of the barriers there afforded less protection than it should and a barrier collapsed. Again, the lack of vigilant monitoring caused a sluggish reaction and response when the crush occurred. The small size and number of gates to the track retarded rescue efforts. So, in the initial stages, did lack of leadership. The need to open gate C was due to dangerous congestion at the turnstiles. That occurred because, as both club and police should have realised, the turnstile area could not easily cope with the large numbers demanded of it unless they arrived steadily over a lengthy period. The Operational Order and police tactics on the day failed to provide for controlling a concentrated arrival of large numbers, should that occur in a short period. That it might so occur was foreseeable and it did. The presence of an unruly minority who had drunk too much aggravated the problem. So did the club's confused and inadequate signs and ticketing.'

Lord Taylor went on to say that the main reason the disaster happened was 'a failure of police control', as set out in his interim report in August 1989: 'It is fair to state that over many years the South Yorkshire Police have given excellent service to the public.

They have handled crowd problems sensitively and successfully at a large number of football games including major matches, during strikes in the coal industry and the steel industry, and in other contexts. Unfortunately, their policing on 15 April broke down in the ways already described and, although there were other causes, the main reason for the disaster was the failure of police control.'

Lord Justice Taylor then went on to chronicle some of that 'failure' in his report: 'Mr Duckenfield leant heavily on Mr Murray's experience. Between them they misjudged the build-up at the turnstiles and did little about it until they received Mr Marshall's request to open the gate. They did not, for example, check the turnstile figures available from Club control or check with Tango units as to the numbers still to come. They did not alert Mr Greenwood to the situation at the fringe of his area of command. They gave no instructions as to the management of the crowd at Leppings Lane. Inflexibly they declined to postpone kick-off. When Mr Marshall's request came, Mr Duckenfield's capacity to take decisions and give orders seemed to collapse. Having sanctioned, at last, the opening of the gates, he failed to give necessary consequential orders or to exert any control when the disaster occurred. He misinterpreted the emergence of fans from pens 3 and 4. When he was unsure of the problem, he sent others down to "assess the situation" rather than descend to see for himself. He gave no information to the crowd. Most surprisingly, he gave Mr Kelly and others, to think that there had been an inrush due to Liverpool fans forcing open a gate. This was not only untruthful. It set off a widely reported allegation against the supporters which caused grave offence and distress. It revived against football fans, and especially those from Liverpool, accusations of hooliganism which caused reaction not only nationwide but from Europe too. I can only assume that Mr Duckenfield's lack of candour on this occasion was out of character. He said his reason for not telling the truth was that if the crowd became aware of it there might be a very hostile reaction and this might impede rescue work. He did not wish to divulge what had happened until he had spoken to a senior officer. However, reluctance to tell Mr Kelly the truth did not require that he be told a falsehood. Moreover, although Assistant Chief Constable Jackson was at hand, Mr Duckenfield did not disclose the truth to him until much later. The likeliest explanation of Mr Duckenfield's conduct is that he simply could not face the enormity of the decision to open the gates and all that flowed therefrom. That would explain what he said to Mr Kelly, what he did not say to Mr Jackson, his aversion to addressing the crowd and his failure to take effective control of the disaster situation. He froze.'

Taylor went on to express his feelings about the police at the inquiry: 'It is a matter of regret that at the hearing, and in their submissions, the South Yorkshire Police were not prepared to concede they were in any respect at fault in what occurred. Mr Duckenfield, under pressure of cross-examination, apologised for blaming the Liverpool fans for causing the deaths. But, that apart, the police case was to blame the fans for being late and drunk, and to blame the Club for failing to monitor the pens. It was argued that the fatal crush was not caused by the influx through gate C but was due to barrier 124a being defective. Such an unrealistic approach gives cause for anxiety as to whether lessons have been learnt. It would have been more seemly and encouraging for the future if responsibility had been faced.'

Since the publication of the Hillsborough Independent Panel report in September 2012, we now know that police statements from junior officers were amended to apparently remove any criticism they had of the South Yorkshire Police operation on the day and to leave in any criticism of the fans, thus creating a series of statements that are more biased against Liverpool supporters. According to the apology given by the current Chief Constable of South Yorkshire Police in the wake of the Hillsborough Independent Panel report, 'In the immediate aftermath senior officers sought to change the record of events. Disgraceful lies were told, which blamed the Liverpool fans for the disaster.' Lord Justice Taylor did not know about this at the time of his report, however, and sadly we'll never know what conclusion Taylor would have reached had he known about the full extent of amended statements, because he passed away in 1997. Within his report, however, Lord Justice Taylor did make a mention of the evidence he received from the police, which makes interesting reading twenty-five years on. In his interim report, published in August 1989, Lord Justice Taylor wrote: 'In all some sixty-five police officers gave oral evidence at the Inquiry. Sadly I must report that for the most part the quality of their evidence was in inverse proportion to their rank. There were many young Constables who as witnesses were alert, intelligent and open. On the day, they and many others strove heroically in ghastly circumstances aggravated by hostility to rescue and succour victims. They inspired confidence and hope. By contrast, with some notable exceptions, the senior officers in command were defensive and evasive witnesses. Their feelings of grief and sorrow were obvious and genuine. No doubt those feelings were intensified by the knowledge that such a disaster had occurred under their management. But neither their handling of problems on the day nor their account of it in evidence showed the qualities of leadership to be expected of their rank.'

Taylor rejected the mass drunken story that South Yorkshire Police had told, and that the British media had broadcast far and wide. He was equally confident that ticketless fans played no significant part in the disaster, as he explains in his report. The Health & Safety Executive had studied the electronically generated numbers for the turnstiles and also looked at video evidence to ascertain how many Liverpool supporters had entered the ground. As Lord Taylor explains in his report: 'First, there was a wide range of witnesses who observed inside the ground that the Liverpool end was at a late stage well below capacity, save for pens 3 and 4. The north stand still had many empty seats and the wing pens were sparse. The match being a sell-out, there were clearly many ticket holders to come and they could account for the large crowd still outside the turnstiles. Had the Liverpool accommodation been full by 2.40 p.m., one could have inferred that most or much of the large crowd outside lacked tickets. Secondly, such figures as are available from the Club's electronic monitoring system and from analyses by the HSE suggest that no great number entered without tickets. They show that the number who passed through turnstiles A to G plus those who entered through gate C roughly equalled the terrace capacity figure of 10,100 for which tickets had been sold. The Club's record showed 7,038 passed through turnstiles A to G. However, the counting mechanism on turnstile G was defective, so the HSE did a study using the video film and projecting figures from the other turnstiles. This gave an assessment of 7,494, with a maximum of 7,644 passing through A to G. Again, using the video, the HSE assessed the number who entered the ground whilst gate C was open at 2,240 with a maximum of 2,480. Accordingly, the HSE's best estimate of the total entering through gate C and turnstiles A to G was 9,734 with a maximum of 10,124.'

The Leppings Lane terrace had a total capacity of 10,100 spectators, so what the Health & Safety Executive study proved was that the number of Liverpool fans who entered the stadium that day was somewhere between 366 less and 24 more than the 10,100 capacity. This surely proves beyond reasonable doubt that ticketless fans were not a factor, despite the South Yorkshire Police accusations?

Lord Justice Taylor also explained the disparity between the access afforded to the Liverpool fans in the Leppings Lane end and the Nottingham Forest fans at the Kop end: 'At the south side of the ground there were 24 turnstiles (numbered 19 to 42 on the plan). Those numbered 37 to 42 led to the Kop and the rest to the south stand. In summary, the south and east sides of the ground accommodated some 29,800 whose access on the day was through sixty turnstiles. The other two sides of the ground, north and west, with a capacity of 24,256 were fed solely from the Leppings Lane entrance where there were only twenty-three turnstiles.'

That means that the turnstiles at the Kop end had to admit an average of 496 spectators each, while at the Leppings Lane end each turnstile had to admit an average of 1,054 spectators. This was because fans with tickets to the North Stand, the West Stand and the terraces had to enter via the cramped Leppings Lane turnstiles. Of those twenty-three turnstiles, only seven were allocated to the 10,100 supporters who had tickets to the Leppings Lane standing terraces, which means that those specific turnstiles (marked A–G) had to admit an average of 1,442 supporters per turnstile. That was nearly three times the average required from each turnstile at the Forest end.

Lord Justice Taylor also stated in his report that the removal of a crush barrier in the years before the disaster should have resulted in a reduced capacity for the central pens: 'The removal of barrier 144 in 1986 should have reduced the notional capacity of pen 3 as already mentioned. But it did more. In the absence of barrier 144, the influx of fans after 2.52 p.m. met no retarding structure as it came into pen 3. The pressure created was free to push fans straight down by the radial fence to the lowest line of barriers. The pressure diagonally from the tunnel mouth down to barrier number 124a which collapsed was unbroken by any intervening barrier. 124a was also vulnerable to pressure straight down the pen through the gap in the barrier above it created in 1985.'

The Taylor Report also states, 'Dr Nicholson calculated that when all relevant factors regarding the configuration and the Green Guide are taken into account, the maximum capacity for pen 3 should have been 822 and for pen 4, 871.' That is a recommended combined capacity of 1,693 for the two central pens, yet on the day the capacity on the day was 2,100, and tragically even that figure was grossly exceeded. Lord Taylor also found that barrier 124a, the barrier that collapsed under the weight of people, was in a poor state of repair: 'Inspection of barrier 124a, and indeed other barriers at Hillsborough, by the HSE showed considerable corrosion of the metal at vulnerable points where water could accumulate. Dr Eastwood agreed that if a significant degree of corrosion was observed on visual inspection, a barrier should be condemned.'

So a 'failure of police control', according to Lord Justice Taylor, was the main reason for the disaster. Taylor had seventy-one hours of video footage at his disposal, hundreds of photographs and thousands of witnesses from all parties involved and had the benefit of reviewing all of this while detail was very fresh in people's minds. A British judge, employed by a Conservative government, found the police to be the 'main reason for the disaster'. A cynical mind might conclude that Lord Taylor, a member of the establishment, might find in favour of the police if there were any grey areas, but he didn't. He was also clear that alcohol played no significant part in the disaster, saying, 'Of those who arrived at 2.30 p.m. or after, very many had been drinking at public houses or had brought drink from home or an off-licence. I am satisfied on the evidence, however, that the great majority were not drunk nor even the worse for drink. The police witnesses varied on this. Some described a high proportion as drunk, as "lager-louts" or even as "animals". Others described a generally normal crowd with an uncooperative minority who had drunk too much. In my view some officers, seeking to rationalise their loss of control, overestimated the drunken element in the crowd.'

Taylor also quoted advice from sixty-five years previously, which was relevant to the build-up of fans outside the turnstiles: 'As long ago as 1924, the Departmental Committee on Crowds stated: "The control of crowds should begin at a point some considerable distance from the entrance to the ground. The advantages of an arrangement of this kind are ... in preventing congestion at the entrances to grounds." This was particularly important at Leppings Lane where the turnstile area was so small and awkwardly laid out. If a large crowd was permitted uncontrolled entry through the perimeter gates, the forming of queues at the turnstiles and control by officers, whether on foot or mounted, would become impracticable. Those waiting at the turnstiles would become a single growing mass. Once that happened, it would be difficult to retrieve the situation.'

The interim report also criticised the practice of allowing fans to 'find their own level' after entering the turnstiles: 'At League matches at Hillsborough, the police practice was to decide in advance how many and which pens would be used. If a modest crowd was anticipated only one or two pens might be needed. It was better to confine the fans to limited spaces (a) to prevent them running about and (b) to reduce the number of police required. The practice was then to fill the pens one by one. This involved making a judgement as to when a pen was full. There would then be a police decision to close that pen and fill another. It was regarded as impractical and unsafe for police officers (just like stewards) to go onto the Leppings Lane terraces with away supporters. This meant that monitoring the numbers in any pen had to be done from vantage points outside it. Here, the police were much better placed than the stewards. There was a good view from the control box and the television screens there. There were officers on the perimeter track. No stewards were placed there because having both police and stewards interfered with the viewing. There were also police in the west stand who could look down on the pens. Intelligence from all these sources could give the police a good appreciation of the state of the terraces. When it was necessary to shut off access to the pens officers on the concourse could be informed by radio and could take the necessary steps. At cup semi-finals, a different approach was adopted.

'All the pens were opened from the start and the policy was "to let the fans find their own level". This phrase was repeated again and again by police officers at the inquiry. What it meant was that no specific direction was given to fans entering through the turnstiles. They were free to go wherever they wished on the terraces. If they became uncomfortable or wished for any other reason to move their position, then theoretically they could move elsewhere. In this way it was hoped that the fans on the terraces would level themselves out and that distribution would be achieved without police intervention. On these occasions, the gates at the top of the radial fences were locked in the open position. It was sought to argue, therefore, that there was freedom of movement from one pen to another enabling fans to "find their level". This argument was bad both in theory and in practice. In theory, the whole object of the radial fences had been to achieve even distribution by directing fans into desired positions. To say then that they could move freely from one pen to another would defeat the object and enable fans to go from a less popular to a more popular area without inhibition. In practice this did not happen because the position and size of the gates was such that once a substantial number of spectators were in, the gates were unnoticeable and inaccessible especially to those towards the front who might have most need of them.'

Having read that paragraph from Taylor's interim report, the recollections from Liverpool supporter Peter Dalling come to mind: 'At this time, a copper came up the walkway [between pen four and pen five] and people were screaming at him to get the gate open, but he didn't have a key.' Peter Dalling was right near the gate in the lateral fence that led from pen four into a sterile area between pen four and pen five, and he remembers that the gate was not in fact 'locked in the open position' at all. It was locked shut. The only way that fans in the dangerously over full central pens could 'find their own level' was to climb out; such was the density of the crowd and the flow of supporters packing the tunnel. When Duckenfield, the Match Commander, asked for a tannoy announcement to be relayed to the fans in the central pens to 'move down and spread along the terrace', he was asking for the impossible. The radial fences stopped sideways movement by design, so to 'spread along the terrace' was an impossible instruction to follow. What was Duckenfield thinking at that time?

Brenda Fox, mother of Steven Fox, remembers when Lord Justice Taylor's interim report was published: 'In August we all received a copy of the Lord Taylor report and in this report he concluded "the main reason for the disaster was the failure of police control". But even though it was in black and white, people outside of Merseyside still believed the fans were responsible and Scousers were still regarded as "drunken yobs". The lies that the newspapers reported were still considered to be the truth. These comments made you feel like you had to defend your loved one, and you were guarding a grave. In September, my husband and I were contacted by the West Midlands police, requesting us to meet them at Birkenhead Town Hall, which we did. But unfortunately, even after nineteen years, this meeting still haunts me. When I think about it or talk about it, it's like I have a television inside my head and I can watch it like I am sitting and watching my television at home. The images are still so clear I wish I could find the off switch, but I can't and have to wait until it clears itself again. The officers informed us that they were gathering evidence to use in disciplinary charges of neglect in duty that would be preferred against the chief officers in control of the operation at the ground. They needed our help as they could not identify Steve on any of the photographs they had of the match, and as his parents we might be able to see what they couldn't. We were given magnifying glasses and stacks of still photographs, scenes from the crush, and scenes from the crowd at the turnstiles. We could not find Steve on any of these pictures. We were then shown the video from the police security cameras on the day of the crush. It was in slow motion and I don't know how many times they had to rewind it before I could see past the horrors of what was before my eyes and to see past the tears and focus on the actual crush. But I did and found a very familiar sight, the side of a head I used to wake of a morning and say, "That's Steve." After watching this video, my question was, if I could see the middle pens were full and the side pens were empty, why couldn't the trained officers watching try to do something about it? For the next couple of weeks, all I could see when I closed my eyes was the video of Hillsborough and the questions whipped through my brain until I eventually cried myself to sleep. I walked around with big red eyes for weeks and when friends asked me if I was ok, I said, "Yes", because I could not explain the terrible scenes that I had witnessed without the tears starting again. My only consolation, which kept me going through this very difficult time, was that Lord Taylor had ordered that the terrible fences had to be pulled down and the grounds would be replaced by seats. No fans would be crushed to death again and no one would have to view those terrible scenes.'

On 18 April 1990, a year and three days after the disaster, Dr Stefan Popper started the process of holding mini-inquests for each of the 95 deceased. The 96th person, who was later to die, was on a life-support machine at this time. Three days after attending the first memorial for those who lost their lives at Hillsborough, families were asked to attend a mini-inquest to hear about their loved ones' last moments. The Director of Public Prosecutions had not yet decided if criminal prosecutions should be followed, but Popper decided to move ahead with the mini-inquest format at that time. According to the Ministry of Justice, a coroner's role is as follows: 'It is a coroner's duty at an inquest to establish who the deceased was and how, when and where the deceased came by his or her death. After an inquest the coroner will send the necessary details to the registrar of births and deaths for the death to be registered when it occurred in England and Wales. An inquest is not permitted to determine or appear to determine criminal liability by a named person or civil liability. It is about what happened, not who was responsible for what happened, for which the civil and criminal courts have jurisdiction.'

Dr Stefan Popper stated that the mini-inquests would deal only with the 'who' had died, 'where' they had died, and at what 'time' they had died. Popper stated that he would not be dealing with the 'how' people died in this mini-inquest format, however. Families of the bereaved were told that they would only hear evidence from a pathologist, and officers from the investigating West Midlands Police force. This evidence was collated by the police, and families and their solicitors would not have the chance to question or cross-reference the evidence. It was essentially evidence stated as fact. After being subjected to media-fuelled police stories of drunken, ticketless fans, this format that allowed no right to reply was a concern to say the least. Summarised evidence would be accepted as fact. Families sat and listened to West Midlands Police officers talk about alcohol consumption and blood alcohol levels, and were not able to question or challenge the evidence.

In August 1990, the Director of Public Prosecutions decided that there was insufficient evidence to prosecute any persons in relation to the disaster and so, in November 1990, the main inquest started. Despite the Taylor Report finding that alcohol played no significant part in the disaster, South Yorkshire Police used the inquest to continue to accuse Liverpool fans of being drunk & disorderly. Dr Stefan Popper caused more anxiety by imposing a 3.15 p.m. cut-off, which meant that anything that happened after 3.15 p.m. on Saturday 15 April 1989 would not be considered. According to the Hillsborough Independent Panel's report (HIP report) in September 2012, Dr Popper's reasoning for this was 'those who died received the injuries that caused their death before 3.15 p.m., even if they lived beyond that time'. His logic was that in each case there was no 'intervening act' (*novus actus interveniens*) that contributed to death. This rationale, however, also suggested that whatever the interventions, or lack of interventions, as part of the emergency response, each death was unavoidable once 3.15 p.m. had been reached. Although this assertion couldn't be challenged at the time, the HIP report in 2012 had studied the medical evidence and found that there was 'clear medical evidence that a significant number of those who died may have been alive after removal from the pens. These individuals might have survived given appropriate and timely intervention, but remained vulnerable while unconscious to the effects of a new event such as being positioned incorrectly or inhaling stomach contents.' The 3.15 p.m. cut-off also meant that some of the major questions families had about the response to the disaster wouldn't be answered. Questions like, 'Why was the major incident plan not implemented?' 'Why did only three ambulances make it onto the pitch when over forty arrived outside the ground?' The 3.15 p.m. cut-off also cast as fact the assertion that actions after this point would not have changed the life expectancy of any of the 96 men, women and children who died.

Kevin Daniel Williams was a fifteen-year-old boy when he travelled to Sheffield to watch Liverpool play in the FA Cup semi-final. His story was one of the reasons why the 3.15 p.m. cut-off was unsafe and unfair in the eyes of his mother, Anne Williams. Saturday 15 April 1989 was the first time Kevin had been allowed to travel to an away game without an adult. Video evidence shows that he entered the ground around 1.30 p.m. and went into pen four, but a little later he saw some other lads that he knew from Formby, where he lived, and so he went to join them in pen three. As the crush worsened, Kevin was moved toward the barrier that eventually broke, and visual evidence shows that he was pulled out of the pens at 3.28 p.m. and laid on the pitch. Tony O'Keefe and Steve Hart were two of the fans who helped carry Kevin on a makeshift stretcher to the north-east end of the ground, where they expected Kevin to get help. Tony O'Keefe said that Kevin had colour at that time and he thought he was alive. At the other end of the pitch, PC Bruder, an off-duty Merseyside police officer, gave Kevin the kiss of life. He said in his original statement that he found a pulse. He was later told that he was mistaken, and his statement was changed. Special

Constable Debra Martin said in her original witness statement that she helped Kevin Williams from the pitch and into the gym: 'I helped carry a young boy into the gym from the pitch nearby. He stopped breathing so I gave him the kiss of life and heart massage and a doctor also helped. He started breathing, and opened his eyes; his only word was "mum" and then he died.'

Debra Martin was contacted by Anne Williams directly, and she spoke about how she was put under enormous pressure to sign a different statement, but she stood by her first statement and said that Kevin woke up momentarily and said the word 'mum' at around 4 p.m. Anne Williams believed that PC Bruder and WPC Debra Martin were put under pressure to change their statements, and that was done because Kevin's story didn't fit with the 3.15 p.m. cut-off point imposed by Dr Stefan Popper. Anne Williams spent twenty-four years trying to get a new inquest for Kevin, and to get truth and justice for the 96, helping and inspiring many others along the way. She felt that the establishment knocked her back time and time again because they knew that if she won, it would 'open the floodgates for other families'. I remember Anne saying the following sentence: 'They used to say you're right, Anne, but you'll not beat the system.'

Sadly, Anne Williams passed away on 18 April 2013, exactly twenty-four years to the day since Dr Stefan Popper held his first mini-inquest, and just three days after the twenty-fourth anniversary memorial service at Anfield. Anne will not see the new inquest that she helped win for her son, Kevin, but she did, at least, see the truth published by the Hillsborough Independent Panel in September 2012. Anne was a mother from Formby, whose love for her son drove her to take on the system and win, and she is an inspiration to so many people because of that. After her passing, she was awarded the BBC Sports Personality of the Year Helen Rollason Award, which is an annual award given 'for outstanding achievement in the face of adversity'. Her daughter, Sara Williams, has written a very moving book for her mother called *With Hope in her Heart*, which is a must-read for anyone who wants to know more about Anne's remarkable story.

In March 1991, the jury returned a verdict of accidental death, much to the dismay of the families who feel that the disaster was foreseeable, preventable and that the two most senior officers in charge, Duckenfield and Murray, are culpable. Barry Devonside lost his son Christopher in the disaster, and attended every day of the inquests: 'I attended every single one of the inquests, and I listened to some of the worst rubbish you could ever hear. The first three weeks of the inquests were all about alcohol. There were licensees, restaurant managers, bar men and women. Having attended every day, I don't really know what I can say other than they were an utter whitewash. I have no qualms in saying that Stefan Popper, the coroner in those inquests, was in my view biased towards the South Yorkshire police. In fact on the last day, when the verdict of accidental death was brought in, there were four people on the jury who broke down crying. They realised the impact of the decision on the families, and I think they realised that they had made a mistake.'

The Director of Public Prosecutions decided against any criminal proceedings against the two most senior policemen on duty – Duckenfield and Murray – but in July 1991, the Police Complaints Authority (PCA) started disciplinary proceedings against them for 'neglect of duty'. Correspondence between the PCA and South Yorkshire Police went on for some time and in one such letter, which can be found on the Hillsborough Independent Panel website, it was written that, 'The incident which gave rise to the tragedy at the Hillsborough Stadium on 15 April 1989 would not have occurred had sensible and simple steps been taken to secure the safety of spectators in Pens 3 and 4 on the Leppings Lane Terraces. It is clear that the basic cause of the disaster was overcrowding in these pens. We have concentrated on this matter.' It was a fairly damning indictment of Duckenfield and Murray from the Police Complaints Authority, which then went on to spell out exactly what it considered Duckenfield and Murray's shortcomings to be: 'Despite these factors it cannot be denied that the police, under the control of Chief Superintendent Duckenfield, assisted by Superintendent Murray, were de facto in control of the ground at the relevant time and had responsibility for the safety of the spectators. In the opinion of this Authority there is sufficient evidence to support disciplinary charges on the following grounds: a. Chief Superintendent Duckenfield, as the officer in overall command, failed to address himself properly to the problems involved in, and the plans for, crowd control even before the spectators arrived; b. failed to monitor the numbers of spectators entering Pens 3 and 4; c. failed to take any action when Pens 3 and 4 became obviously overcrowded; d. authorised Gate "C" to be opened and, together with Superintendent Murray, failed to take any steps to control the movement of those who entered the ground through this gate at a time when it was, or should have been, clear to both of them that Pens 3 and 4 were, or were likely to become, overcrowded.'

So we now have a situation whereby the South Yorkshire Police had blamed Liverpool fans in the Taylor Inquiry, and failed to convince Lord Justice Taylor. Despite the Taylor Report findings, the accusations continued through the inquests and now the Police Complaints Authority were convinced enough that Duckenfield and Murray were in 'neglect of duty' to bring charges. Chief Superintendent David Duckenfield retired on medical grounds in November 1991. As a result, in January 1992, it was decided that proceeding against Murray alone would be unfair. Many people were outraged that Duckenfield was allowed to retire on a full police pension and avoid any culpability as a result. It seemed unfair that retirement protected officers from facing potential charges. One fan said, 'If I were an architect, and one of the buildings I worked on fell down and killed people as a result of my negligence, I couldn't retire and expect that to get me off the hook, so why is it different for the police?'

The Hillsborough Family Support Group, the Hillsborough Justice Campaign and Hope for Hillsborough continued to explore all avenues possible to get truth and justice for the 96. Bereaved families, survivors, friends and football fans from Liverpool and beyond stood shoulder to shoulder to support the fight for justice. Many fans from other clubs knew that it could have quite easily have been them and their fans suffering, and there still remains a feeling of 'there but for the grace of God go I'.

Steve Hart remembers that a few years later he found a picture of himself on the front page of the *Liverpool Echo*, and the events that followed: 'I think it was about five years later, there was a front page on the *Liverpool Echo*, with a picture of me and others carrying Anne's son, Kevin Williams, on an advertising hoarding. I think the headline was "Do you know these people?" Obviously the house phone is going off its rocker then, and Denise said to me, "You're on the front page of the *Echo*." I thought, oh yeah right, come on, I mean only people who rob banks are on the front page of the *Echo*! Anyway we went down and bought a copy, and I thought, wow! So I called Anne, and she already knew who I was by that point because she'd had that many people call her and say that they knew me. Anne asked me if I'd meet her, and I think it was the next day or the day after that we arranged to meet. All the way down there I remember thinking that this is going to be a case of thanks for saving my lad, or getting him help, or whatever. I was convinced of that, so I went down there in quite a jovial mood. Until that point I had put Hillsborough on the back burner, I had been in quite a deep, dark place and just tried to shut it out.

'So when I went to meet Anne, she introduced herself and literally pulled this picture out and asked if I recognised him. I said, "Yeah, that is the lad who was on the stretcher," and I am still at this point for some weird reason thinking that he's going to come walking out of the back room or something. Anne asked me, "Was he alive?" Straight away I thought, wow, where's this going? I said when we put him down he was, yeah. She then told me that he was dead, and that was a massive shock. Everything that I hadn't thought about, and managed to stick subconsciously away starts coming back. I could remember vividly what had happened with Kevin, because at the end of the day he was just a kid and I had four kids of my own. We stay there for a bit and went through the story, and she introduced me to some people who turned out to be part of the production team from The Cook Report, which was quite a hard-hitting programme in its time. They asked if I would be interviewed, and I said yeah, but I think deep-down that I might not want to do this. I hadn't spoken about Hillsborough to anyone, and managed to put it locked away. I agreed to do the interview, and we did the shoot in a hotel in Formby. The wife came down with me, and Anne was in the room. I tried to do the interview but there was only so much

I could do and I just broke down. So Roger Cook suggested to my wife and Anne that they should both go for a walk down the beach, as it might be easier for me to talk without them there. They went, and I managed to do the interview, and from that day until the day she died, Anne and I were very close friends. We've done countless interviews, and as I got to know her I started to learn what evidence she had. As we got deeper into it I found it easier to talk about it, and I thought people needed to know more of the truth. Too many people have probably said too little for too long really, and who could we speak to? Nobody was our voice. The more I learned the more I came to see the injustice of it all, and how badly the story needed to be told.'

In June 1994, The Cook Report broadcast a thirty-minute programme across the nation that highlighted the plight of Anne Williams, and the fight for justice for Kevin and the other 95. It focused on testimony from WPC Debra Martin, who said she looked after Kevin and heard Tony O'Keefe, who helped to carry Kevin on an advertising hoarding. The programme focused on the fact that those who touched Kevin from the time he was pulled out of the pens, until the time he died in the gym, believed that he was alive; the inference being that if Kevin was alive at 4 p.m., then the 3.15 p.m. cut-off point imposed by Dr Stefan Popper was unsafe.

Another programme about Hillsborough came to British screens in 1996, this time a hard-hitting docudrama by Jimmy McGovern starring Christopher Eccleston and Ricky Tomlinson. This moving docudrama focused on the story of the day and the inquests, and followed the Hicks, Spearritt, and Glover family stories. These programmes helped move Hillsborough back into the public eye, and got people talking about it again.

In May 1997, the incoming Home Secretary, Jack Straw, told the families that there would be a judicial review, and he appointed Lord Justice Stuart-Smith to conduct a 'scrutiny of the evidence' to see if there was any evidence in existence that was not available to the Taylor Inquiry. This review was a part of a pledge made by the Labour government to the Hillsborough families before they got into power. It had come to light that police statements had been amended, and it was these amended statements that were thought to be new evidence that was not available to the Taylor Inquiry. Some of these amended statements seemed to favour the South Yorkshire Police and some of the lines that were deleted could have put the force in a difficult position. For example, PC Woodcock said, 'I saw Inspector Harry White at the debrief. He told me that his serial usually got the job of putting the crowd in the different pens at the rear of the goalmouth, working from the outside to the centre, but for some reason he'd been told to let the fans find their own level, on this occasion, resulting in too many going into the area immediately behind the goal. I could tell he was distressed by what had happened.'

Had this part of the statement been allowed to remain, then questions could have been asked about why the fans were left to 'find their own level' on 15 April 1989, especially if 'usually' a serial had the job of filling the pens from the outside in, and especially as the man who 'usually had the job', Harry White, didn't appear to know why the decision had been made.

PC Powell had originally written: 'The first thing I said was, "Where are all the bobbies? There's hardly anybody there." I saw numerous people climbing over the tops of the turnstiles and the few police officers that I saw appeared to be doing nothing about it. My main observation at this point was the lack of police presence. I couldn't understand how such a large crowd could have possibly gathered. I recall in previous games there was usually a large police presence concentrated on this part of the ground, usually forming some sort of cordon.'

PC Powell of South Yorkshire Police seemed to have observed what many fans who had been at both the 1988 and 1989 semi-finals had seen, and this was that the organisation outside the ground was different. The paragraph in PC Powell's statement would possibly have corroborated what the fans had said, and called into question Duckenfield's management of the 1989 semi-final. It was deleted. Lord Justice Stuart-Smith met with Stuart Denton of South Yorkshire Police, and thanks to the work carried out by the Hillsborough Independent Panel, we are able to read the minutes of that meeting. Lord Justice Stuart-Smith said to Donald Denton:

'Q [LJ Stuart-Smith]: One of the things that strikes me about the alterations that I have looked at – and I have not looked at all of them – is that there tends to be a removal of criticisms of senior officers but no corresponding removal of criticism of the fans.

A [Donald Denton]: I think one has to look at the light in which this was being done, sir.

Q [LJ Stuart-Smith]: In what light is that?

A [Donald Denton]: This, as you say, was in fact being done in a way which anticipated an inquiry and anticipated actions against the Club, against the Police, and I think it would be fair to say that throughout the whole of this exercise – whilst there was nothing distinctly deliberate about it – the South Yorkshire Police at that time had their backs to the wall a little bit with public opinion against them. I think it was absolutely natural for them to concern themselves with defending themselves.'

One officer who had his statement amended said: "One officer stated he had accepted the changes only because he was suffering from depression and post-traumatic stress. He considered it an 'injustice for statements to have been "doctored" to suit the management of South Yorkshire Police'. Another officer had accepted the process, but had not realised how much of his statement had been removed.'

At the end of the 'scrutiny', Stuart-Smith decided that there was no reason to launch a new public inquiry and that, 'In no case does what is excluded render the rest of the statement misleading. In those cases where factual matter has been excluded I accept that the solicitors had to exercise judgement as to whether material unhelpful to the police case should have been excluded ... at least in some cases it would have been better if it had not been. But I would categorise this at worst as an error of judgement. I certainly do not think the solicitors were guilty of anything that could be regarded as unprofessional conduct.'

Once again, the families of the 96 Hillsborough victims felt as if the door of justice had been slammed in their faces. As quoted in the Hillsborough Independent Panel report, 'Some 116 of the 164 statements identified for substantive amendment were amended to remove or alter comments unfavourable to SYP', yet

Lord Justice Stuart-Smith felt that there was no need to open a new inquiry.

The Hillsborough Family Support Group decided then to bring private prosecutions against former Chief Superintendent David Duckenfield and former Superintendent Bernard Murray. The charges against the pair included 'manslaughter' and 'misconduct'. Duckenfield had a further charge against him of 'perverting the course of justice'. The trial was held in Leeds, and Judge Hooper presided over it; however, Judge Hooper courted controversy before the trial had even started by telling Duckenfield and Murray that, if they were found guilty, they wouldn't go to prison. This was a most irregular practice by Judge Hooper, who seemed to the layperson to have started the sentencing procedure before the defendants were put on trial. The trial started in June 2000. In July, the jury returned a verdict of 'not guilty' against Bernard Murray, and they could not reach a verdict on Duckenfield, so the jury was discharged. A retrial against David Duckenfield was refused on the basis that he could no longer receive a fair trial.

The fight for truth and justice has never stopped. The three groups – namely the Hillsborough Family Support Group, the Hillsborough Justice Campaign and Hope for Hillsborough – have continued to fight to get truth, justice and accountability for the 96 men, women and children who died at Hillsborough on 15 April 1989. Lord Justice Taylor seemed to get the story pretty much right at the first time of asking, but still no individual or organisation has been held properly accountable for the tragedy. Every legal avenue that the families travelled down was blocked, but with the support of people all over the world the fight continues.

A major breakthrough in the fight for truth and justice was set in motion at the twentieth anniversary memorial service at Anfield on 15 April 2009, when over 30,000 people gathered in the stadium to pay their respects. Andy Burnham, who was then Secretary of State for Culture, Media and Sport, was invited to come and address the Kop. Andy grew up on Merseyside, and on the day of the Hillsborough disaster he was at Villa Park supporting Everton in the other semi-final against Norwich:

'We headed down the M6 to Villa Park – lovely, sunny day. For once, this was a semi-final that didn't put us through the mill. It was a scrappy game, but we won quite comfortably. I have a recollection that the scoreboard at Villa Park flashed up "6 dead at Hillsborough" and then word started to spread, and the Everton end of the ground became completely subdued, having just won an FA Cup semi-final. In the era before mobile phones, we were wondering how we could get hold of somebody we knew who was there. We stopped at a service station and I called one of my best friends and I got his mum on the other end of the line, who was just frantic because she hadn't heard from him. Incredibly, incredibly difficult.

'I remember the conversation in the car on the way home. Everton had been at Hillsborough the year before; I can't remember if it was a third- or fourth-round game, but it was a day that we'll never forget. It had been an incredibly uncomfortable experience in those central pens, and I don't remember a single thing that happened in the second half of that game. That was because I was in terrible discomfort, and I was looking out for my dad and my brother. I was eighteen at the time, and my brother was fourteen, and I was thinking if I feel this bad what must they be going through?

'Hillsborough was an unsafe ground, and a disaster waiting to happen, sadly. There were repeated warnings down the years that weren't acted upon and that is utterly unforgivable. I'd been to Hillsborough a few times in that era. We had a lot of replays against Sheffield Wednesday, and I'd have gone to Hillsborough three or four times in that era. I have a very clear recollection of the ground, and the sheer inadequacies of the ground. The turnstiles outside the ground, and the tunnel leading down to the away end. We never had the weight of numbers because the games I went to were not as high profile, but it was always uncomfortable. Chaotic. That was always the experience, and when news started to filter through on that terrible day, we immediately went back to the bad experiences we'd had there.

'I think football fans who had been there would have immediately known what had happened more than maybe the wider public would have. That night we went to the pub where we always drank, and just didn't know what to do really. We'd watched the evening news. We still hadn't heard from so many of our friends, and one by one people were starting to appear, having found their way back from Sheffield. There was a sense of relief as they turned up. There was a growing sense of anger that night as those who were there told us what happened. They were saying things like, 'We were screaming and the police were just walking by, just a yard away,' and I remember it was making me feel really angry. In that era it was very much us and them. The Thatcher government called us "the enemy within" and all that, and every football supporter was treated as if they were a hooligan. That was the era that we were in and the sense of injustice about that was strong anyway, even before Hillsborough.'

Mr Burnham shares the deep sense of injustice that is felt by the families of the bereaved, the survivors and the wider Liverpool city and supporter base where Hillsborough is concerned, and as a politician he hoped to be able to make a difference: 'In the 1997 Labour manifesto, we said that we would reopen Hillsborough, and we did, but what happened with the Stuart-Smith inquiry was a disaster. From anyone on my side of politics it was painful. It felt like a lid was placed on Hillsborough after that. It was only when I was in the Cabinet coming up to the twentieth anniversary of Hillsborough that I felt that I had the chance to do something. Some people might not know this, but I actually made a call for full disclosure before the twentieth anniversary alongside Maria Eagle.'

Andy Burnham was invited to speak at the twentieth anniversary and it wasn't an easy invitation to accept, as he recalls: 'I agonised about whether I should go that day, I agonised about what I should say. I made the decision in consultation with my brothers that I had to go; I wouldn't have been able to live with myself if I hadn't. My main worry was would I be able to get through it without crying. Strangely, I had a feeling that something was going to happen. I almost wanted it to happen. I've always said that had I not been the minister, I would have been one of them shouting at the minister. I understood how they felt. My younger brother, text me as I was going in that day, and it said, "I don't want to worry you but I am in the Anfield Road end, and there are so many people here. I got the feeling that something was really happening here.'

Andy Burnham addressed the Kop and praised the fans for their efforts at Hillsborough, before conveying a message from the then Prime Minister, Gordon Brown. A lone voice from the Kop cried out, 'Justice!' and within seconds the entire crowd were on their feet singing 'Justice for the 96!' It is a chant heard at many a Liverpool match, and Andy Burnham stood silent, dignified and alone in front of the crowd, as they chanted loud and full of a passion that had burned for twenty years.

'Justice for the 96!'

After the ceremony, Andy recalls another supportive text from his brother, who was also an Evertonian and at Anfield that day, which read, 'Don't worry, we've had many bad afternoons at Anfield, and we'll have many more after this!' Andy just felt like going afterwards, but Steve Rotheram convinced him to go and meet with the families. As Andy recalls, 'I felt overwhelmed and just wanted to go home, but Steve Rotheram convinced me to come down to the town hall to see the families. I didn't want to go, but he dragged me there and I am really glad he did because I got the chance to speak openly with the families and I told them that I would do everything I can to get them the truth.' Andy Burnham was true to his word. The Hillsborough Independent Panel was set up to oversee the full disclosure of all documents relating to the Hillsborough disaster. In their own words, 'The Hillsborough Independent Panel was established by the UK government in January 2010 to oversee the release of documents related to the 1989 Hillsborough football disaster. The panel's role is to ensure that the Hillsborough families and the wider public receive the maximum possible disclosure of all relevant information relating to the context, circumstances and aftermath of the tragedy. It is also the panel's role to research and analyse the documents and provide a comprehensive report on what their disclosure adds to public understanding. Throughout its work the panel has consulted with the families of the deceased and its work has been informed by their views and priorities. Disclosure took place first to families and then to the public.'

On 12 September 2012, the Hillsborough Independent Panel met with the families at the Anglican cathedral in Liverpool to deliver their report before it was released to the wider public.

Families were told that '41 of the 96 had the potential to survive had the emergency response been more appropriate'. The panel went on to say: 'During the inquest, the coroner ruled that there should be a cut-off of 3.15 p.m. on the day in relation to medical evidence, arguing that the fate of all those who died after this point had already been determined by earlier events. The panel's access to all of the relevant records has confirmed that the notion of a single, unvarying and rapid pattern of death in all cases is unsustainable. Some of those who died did so after a significant period of unconsciousness, during which they might have been able to be resuscitated, or conversely may have succumbed to a new event such as inappropriate positioning. It is not possible to establish with certainty that any one individual would or could have survived under different circumstances. It is clear, however, that some people who were partially asphyxiated survived, while others did not. It is highly likely that what happened to these individuals after 3.15 p.m. was significant in determining that outcome. On the basis of this disclosed evidence, it cannot be concluded that life or death was inevitably determined by events prior to 3.15 p.m., or that no new fatal event could have occurred after that time.'

Families were also told that '116 of 164 police statements were amended to remove or alter comments unfavourable to South Yorkshire Police'.

With regard to the lies that were run by the media, the panel said: 'The documents disclosed to the panel show that the origin of these serious allegations was a local Sheffield press agency informed by several SYP officers, an SYP Police Federation spokesperson and a local MP. They also demonstrate how the SYP Police Federation, supported informally by the SYP chief constable, sought to develop and publicise a version of events that focused on several police officers' allegations of drunkenness, ticketlessness and violence among a large number of Liverpool fans. This extended beyond the media to Parliament. Yet, from the mass of documents, television and CCTV coverage disclosed to the panel there is no evidence to support these allegations other than a few isolated examples of aggressive or verbally abusive behaviour clearly reflecting frustration and desperation.'

So, after twenty-five years, the truth is finally in the public domain. Those at Hillsborough that day have always known the truth, and have had to defend themselves against allegations of drunken, loutish behaviour for a quarter of a century. Families of those who died have had to deal with the pain of bereavement, and had that compounded by the fact that those responsible would not take responsibility. Yet, despite the apologies that followed the Independent Panel's report from the Prime Minister, South Yorkshire Police, Sheffield Wednesday Football Club, the Football Association and many more besides, no person or organisation has ever been held accountable for the disaster. So justice must surely follow the truth, if the families of those who died are ever to get any sort of peace?

There are three investigations underway that the families hope will deliver 'justice for the 96'. There is an Independent Police Complaints Commission (IPCC) investigation running, whose terms of reference are to look at 'events prior to, and on the day of, the disaster'. The IPCC are investigating the action of the police, as their site states: 'A team led by former Durham Chief Constable Jon Stoddart is investigating a range of organisations involved in the preparation for the event and what happened on the day. The IPCC is managing the aspect of this investigation which is examining the actions of the police.' Operation Resolve is the criminal investigation into events before, during and after the 15 April 1989 and, according to their site, 'Ultimately, the investigation will either prove or disprove that 96 people were unlawfully killed.' Lastly, the new inquests into the deaths of the 96 will start in March 2014.

Andy Burnham believes that the lies printed as truth in the aftermath of Hillsborough were an early warning sign for things that have transpired since, when the media and the police appear too close for comfort: Things that have happened since Hillsborough have put it in a new light. The Leveson Enquiry and phone hacking for instance, and Hillsborough was an early warning sign, it seems to me, of unacceptable collusion between the press and the police, working against the interests of ordinary people. People in Liverpool were screaming loudly, telling us that lies have been told in the midst of tragedy, and no action was taken against *The Sun* so I think questions need to be asked. To have 'The Truth' printed over utter lies is the lowest of the low of British media.

Speaking specifically about the scurrilous lies printed in *The Sun* under the headline 'The Truth', Andy Burnham said, 'I can find no justification for *The Sun* newspaper and that individual in particular. The phone call made to Kenny Dalglish then proves that they knew they had done something terrible, yet the arrogance of the institution was they couldn't find a way to immediately correct what they'd done. The damage that caused was incalculable.'

He goes on to say, 'I describe Hillsborough as one of the greatest injustices of the twentieth century. I say that because it wasn't just one of the largest ever peacetime tragedies, and it wasn't just that it was entirely man-made, it was also the fact that in the immediate aftermath of ninety-six people having died, in the most unbearable circumstances, the full weight of the authorities was turned against the victims and the survivors were blamed. That is what sets it apart; the victims and the survivors were blamed and I can't find a precedent for it. That is why I think it stands apart as one of the greatest injustices of the twentieth century.'

Nothing will bring back the 96 men, women and children who died at Hillsborough, and nothing will take away the guilt, nightmares and flashbacks that many fans still suffer to this day. Survivor guilt is a horrible cross to bear; common sense and logic tell you that you could have done nothing more to help your fellow fans, yet you still feel guilty that you survived and somebody else didn't. No justice will make that go away, nor bring back those who have taken their own lives since, unable to live with the horrors in their mind any longer. Most of those worst affected by the tragedy believe that the real truth, on record, and without reservation, is the least they deserve alongside seeing those who caused the disaster being held properly accountable. Let's hope that the current investigations can deliver that basic human right and, after twenty-five years, finally deliver 'justice for the 96'.

5

Fresh Inquests

The previous chapters in this book were researched, written and ready to print by March 2014, but because new inquests were about to commence, the Attorney General had given advice on what the media could and couldn't say. It was that advice that led to the book being put on the shelf. This final chapter was written two years after the rest of the book, and so it will be interesting to see how the evidence presented to the new inquests, which will be summarised in this final chapter, marries up with the evidence presented earlier in the book.

On Tuesday 1 April 2014, the new inquests were started in Warrington, with Sir John Goldring, the coroner, presiding over events some twenty-four years, eleven months and seventeen days after the disaster.

At the outset the jury was sworn in and given the brief overview about the disaster by Sir Goldring, which included the following statement, 'Why are the inquests taking place now? This happened twenty-five years ago. Why, in 2014, are we investigating something that happened in 1989? I shall explain in more detail later, but the short answer is this: between 1990 and 1991, there were inquests in respect of ninety-five of those who died. Ninety-five, because one person who subsequently died, had not by then done so. Those inquests were conducted by the then Coroner for South Yorkshire. In December 2012, following a campaign by the bereaved families, the High Court set aside the determinations reached. This fresh hearing was ordered. The decision was made because a new inquiry was needed. We are conducting that new, or fresh, inquiry. In doing so, we are not concerned with whether what was decided at the previous inquests was right or wrong. As Lord Judge, the Lord Chief Justice, explained, there were significant lines of enquiry which remained to be pursued. As he put it, and I am quoting what he said, "The interests of justice must be served. Within the limits of the coronial system, the facts must be investigated and reanalysed in a fresh inquest when, however distressing or unpalatable, the truth will be brought to light. In this way the families of those who died in the disaster will be vindicated, and the memory of each victim will be properly respected." That is now our task, ladies and gentlemen, to investigate the facts, to reveal the truth in a public forum and to reach conclusions on the basis of the evidence presented.'

This book couldn't possibly cover the two years of evidence which the jury heard in any great detail, that would take a book in itself; so it will follow the summing up made by Sir John Goldring. The summing up itself lasted for several weeks, which gives a sense of just how much evidence the jury heard.

All quotes used in this chapter were heard in open court. This is all available online and can be found at www. hillsboroughinquests.independent.gov.uk. For clarity, because the evidence in this chapter is from the summing up, it is usually quoting the coroner, Sir Goldring, who is in turn quoting whoever previously gave the evidence.

At the outset of the new inquests, the jury started to hear a background statement about each of the ninety-six victims. Each emotional pen portrait, as they were called, was read by a family member, accompanied by a photograph of the deceased, and each and every one served as an emotional reminder of the human life behind the number ninety-six. Not just a number; rather a loved one taken too soon.

Sir John started, 'Let me start by explaining the purpose of my summing-up. First, it is to give you legal directions; second, to summarise the evidence that you have heard over what is nearly two years. I hope that my summing-up will help you in reaching the decisions, which you have to take; the determinations, as they are called. I shall take matters in the following order. First, the legal directions. I will introduce you to the twenty-five documents that you will use in giving your determinations: the questionnaires and the records of inquest. I shall say something about how to approach evidence of different kinds. I hope that I shall be able to complete that part of the summing-up today. Next, I shall summarise the evidence, and that will obviously take most of the time. I shall cover the topics in the order in which we heard the evidence: (i) Stadium safety; (ii) Preparation and planning for the 1989 semi-final; (iii) The events of 15 April, including the emergency response; (iv) The gathering of evidence by South Yorkshire Police; (v) The ninety-six people who died, their experiences, the injuries they suffered, and the treatment they received. You will have much of that evidence in agreed form in writing. Lastly, I shall return to the questionnaires and the law and give you some final directions.'

The jury was given a general questionnaire, with fourteen questions to answer. Finding answers to these questions would assist them in reaching their final verdict. The questions, as listed in the court transcript, were:

Question one

Do you agree with the following statement: On April 15 1989, ninety-six people died in the disaster as a result of crushing in the central pens of the Leppings Lane terrace, following the admission of a large number of supporters to the stadium through the exit gates.

Question two

Was there any error or omission in police planning and preparation for the semi-final on April 15 1989, which caused or contributed to the dangerous situation that developed on the day of the match?

Question three

Was there any error or omission in policing on the day of the match, which caused or contributed to a dangerous situation developing at the Leppings Lane turnstiles?

Question four

Was there any error or omission by commanding officers, which caused or contributed to the crush on the terrace?

Question five
When the order was given to open the exit gates at the Leppings Lane end of the stadium, was there any error or omission by the commanding officers in the control box which caused or contributed to the crush on the terrace?

Question six
Are you satisfied, so that you are sure, that those who died in the disaster were unlawfully killed?

Sir John told the jury, 'In order to answer "yes" to that question, you would have to be sure that David Duckenfield, the Match Commander, was responsible for the manslaughter by gross negligence of those ninety-six people.

'When answering this question we are looking at Mr Duckenfield's conduct and his responsibility.'

He said they would have to be sure that Mr Duckenfield owed a duty of care to the ninety-six people who died, that he breached that duty of care, that his breach caused their deaths and that the breach amounted to 'gross negligence'.

Question seven
Was there any behaviour on the part of the football supporters which caused or contributed to the dangerous situation at the Leppings Lane turnstiles?

Question eight
Were there any features of the design, construction and layout of the stadium, which you consider were dangerous or defective, and which caused or contributed to the disaster?

Question nine
Was there any error or omission in the safety certification and oversight of Hillsborough Stadium that caused or contributed to the disaster?

Question ten
Was there any error or omission by Sheffield Wednesday and its staff in the management of the stadium and/or preparation for the semi-final match on April 15 1989, which caused or

contributed to the dangerous situation that developed on the day of the match?

Question eleven

Was there any error or omission by Sheffield Wednesday and its staff on April 15, 1989, which caused or contributed to the dangerous situation that developed at the Leppings Lane turnstiles and in the west terrace?

Question twelve

Should Eastwood and Partners (structural engineers) have done more to detect and advise on any unsafe or unsatisfactory features of Hillsborough Stadium, which caused or contributed to the disaster?

Question thirteen

After the crush in the west terrace had begun to develop, was there any error or omission by the police, which caused or contributed to the loss of lives in the disaster?

Question fourteen

After the crush in the west terrace had begun to develop, was there any error or omission by the ambulance service (SYMAS), which caused or contributed to the loss of lives in the disaster?

The jury was reminded that it was not for them to find criminal or civil liability in respect of any individual or organisation. The jury was also advised that they should make their deliberations based on the 'balance of probabilities'. In court, Goldring said, 'That means no more than this: if you decide that it is more probable than not that something happened, you have decided on the balance of probabilities that it did. In short, you ask, did it probably happen? If you are satisfied it probably did happen, you have decided on the balance of probabilities that it did. If not, you have decided on the balance of probabilities it did not.'

The next day in court, the evidence of John Cutlack, a structural engineer expert witness, was recalled. Sir Goldring continued his summing up by recounting the evidence of

Mr Cutlack who had previously given damning evidence about the suitability of the crush barriers on the Leppings Lane terraces. He told the jury in court, 'Mr Cutlack expressed it in these terms, that these barriers were "substantially" and "grossly" too low.' He noted that the range of heights recommended in the Green Guide allowed for a barrier to be 8 cm below the ideal height. Barrier 136 was 83 cm high, when measured from the nosing of the step behind; around 27 cm lower than the preferred height. As Mr Cutlack put it, that was 'almost 300 per cent outside the guidance'. He said that it was 'quite ridiculous' that this could be considered a 'marginal deviation' from the Green Guide. He found it 'very surprising' that this line of barriers had been kept at Hillsborough, particularly given that barriers on the Spion Kop, which were too low, had been replaced as part of the certification process in 1979. Mr Cutlack was asked what approach an engineer should take to a barrier that is too low when assessing capacity on a terrace, he answered, 'He has one of two options. You either have the barrier replaced and a new one put in at the correct height; or you discount the barrier and you assume that it is just not there at all and you calculate the available area for people to stand in on [that] basis. So, in other words, you calculate capacity ignoring the barrier altogether.' The jury was also reminded that Mr Cutlack had given evidence to say that 'a basic error' was made by Eastwood's, the club's structural engineers, in 1979 when they calculated the capacity of the Leppings Lane terracing.

On Friday 29 January, the allegation of 'ticketless fans' was addressed, as Sir John Goldring recounted the evidence of John Cutlack, and the Health and Safety Executive (HSE). After the disaster, the HSE conducted a review of how many fans entered the ground at the Leppings Lane end. It used CCTV footage to count spectators entering the ground, including those who entered through Gate C after the police had opened it, and those that climbed over the turnstiles to escape the crush outside. Goldring reminded the jury ... he concluded that some 14,264 people had entered the west stand, west terrace and north-west terrace.

That was 300 lower than the number who would have had tickets for those areas. Mr Weatherby made the point to various witnesses in view of the period of time for which Gate C was open, anyone outside the Leppings Lane turnstiles who wanted to gain access to the west stand and terraces could have done so. As the numbers going through the entrances for those areas were no more than the capacity figure for the areas, it was suggested that there probably were not many people without tickets at that end of the ground.

On day six of the coroner's summing up, Sir John turned the jury's attention to the tunnel that led supporters from the turnstiles and onto the back of the Leppings Lane terracing. Liverpool supporters who had been to Hillsborough before had remembered that on previous occasions, the gates to that tunnel had been closed when the central pens were full, and a cordon of police officers or stewards had directed fans away to the less obvious side entrances to the Leppings Lane terrace.

Sir Goldring restated previous evidence saying, 'We were looking at the closing of the tunnel, and I was about to remind you of the evidence of former Sergeant Miller, who had considerable experience policing football stadiums. He was part of a Tango mobile unit. He was present at the 1981 crush. He said the practice was that, once the terrace was full, "We would stop anybody else going down the centre pen and then filter traffic left and right to the other pens."' Despite some officers admitting that it was a part of a known 'practice' to close the tunnel gates when pens three and four had reached capacity, other senior officers had claimed to have no knowledge of this tactic to divert fans away from full central pens.

By Thursday 11 February, Sir John Goldring started to sum up the conflicting reports about the behaviour of Liverpool fans outside the turnstiles. For me, one of the most curious parts of the police accusations against Liverpool fans that day was that there was no visual evidence to back it up. The BBC and police cameras were filming outside the Leppings Lane turnstiles, with the former likely hoping to pick up the atmosphere of a big game and the latter looking to manage the crowd. Yet there is no video evidence that I have seen that depicts a large number of fans turning up late, drunk or without tickets, and causing a crush outside the turnstiles. The coroner recounted the evidence of Police Constable Duffy, who was part of serial 16, under the command of Sergeant Payne.

The court was shown video footage shot outside the Leppings Lane end of the ground at 2.32 p.m. on the day of the disaster. The coroner told the jury, 'It was footage in respect of which Mr Duffy agreed that it depicted what would be no different from what would be seen at any other big game approaching kick-off, in terms of the behaviour of the fans.'

The next footage shown to the jury was shown was shot by a BBC handheld camera from 2.35 p.m. The coroner, recalling the evidence of PC Duffy, said to the jury, 'He looked at some footage a little later on, from 2.35 p.m. He agreed, in the context of it, that there was no hope of those people at the back of the group in the service road getting through the turnstiles in time. He agreed that the demeanour of the fans gave no cause to criticise. This footage was timed from 2.37 p.m.'

The coroner called for 'clip five' to be played next, which was filmed by police camera one and was timed from 2.37 p.m. When shown this evidence, Mr Duffy had agreed that 'it depicted a fair degree of chaos, but no misbehaviour'. Clip six was called for next in court, which overlapped with a clip the court had already been shown. Sir Goldring said, 'Mr Duffy agreed that AV material from just 2.44 p.m. showed a considerable number of supporters coming over the bridge. He agreed some space was created when the perimeter gates were closed. He agreed no loutish behaviour was depicted. There was nothing to suggest shoving into the backs of people.' Sir John Goldring continued, 'Mr Duffy was shown some footage from just after 2.54 p.m. We have already seen that footage, and I am not going to trouble with it again. It was the footage which showed some of the perimeter gates opening … Mr Duffy agreed that the police had effectively lost control of the perimeter gates.'

The coroner then read to the court what Mr Duffy had said back in 1989, which seemed to run counter to what had just been described. He said Mr Duffy's 1989 statement read, 'I formed a definite opinion that a deliberate effort on the part of a section of the crowd had been made to cause chaos at the turnstiles so that persons could gain entry without tickets.' He said that he came to that conclusion from the way the crowd went from being very busy but manageable to being 'horrendously unmanageable ... in seconds ... The crush suddenly changed from being one that I was, to some degree, happy with to one that I was extremely unhappy with ...'. It is worth remembering that the match-day ticket itself was printed with a request that supporters should try to be in their place by 2.45 p.m., so when Mr Duffy ascertained that, at 2.35 p.m. 'there was no chance of those at the back getting in by 3 p.m.' and that the scene at 2.37 p.m. 'depicted a fair degree of chaos, but no misbehavior ...', it seems crazy that those fans can be deemed as being late.

No police or BBC camera had apparently filmed the behaviour that Duffy had assumed, because if they had then surely the police would have brought forward such evidence to support their claims? However, in 1989, Mr Duffy said that he 'assumed' that the 'push to the people who were behaving in a perfectly reasonable manner came from behind'. He thought a large number of people had rushed to the back to cause the pressure at the front.

The next day the coroner turned his and the jury's attention to the evidence of Police Constable Larkin, who was a part of serial 11 and who was deployed at the rear of turnstiles one to eight in Leppings Lane. The coroner read to the jury to summarise the evidence given by PC Larkin: 'He said there was nothing out of the ordinary until about two o'clock. The fans were good natured and looking forward to the match. At about that time, a steward opened a gate and moved a temporary barrier to allow spectators entering through turnstiles nine and ten to access the north stand. The detail, I think, does not matter. Some time after that, a large crowd built up outside the turnstiles. There was a lot of pressure on the turnstiles. The fans who came through were visibly distressed, upset, annoyed, red in the face, as though from exertion. They said that the turnstiles were not operating quickly enough; something should be done to relieve the pressure. One fan described it as "f***ing murder out there. Open them f***ing gates or you are going to be held responsible for their deaths …". Police Constable Larkin said that these were decent people, middle aged and young. The situation was very tense. He felt apprehensive. Something was not right. He was very much concerned for the wellbeing of those on the other side of the turnstiles.'

On day eleven the jury was reminded about the changes made to various statements. First up, he recalled the two logs produced by Constable Bichard and in particular the difference between the first log he produced and the second. Sir Goldring told the jury that in his evidence, PC Bichard had said that 'in broad terms, what was recorded in the log happened,' and he had ticked the entry as correct.

The first log that PC Bichard had produced, on the day after the disaster, included the words, 'Shut the gates at the back of the tunnel', and the words were in speech marks as if it was recalling something somebody had said and it was timed at 2.55 p.m. The initials 'PR' were marked next to this log, which stand for personal radio. Christina Lambert QC, representing some of the bereaved families, had suggested to PC Bichard that this entry was the only entry omitted from the second log, which had been included in the first. Police Constable Bichard said he had no idea why. He also suggested that the log entry could have been from an officer on the inner concourse of the Leppings Lane end, and could have referred to the closure of Gate C, rather than the gates at the mouth of the tunnel.

Police Constable Bichard was asked what he saw after Gate C had been opened. He was operating a camera from the police control box, and the jury was shown footage from that camera with a timestamp of 14:59:08 to 15:00:30. Police Constable Bichard had said, 'The first real significant thing I recall was seeing fans getting from the terraced area onto the seating area above and being helped up there … that had happened the previous year, people had bunked up to the seated area to watch the match. So that initial thought was, these people were climbing up there to get a better view of the match from the seated area.'

The jury was shown footage which showed Chief Inspector McRobbie on the pitch and PC Bichard confirmed that he continued to believe at that time that it was a 'public order situation'. Goldring then reminded the jury of previous questioning from the inquests: 'Question: Why did you think it might be a pitch invasion when, putting it bluntly, the pitch was not being invaded? He answered, 'Well, hindsight is a wonderful thing … that's what the thought was at the time …'

At 3.03 p.m. PC Bichard made a request for dog handlers to attend the stadium. The video, in Goldring's words, showed that 'the pitch was not being invaded', yet the prevailing attitude, while people were dying, was to assume that the fans trying to escape the central pens into the seated area above, or onto the perimeter track, were doing so because they were misbehaving. This despite no pitch encroachment, and despite the fact that pitch invasions did not usually happen just a few minutes into a game, especially a game that was still scoreless. It has always been staggering and frustrating to survivors who have seen that video footage, as it seems so very obvious, maybe with the benefit of hindsight, that it was not misbehaviour.

The jury was then reminded about another statement which seemed to change over time. Club Steward, Malcolm Bain, made a statement in May 1989 in which he said, 'Quite a lot of the late arrivals had been drinking … you could just smell the drink on them.' Sir Goldring told the jury that having a drink before a football match was not unusual. However, Mr Bain had not mentioned alcohol at all in his earlier statement given to the club and when questioned he agreed that he must have been asked his views about alcohol consumption by the West Midlands Police.

Next, the jury was reminded of the evidence of former sergeant, John Morgan, who had said he felt that criticisms of the police were removed. Morgan's first statement had said there was 'panic and utter chaos' but that was removed. Sir John Goldring said, 'It was Mr Metcalf who suggested that part of the statement be "reviewed". Mr Morgan said that he thought that the review had resulted in his statement having been "sanitised", to take out criticism of senior officers. He said he had no idea in whose writing the amendment was. Mr Morgan said he thought he had never been asked about the amendment. He said he was shocked and stunned when he learned that it had been.'

On Tuesday 23 February, Sir Goldring started to summarise the evidence of Mr Houldsworth, an electrical engineer. Mr Houldsworth had done some work on the club's computer systems and CCTV cameras and was stationed in the club control room on the day of the disaster in an advisory capacity. The club control room was situated in the South Stand, around the area of the players' tunnel. This viewpoint gave him access to the pictures being recorded by both the club's CCTV cameras and also the pictures from the police CCTV cameras. Perhaps surprisingly, a man positioned with such a key vantage point was not asked to give evidence to the Taylor Enquiry.

According to Goldring's summary of Mr Houldsworth's evidence, Houldsworth had told the court, "It was possible to display footage from one of the police cameras on one of the monitors in the club control room. They could choose which one to look at. They could not control what it showed. They saw, in other words, whatever PC Bichard in the police control box chose, himself, to look at. Mr Houldsworth described it in terms of "passive viewing".'

Of the club's computer counting system, the court was reminded that the system, which counted the numbers entering the ground through the turnstiles, was, 'Primarily, we were told, to avoid fraud, not for reasons of safety: to prevent turnstile operators allowing people in without a ticket for cash, which they then kept. An electronic switch recorded when a person went through the turnstile." It also recorded things at eye level within each turnstile and would show anyone trying to pay cash to gain entry. This information was all relayed to a screen in the club control room. The court was reminded that the turnstiles were grouped into three areas, with the Leppings Lane terrace being counted as one area. Once an area of the ground reached 90 per cent capacity, the area in question would change colour on the screen and an audible alarm would sound. Houldsworth had given evidence that the alarm pertaining to 90 per cent capacity had not sounded for the Leppings Lane turnstiles on the 15 April 1989.

Talking next about the communication between the club control room and the police control box, the court was reminded that, according to Houldsworth's evidence, PC Guest was seated in front of the control room and was 'primarily responsible for monitoring the computer system', and that it was PC Guest's job, he said, 'to pass information to the police control box or to respond to requests for information from there'. There was, he said, 'An internal landline. There was the police radio and the club radio.' Houldsworth's evidence also confirmed that anyone in the control box would have been able to see the crowd outside the Leppings Lane turnstiles through the pictures generated by a club camera which was on top of the West Stand, and that, 'It was possible to calculate at an all-ticket match how many people were yet to come into a particular area. All the information would be displayed on the screen'. Mister Houldsworth was employed by Sheffield Wednesday FC to carry out necessary checks and maintenance three times a year. The coroner reminded the jury that Mr Houldsworth had said in his evidence that he had carried out such checks the week before the disaster.

Sir Goldring reminded the jury that while the electronic monitoring system allowed the club and police to know how many people had entered a certain 'sector' of the ground at any given time, it did not monitor where those people went after entry. In an area such as Leppings Lane, that had been modified over the years to have lateral fences that broke the terrace up into pens, it was not possible using the system to know how many of those that entered through the Leppings Lane turnstiles had entered each pen.

The jury was also reminded of Houldsworth's evidence with respect to camera five, which had powerful zoom facilities and was aimed at the Leppings Lane terraces. Police officers had previously said that camera five had not been working as it should on the day of the disaster, but Houldsworth disagreed with that. Sir Goldring said to the jury, 'Mr Houldsworth said camera five was working satisfactorily on 15 April. There had been problems with it when the scoreboard was on and the kitchens were busy. You remember I summarised some evidence relating to different accounts that the South Yorkshire Police gave about camera number five. He said he'd spent some time the week before the match investigating it. He checked the camera on the Saturday morning. Its problems had been resolved. He told PC Bichard and PC Ryan. The police, he said, were wrong if they said anything to the contrary.' Mr Houldsworth also gave evidence to say he saw the pictures generated by camera five displayed on a monitor in the police control box. This had been a contentious issue, because officers were asked how they managed to miss the distress in the central pens when they had a camera (five) with such powerful zoom facilities.

As the kick-off drew nearer, Houldworth's evidence turned to the pictures they could see on the screens in the club control room. Sir John Goldring summarised, 'We know, members of the jury, that by about 2.30 p.m., between 4,750 and just over 4,800 spectators had entered through gates A to G. Over 5,000 were still to come in. You will remember Mr Cutlack's evidence about that. Mr Houldsworth said he told PC Guest at about 2.50 p.m. or later that, "This is not right. The amount of people outside externally ... the build-up in the Leppings Lane reservoir area and ... what was coming through the turnstiles, there was no way they were going to get them in". He said there was a discussion then about whether the kick-off would be delayed, and I'm quoting his account, " 'Surely, by God, they'll delay the kick-off?', said someone". Mr Houldsworth said that, during the period leading up to the opening of the gate, "we were swapping around from camera to camera by use of the switcher". That included, he said, camera five. They could see there was going to be trouble when Gate C was opened. He said there were spaces in the wing terraces, but the fans were not directed to that area.'

Sir John Goldring continued to summarise the evidence Mr Houldsworth gave at the time that exit Gate C was opened, 'Mr Houldsworth said the police cameras three and five showed the pens were packed. "The focus of cameras three and five occurred after Gate C was opened", said Mr Houldsworth. He was concerned that there would be injury, but not to the extent that occurred. He said he thought it was dangerous because there was such an influx of people when Gate C was opened. He could see that there would be a problem, especially in the tunnel area. He agreed that, apart from PC Guest trying his best to get through to the police control box, nothing was done by those in the club control room. He agreed that in retrospect he or the others in the club control room might possibly have gone down to the police control box.'

By Wednesday 24 February, Sir John Goldring started to summarise the evidence from fans that had been in the central pens. This evidence is from members of the public, not professional people like others I have quoted, and while this evidence is online in the official court transcripts, I don't think it is fair to reproduce their harrowing stories in this book without their consent, so I will summarise the evidence and remove the names to protect their privacy. The following words are a summary of how Sir Goldring recounted these fans' evidence.

'One fan talked about getting into the central pens at around the time the players on the pitch started their warm up. He talked about how the pen seemed to get "busier and busier" until the point that he was concerned that the glasses in his pocket might break and puncture his heart or lungs. He talked about one young fan being pushed back into the pens by the police as he tried to escape the crush by scaling the fence. He also said that the police didn't seem to realise that people were in danger and expressed his shock that they were not able to see. He talked about how the police on the perimeter track didn't appear to know that the pressure of fans that were flowing through the tunnel at the back of the terrace were slowly pushing people forwards, and the police pleas for people to "get back" were impossible to comply with.'

'Another fan talked of how he saw no loutish behaviour. He said that "at around 2.55 p.m. it became very difficult to move". He talked about how his friend was "bent very far forward over the barrier. His face was very, very red; eyes were very wide; significant distress and panic on his face." He asked for help to get him off the barrier. He talked about how people were trying to help, "Even given the distress that people were in themselves, they were still doing everything they could to help others." This supporter also said that the fans had been screaming at the police to open the gates for what seemed like "a very, very long time" before the small gates in the fence at the front were finally opened.

He said he thought that the police were under the impression that the fans could simply move back to relieve the pressure on the people in front. "People were screaming, 'Open the gate. Open the gate'. They were shouting that people were dying." Of course, we now know that the steady stream of supporters filing down the tunnel, from the open exit Gate C, was preventing supporters from being able to move back.'

'Another fan talked about how the crowd started to build up at around 2.30 p.m. until the point where he couldn't move. He described being stuck at the front with his arms pinned to his side, and his face being crushed against the fence [at the front].'

'One fan, an off-duty police officer, gave evidence that he was shocked that pen three was "very, very full" when he entered because he knew how many fans were still outside. He was moved by the crowd towards the front where he came to a halt. His evidence was that he wanted to move to the right, but the density of the crowd made it so that "there was just no room to move". He saw a man next to him who "appeared to be dead". He describes his escape, "Suddenly, a breathing space developed". He could only assume people at the front had gone down, or something. He did not know if a barrier had been broken. He was able to get onto the perimeter fence. He had the impression that one of the officers at the perimeter fence was trying to stop him getting over.'

'Another fan talked of the pressure that moved him down the terrace towards the front. He gave evidence that there was no movement in the crowd around him and that "he couldn't breathe". The supporter said that he was pushed up against people. The young man's knee was trapped against the barrier. He was pushed into the young man. Someone said the barrier was about to go; it went. He heard the young man's knee crack. He screamed. He said the police on the pitchside were doing nothing. He said that long before the young man's knee was trapped against the barrier, they were screaming to the police there were people dying in the terrace. The supporter said the police could hear them. They were not reacting. When the barrier went, he landed face down on top of the young man. He could then breathe slightly, although it was difficult.'

'Many of the fans in pens three and four gave evidence that they saw police officers push fans back into the pens as they were frantically trying to escape the 'suffocating crush'. One fan said, "Each time people forced their way out, the police officers grabbed them and threw them back into the crowd." '

Richie Greaves evidence was recalled by Sir Goldring, saying, 'He said to us that the fans at the front were seeing the same thing as the police. The fans were pulling people out, the police were pushing people back in. He said that fans were putting their arms through the fencing and using their hands to provide platforms or fans to climb up and out of danger'.

Another fan's evidence was read to the court. He said he 'pleaded with a policewoman to help'. He told the Taylor Inquiry that he thought she could hear him. She was six or seven feet away. She did not ignore him. She was looking straight at him. As far as he could see, she was panicking. She did not know what to do. He was screaming, 'I have got a girl who has fainted here. Can you help her?' He said he could not remember if she said that she was unable to do anything. He did not think, he said, 'that she understood how bad the situation was'.

Another fan at the front recalled the dialogue with the police officers on the other side of the fence. He said that he was 'confident the officers were addressing those in the area he was', and that they 'were probably five or six feet away.' He said 'As I recall, several officers were telling those at the front to push back, push back, push back.' He replied, 'We can't push back. It's not possible. Please open the gates', before he lost consciousness.

Woman Police Constable Nicol's evidence was summarised for the jury on Wednesday 24 February and Thursday 25 February 2016. She had policed the Hillsborough Stadium on many occasions, but her evidence said that usually she was stationed outside the Leppings Lane turnstiles. On the day of the disaster, WPC Nicol was stationed on the perimeter track, between the Leppings Lane central pens and the pitch.

Sir Goldring reminded the jury of WPC Nicol's experiences outside the Leppings Lane turnstiles in previous years. The evidence includes the closure of the large perimeter gates in order to 'create a sterile area' in the small area between those outer perimeter gates and the turnstiles. Goldring said that WPC Nicol had given evidence to say this 'happened more than once'. WPC Nicol had also given evidence with regards to the tunnel, and the police management of supporters heading towards it. Goldring said that WPC Nicol had testified that, 'The sergeant told officers to line up in front of the tunnel and send the fans to the pens at either side'. She understood that was because the central pens were too busy. She said she only remembered doing it once, but she stood at that time with a colleague who had done it before. It would probably have been a couple of years before 1989.

Recalling the pre-match briefing by Chief Superintendent David Duckenfield on the day of the disaster, WPC Nicol recalled that officers were not to open the gates in the perimeter fence. Sir Goldring quoted WPC Nicol's evidence, '... It was specifically mentioned at the briefing, we weren't to open the perimeter gates under any circumstances, unless we spoke to a senior officer first. There was nobody allowed to come on to the pitch, no matter what. I remember having that clear in my mind', she said.

On the day of the disaster, WPC Nicol had been asked by a scout leader if his group could be let out of pen three, as it was crowded. In WPC Nicol's evidence, she told the scout leader that 'she was not allowed to open the gate', but did so when she noticed one of the boys looked 'very upset'. She then walked the group towards the area of pen one and two. Sir Goldring said to the jury, 'Ms Nicol said that, as she looked back, she saw more and more people had come out onto the track. There was, she thought, another police officer standing by the gate, trying to shut it. She went back to try to help. She said she saw a man's face in the crowd. She said "It was just terror".'

Sir Goldring continued to summarise the evidence of WPC Nicol, 'Ms Nicol went up to pen three. Other police officers were there by then. On the AV footage she identified someone who was likely to be her standing on the fencing on the far left looking at pen three at 15:08. Members of the jury, let's look at that bit of footage and I will then tell you what she said.' After the jury was played the video footage, Sir Goldring continued, 'Ms Nicol said she was sure the gate was opened. There were "dozens of people just completely squashed against the fencing. There were people on top of people. Nobody could get out of the gate. The gate was completely blocked". She said, "I climbed up onto the perimeter fence and I could clearly see a space towards the back ... I was screaming 'Move back, move back' ... the people towards the back didn't seem to know what was happening. They were still looking towards the other direction, which I presumed was the football match going on ..." She said the reason she shouted "get back" was because another police officer had shouted, "Move back, move back".'

WPC Nicol also gave evidence as to what role the senior officers in the police control box would have assumed, in her opinion. Sir Goldring recalled this for the jury, 'She said she did not push fans back. She did not see any of her colleagues doing so. She never saw the gate to pen three opening and shutting. She never saw the gate shut. She said, "We were all too late ...everybody realised far too late". Mr Menon put to Ms Nicol that, ultimately, the senior officers in the police control box had overall responsibility because of their bird's-eye view of the central pens, and she said, "I would have thought that was their role, yes".'

WPC Nicol also gave evidence about how she was asked to give a statement on the Monday after the disaster. The coroner reminded the jury that WPC Nicol had been asked to go to Snig Hill police headquarters. She was shown up to the fourth floor, where the senior officers had their offices. WPC Nicol's evidence was that there were a team of people in the foyer who asked her to put in a report of her experiences. She said she was 'sent to a small, windowless room, given some plain paper and told to write on it'. WPC Nicol had said she was in the room 'for quite some time' and that other plain clothes officers kept coming in, reading what she was writing, or taking it away. They were, she said, 'Obviously reading it outside ... they kept shutting the door on me, so I don't know what the conversation was'. She said she understood one officer was a chief superintendent. He was the one who spoke to her first. She did not know any of the other officers. She was quite, she said, 'overwhelmed'.

Sir Goldring reminded the jury about WPC Nicol's description of the central pens being challenged, 'Ms Nicol explained that in the statement which she made the gate numbers that she referred to were confused, and where, as it did in the statement, it said, "Gates one to four half full", she was intending to refer to gates one and two, which were, she said, half full. Where it said, "Gates two to three, three-quarters full", this was a reference, she said, to gates three and four. She recalled, she said, writing that they were "full", not "three-quarters full", as it states. Ms Nicol said, and this is referring in part to her statement, "I wrote 'full' ... I put the word 'full' and on one of the occasions when they came in to read it and then brought it back again, I was asked to look at the word 'full' and to say if it was full and how could I tell it was full from where I was standing. It's not an amendment. I have not crossed it out. I actually rewrote the page rather than crossed it out. That's not because I was told to rewrite the page. It's because I've got terrible handwriting and I would have tried to make it look neater." She said that that particular wording was picked up on, "As I said, they used to take what I were writing out and come back in again. And that particular wording, the word 'full' – it made sense to me at the time from where I was – obviously I couldn't see the pens very well and using the word 'full' means they were, like, packed out, extremely full, and they weren't, because there was still movement in the crowd so people could still move around. I did agree that they weren't, I think it was the use of the grammar of the word 'full' more than anything else. But I couldn't think of any other word to put, that's why I've put three-quarters full ..." She said there was discussion as to whether or not she could see from where she was whether the pens were full. She said that three-quarters was just a figure that she used. "When I look at it now", she said, "That's not right. I would have said it was fuller, the fullest, but not over[full]." She said that at the time what the officer was saying to her made sense. She was not told what to write or what to put in the document, but it was the environment she was in at the time, on her own in the room. It was not very pleasant. She finally said to Ms Lambert she felt uncomfortable. The circumstances were probably intimidating. She said that the change of "full" to "three-quarters full" in her statement has bothered her for the last twenty-odd years. She said she was not forced, but encouraged, to change it.'

WPC Nicol's evidence was also that she felt that the senior officers within South Yorkshire Police had tried to blame her and other 'officers on the ground' for what had happened. Sir Goldring said to the jury, 'Ms Nicol said that she believed that she and Police Constable Smith and Police Constable Illingworth seemed to be picked out, scapegoated, she said, by the hierarchy of the South Yorkshire Police in the lead-up to the Taylor Inquiry. She believed, she said, there was an attempt to divert the blame from what happened onto the officers on the ground and the fans.'

Sir Goldring then picked up on the evidence of PC Walpole, who was a community officer and a part of serial one that day. The coroner reminded the jury that PC Walpole had 'regularly policed Hillsborough'. PC Walpole had estimated that he had policed Hillsborough about one hundred times before 15 April 1989. Sir Goldring reminded the jury that PC Walpole had told the court in his evidence that, 'I can't remember exactly what was said, but I can clearly remember Mr Duckenfield saying, under no circumstances will fans be allowed onto the track and the match will kick off at 3 p.m. and won't be delayed under any circumstances.' He said he remembered that clearly. He said he 'thought it surprising, because you never know what is going to happen at a football match. The match will kick off at 3 p.m. and won't be delayed under any circumstances.'

With regards to PC Walpole's evidence from the day itself, he had told the court that his radio 'was working perfectly between 2.45 and 3.10. He clearly heard every message that came over.' Sir John Goldring reminded the jury further of what PC Walpole had said he heard over the radio from inside the ground, 'He heard from Marshall, Superintendent Marshall, whose voice he said he recognised, very distressed. He said he radioed through saying there were thousands of fans arrived pretty late on, and there was a boundary wall swaying and he thought that that might collapse and he felt that someone might be killed and he was asking for … a gate to be opened to relieve the pressure. Mr Walpole said he heard Mr Marshall repeat this three times over the next five minutes. He could not remember whether Sergeant Goddard in the control room said, "Stand by" or if the radio was just quiet. After the third request, he said Sergeant Goddard came over the radio and his words were, "If it looks like someone might be killed, then we'll have to open the gates". Mr Walpole said he heard those words very clearly. It went through his mind that Mr Duckenfield would no doubt delay the kick-off, as it was, in his view, as he put it, "a no brainer".'

PC Walpole's evidence continued to be summarised by Sir Goldring, 'In his 2013 Operation Resolve statement, Mr Walpole said that he "remembered thinking, they must be going to shut the gates into the tunnel because there was no more room in the central pens". He told us that he presumed that the police officers at the Leppings Lane end would disperse the crowds to the sides. He said it would have been pretty obvious to everybody in the police control box that the two central pens were "packed solid". At about 2.55 p.m., Mr Walpole said he heard PC Buxton asking for the kick-off to be delayed. He said Sergeant Goddard immediately said, "We've no chance. One of the teams is out".'

The coronor continued with the evidence of PC Walpole, and now focused on the PC's subsequent statement. PC Walpole had given evidence that he was asked to 'review' a part of his statement, 'Mr Metcalf, members of the jury, the solicitor, advised that that section at the end be removed and suggested "reviewing" a statement that the officer had not heard any radio message asking for the central pens to be closed off although it was packed solid.'

Goldring continued to address the jury, 'Mr Walpole said that Sergeant Watts produced a statement for him to sign. The reference to Mr Buxton had been deleted; so, too, had some other comments. Mr Walpole said he refused to sign it. He made a note in his pocketbook about it. As he put it, "because this was one of the most important facts of my evidence that had been removed". Having, as he noted in his pocketbook, at 3.30 p.m., spoken to the Police Federation, he said he told Sergeant Watts he would not sign a statement "which has been doctored or changed". He said the document he was asked to sign was a clean, typed copy. We do not have a copy of it.'

He continued, 'Mr Walpole, PC Walpole, as he then was, said he met Chief Inspector Foster at 2.40 p.m. at headquarters. On his way, he gathered PCs Smith and Groome. They were also refusing, he said, to sign their amended statements. He thought that they had mentioned that their statements had been altered. He thought that he was the first to see Mr Foster. Mr Walpole said, "He [Mr Foster] said it was about the Hillsborough disaster statements, and he had got a copy of my original typed statement, and there were marks all over it that he had put on it. He was indicating to me matters that were going to be removed, and he said this was all opinions and criticisms that weren't allowed and that I would be getting a retyped version that would be sent through for signing. Obviously I told him I wasn't happy about this and I thought police officers' opinions and criticisms in the circumstances were very important. But he told me that wasn't going to happen. I also brought up to him the point about PC Buxton asking for the match to be delayed had been taken out, and he agreed that that would be allowed to be kept in it. So, basically, he was ordering me that a retyped statement be sent to me and I would be expected to sign that without further delay." Sir Goldring then said, 'As you will recall, these matters were looked into by Lord Justice Stuart-Smith. In his response to the Stuart-Smith Scrutiny, Mr Walpole said, "Since I, like most others, was suffering from post-traumatic stress and depression, I agreed to the deletions to my final statement under the conditions I was placed under."'

On Monday 29 February Sir Goldring was summarising the evidence of Superintendent Greenwood who was stationed inside the ground on the day of the disaster. The evidence recalled for the court was that Mr Greenwood conducted a tour of the ground between 11 a.m. and 2.30 p.m., speaking to officers who were responsible for the perimeter track, Inspector Darling and Sergeant Chapman along the way. Mr Greenwood told the court that he 'did not recall any discussion about the order prohibiting access from the pens to the track.' His evidence was that, 'He thought it was common knowledge that once a pitch perimeter gate was opened, it was like a tap that could not be turned off.' Mr Greenwood did not recall having any specific conversations with officers about monitoring the density in the pens but said 'they were experienced officers who did it week in and week out.'

Superintendent Greenwood had told the court that he thought that he would have contemplated what to do if the pens became over full. Greenwood went on to explain that one plan would have been to 'open the gate and let people move to other areas'. He also explained that there were gates in the radial fences, right at the back, between the pens, and officers could move people at the back through the radial fences to the less full side pens or divert people back up the tunnel.

The evidence heard so far, including the eye witness accounts in this book, would suggest that after exit Gate C was opened there were too many people coming down the tunnel for officers to have been able to access the back of the terrace. Also, at least one fan gave evidence that the gate in the radial fence between pen four and a sterile walkway that separated pen four and pen five was locked. Earlier in this book, you heard the evidence of Peter Dalling who had struggled to work his way back up the terraces towards the back of the terrace, thinking that if he could get his back against the wall at the very back of the terrace then he would be safe. He said, 'At this time, a copper came up the walkway and people were screaming at him to get the gate open, but he didn't have a key.' If Peter was correct, that the gate was locked, and he is adamant that he is, then the idea that fans could 'find their own level' by moving between pens was seriously flawed. Also, the gates were not easy to see in a densely packed pen.

Superintendent Greenwood also admitted that, if the central pens were full, he would have opened the gate in the fence between the pens and the pitch. Sir Goldring reminded the jury of the evidence of Superintendent Greenwood, 'If it's over full and there is a safety consideration, then I would do what I did in 1981 and open those gates ... I have to say ... that the pressure that was exerted on myself in 1981 as a result of doing that, both from ... the police and, more than that, from the Club ... put a lot of pressure on people in terms of opening those gates, because you can't stop the tap, the flow keeps coming.'

Greenwood had also indicated to the court that closing access to the pens from the back of the tunnel was a tactical option, and went further, 'Even if it was not', he said, 'it was common sense.'

Superintendent Greenwood had been stationed outside the Leppings Lane turnstiles at the semi-finals in 1987 and 1988, but was inside in the stadium on the day of the disaster in 1989. Greenwood said that things outside the ground had gone 'very smoothly' in 1987 and 1988, and in court he was shown video footage from outside the Leppings Lane turnstiles in 1989. He was shown a clip of video footage timed at 2.37p.m. and he commented that 'the situation by gate A was not ideal.' Superintendent Greenwood told the court that he had used the outer perimeter gates to control access to the area in front of the turnstiles in previous years. He also said that, 'People seen spreading into the service road were not allowed to congregate in that area in 1988'. He said, 'technically speaking, they should not.'

On the day of the disaster, Superintendent Greenwood said he was near the players' tunnel as the players started to come onto the pitch at 2.54 p.m. He described that position as 'the best vantage point in the ground'. He was shown video footage that confirmed he was indeed in that area at that time. Sir Goldring recalled the evidence for the jury saying, 'Shortly after kick-off he said he saw people coming over the fence at the Leppings Lane end: "My view was ... that from my experience it wasn't a pitch invasion. It was too early in the game, so it had got to be something else, but not a pitch invasion." Mr Greenwood said he went along the perimeter track to the Leppings Lane end at about three o'clock, which was backed up by video footage that had been shown to the court.'

Greenwood had said that when he reached the area he surveyed it. This was between 3 p.m. and 3.01 p.m. He said from ground level he could see there was some pressure on supporters at the front of the pens.

In Greenwood's statement in 1989, he had said that as he arrived in front of the pens, 'From ground level, I looked at the crowd in pen three behind the goal and saw quite clearly that supporters were being squashed against the fencing.' During the new inquests, Greenwood said at this time he thought that the situation was 'recoverable' and that he climbed up onto the fence and motioned to the crowd to move back. Sir Goldring said, 'He agreed that when he first looked through the fencing, he saw people being pressed against it. He thought they were at risk. He did not see a scene which was as troubling and distressing as depicted in the later photographs: "If that had been the case, [Greenwood said] I would have stopped that match there and then, but my view was that it was recoverable and we could minimise the risk."'

Mr Greenwood was shown a distressing photograph of a lady being pressed up against the wire mesh, taken at 3.01.30 p.m. He was then shown another photograph which depicted Mr Greenwood in the immediate vicinity of the lady in distress, and Greenwood agreed he was 'about an arm's length from the woman in the light blue top pressed up against the railings.' Mr Greenwood agreed that he must have been able to see the position of those people in the open pens. Two of the people in the picture are the Hicks sisters. He repeated that his judgement at the time was that the situation was 'completely retrievable'. Sir Goldring recalled for the jury that Greenwood had told the court, 'I made a judgment. If I was wrong, then I was wrong. But I stand by it today, that there was room for the crowd to move back ...'. Greenwood admitted that, in hindsight, the situation was not retrievable by about 3.02 p.m.

Once Greenwood realised that the situation was not retrievable, and that the game needed to be stopped, he contacted the police control box. Sir Goldring said, 'When he contacted the police control box by radio, he said he received no response. He said he signalled to the control box. He could not say whether that had any effect. Greenwood ran onto the pitch. We know, members of the jury, that was at 3.05 to 3.06. He told the referee they had an emergency running. The referee complied with his request to take the players off the pitch.'

Greenwood had told the court that he knew nothing of the order to open exit Gate C at the time. Recounting Greenwood's testimony, Lord Golding read, 'Mr Greenwood said he would have wanted to know about an order to open the exit gates. If he had been, he would have gone to the Leppings Lane terrace to monitor the situation; in other words, if he'd been told about an order to open the exit gates. It might have taken him some time, he said, to get there. He would have wanted to make an assessment of what the capacity level was in the terrace as a whole and the individual pens. He would have wanted to have some knowledge of what he was likely to be confronted by in terms of the mood and behaviour of the supporters. He would be looking at whether to deflect supporters into other parts as well. He would ask how many officers he needed to deal with this or whether the horses were available to deal with it. When asked whether it would have occurred to him to close off the tunnel, he said not necessarily. It would depend on the capacity of the pens. It would depend on "find your own level". He said there were other popular areas of the ground other than behind the goal through the tunnel.'

Greenwood also accepted that the concept of letting the supporters find their own level required 'observation and monitoring to ensure that the pens did not overfill.' Greenwood accepted, with hindsight, that this should be covered in the operational order. Superintendent Greenwood also admitted, 'That it was possible the policy would break down if a very large number of people, hundreds or thousands at one go, were admitted'. He said, too, that he would expect the officers in serial thirteen on the west stand, the front of the west stand, to 'keep their eyes open and report on problems in the pen'. Except in an emergency, he would not expect the tunnel to be closed without an order from the police control box. If Inspector White were to divert people from the tunnel as they entered when Gate C was open, he would need to know that Gate C was going to be opened. The real responsibility for managing the consequences of the decision to open Gate C rested with those who made it. Greenwood seemed to point the finger of responsibility of closing off the tunnel at Duckenfield, as he gave the order to open the exit gates.

Greenwood also admitted that, 'If confronted with full pens and having been told that a large number of people were being allowed in through exit Gate C', he would have considered it the 'obvious expedient' to prevent them entering the pens by closing the tunnel. But Greenwood said he did not know that the order to open Gate C had been given.

When giving evidence in 1990, Superintendent Greenwood had said that 'The control box was responsible for monitoring the numbers of supporters. There was also an inspector [that's Mr Bullas] together with a serial who would be able to assess the build-up and who would report direct to the control box as required. I considered the role of serial men and inspectors was to be supplementary to the role of the control box in terms of monitoring the crowd … It is my understanding that the control box would be specifically monitoring the crowd visually and with screen.' Sir Goldring continued summarising Greenwood's evidence, saying, 'It was not for me or my officers to monitor the numbers in the pens. It was the job of the control box.'

Sir Goldring next moved on to summarise the evidence given by Assistant Chief Constable Walter Jackson. The coroner reminded the jury that there had been some medical evidence given that Mr Jackson 'had a difficulty recollecting things' and that the jury should bear that in mind when assessing his evidence.

The coroner reminded the jury that Mr Jackson had become Assistant Chief Constable in 1985, and that he had 'considerable experience policing football grounds'. Mr Jackson was one of two assistant chief constables, and was 'in charge of operations. He had responsibility for all major events.' As a part of Mr Jackson's role, which also included crime, traffic, and anything to do with major events, the coroner reminded the jury that Mr Jackson 'was responsible for operational orders generally'. His evidence was, however, that he 'could not realistically attend each of the venues and know the detail of them, each of the venues for which he had ultimate responsibility.'

Mr Jackson had told the court that he was present at the 1987 semi-final at Hillsborough between Leeds United and Coventry City. That day, Mr Mole was the Match Commander and the kick off was delayed on that occasion. In an interview Mr Jackson had given to the West Midlands police in 1990 he had said that he had seen 'a big crowd build up … a big traffic build-up and I radioed into the ground commander making a suggestion that he might look at the business of delaying the match, which he did for fifteen minutes.'

Mr Jackson's evidence was that he did not attend the 1988 semi-final, but he had received a report about the match afterwards with was 'generally positive' although notes were made that the police communications in 1988 had been disrupted 'by a breakthrough from a local radio station'. Mr Jackson said he had been to various meetings concerning the policing of football matches, and on 20 March 1986 he produced a memo giving recommendations following the publication of the interim Popplewell Report. The main focus of the Popplewell Report was to look into events at the Bradford City Valley football ground on Saturday 11 May 1985, when a fire claimed the lives of fifty-six supporters.

Goldring continued, 'He was asked about the operational order which we've looked at more than once, and he was asked about the instructions to the serials outside the turnstiles. He agreed that preventing the funnel area on Leppings Lane becoming over full would normally require some sort of filtering system before the fans reached it. He agreed that the operational order did not contain a tactical plan for managing crowds through any sort of filter system. There was nothing about using the outer perimeter gates to help with that. There was nothing about stationing officers further from the ground. Mr Jackson said it would be a matter for the superintendent in that area to decide how to manage the crowds. He agreed that, "perhaps in hindsight, it would have been useful to have had a reference in the order to a kind of filtering system."'

It was put to Mr Jackson that there were in fact seven major failings of the police operation order. 'First, it stated that the three serials responsible for patrolling outside the turnstiles at Leppings Lane and the further serial with responsibilities to patrol Leppings Lane itself were under the command of Superintendent Greenwood, the inside commander, whereas the reality was that they were under the command of Superintendent Marshall, the outside commander.' Mr Jackson responded by saying that 'Chief Inspector Creaser was particularly allocated to deal with the turnstiles', and that 'the briefing at the ground would make it perfectly clear what the responsibilities are'.

The second of the suggested major failings was that 'the responsibility to ensure orderly queues set out in the operational order was completely unrealistic'. Mr Jackson said that 'nobody told him it was unrealistic', and that 'he was not aware of any previous problems with the formation of queues at Leppings Lane'.

The third suggested failing levelled at the operational order was that there was 'nothing about how the outside serial, serial nineteen, was to control the crowd before they came through the outer perimeter gates'. Mr Jackson said the senior officers had considerable experience in dealing with the issue. They would deal with any problem. He agreed that the only way to prevent overcrowding outside the turnstiles was to keep control of the fans coming through the outer perimeter gates. He said that 'the superintendent and chief inspectors were well aware of working at Hillsborough and would deal with that situation.'

Fourth, it was suggested that the operational order should have reflected the change in turnstile arrangements for the April 1989 match. Mr Jackson said that would be dealt with locally.

The fifth point raised for the match in April 1989 was that there was 'no mention in the operational order of the possibility of having to close the tunnel to the central pens'. Mr Jackson agreed. He said 'he did not know about the tunnel arrangements. That was a local issue. If closing the tunnel when the pens were becoming full was a recognised practice, he would have liked to see something about it, he said, in the briefing notes.'

Goldring continued to recount the suggested failings to the jury: 'Sixth, Mr George suggested there was nothing about any role for serial one on the perimeter track in monitoring the build-up of the crowd in the pens. Mr Jackson agreed that would possibly have been helpful. He said the briefing at the ground would probably deal with all these issues. He thought the officers would be well aware of the requirements.'

Finally, it was suggested there was no direction to the officers in the West Stand to have any role in monitoring the build-up of the pens, and Mr Jackson said, 'Perhaps an emphasis might have been helpful, but the officers are well experienced in dealing with football matches, and if they had seen anything wrong, they would deal with it.' Some officers certainly were experienced, but by his own admission, the Match Commander, Chief Superintendent David Duckenfield, was anything but.

Mr Jackson also agreed that the commanders in the control box, [led by Chief Superintendent David Duckenfield on the day] had 'the primary responsibility for looking out for problems connected with density in the pens.'

'As we have already heard, Duckenfield had already led representatives from the Football Association and Sheffield Wednesday Football Club to believe that the gates at the back of the Leppings Lane had been forced open by the fans. These mistruths were among the details given, unwittingly, by those first asked to comment on the situation and picked up by TV companies broadcasting globally. In Mr Jackson's evidence, he said that "at some time after five o'clock, in a car on the way to the police station, Mr Duckenfield said it was on his authority that the gate was opened". In the car going to the police station were Mr Jackson, Mr Duckenfield, Mr Marshall and somebody called Superintendent Pratt, who was the press officer of South Yorkshire Police. They were going there because Mr Jackson said he felt it important that Mr Marshall and Mr Duckenfield should speak to the Chief Constable to give their views of what had happened. Mr Jackson told the West Midlands Police in 1990 that he thought it would help prepare the Chief Constable for the press conference which was to take place. Mr Jackson said he did not want to exacerbate the situation. He did not ask Mr Duckenfield about the difference between his account in the car and his earlier account that the gates had been stormed. Mr Jackson said that people were very, very shocked.'

Sir Goldring was now to summarise the evidence of Match Commander, Chief Superintendent David Duckenfield. The court was reminded that Duckenfield had been promoted on 27 March 1989, just a few short weeks before the semi-final at Hillsborough. Duckenfield had given the court an overview of his experience in relation to football, which Sir Goldring read to the court: 'In the mid-1970s, when a uniformed inspector, he had worked at Bramall Lane, the Sheffield United ground. He thought that was probably for one season. During the 1979/1980 season, when a Chief Inspector, he said he'd worked at Hillsborough. He was generally, he said, at the players' tunnel. He was at the semi-final between Liverpool and Arsenal. When a superintendent between 1985 and 1989 and at West Bar Police Station, he only policed on the periphery at Bramall Lane if there was a major match. He did not go as a spectator. Bramall Lane involved relatively small capacity crowds. His knowledge of Hillsborough was "very general". He had no experience of planning, he said, for football matches or in the formulation of operational orders.'

The coroner reminded the jury that Duckenfield had also told the court, 'With hindsight ... I should have thought about my limited knowledge of the role of a commander in a major event that was an all-ticket sell out, when I had not been ... in that responsible position, previously ...' He said that, having reflected on it for many years, he was probably not the best man for the job, although he did not think, he said, he was overconfident.

Sir John Goldring reminded the court of Duckenfield's evidence relating to offers of help and the culture in the police force back then: 'He did not turn down offers of help because he was desperate to be his own man. It never crossed his mind, he said, that if he asked for Mr Mole's help, he would have lost face or been diminished in the eyes of his colleagues. He said the culture at the time in the police service was that one moved without an overlap. You learned on the job. He said, "With hindsight, it was a serious mistake" to accept the role of Match Commander.'

The coronor reminded the jury that Mr Duckenfield had been asked in open court about the South Yorkshire Police Standing Instructions, and the jury was directed towards their copy of this document. Duckenfield told the court that 'he could not recall if he read them', but he accepted 'that he would have fallen into the intended readership of the guidelines'. Duckenfield was then asked about some of the contents of this document which included the line '...effective turnstile policing is key to prevention of disorder [outside] the ground. Officers should be encouraged to talk to those waiting to enter in order to identify non-local accents, drunks, etc.'

He was asked about section 1.43: 'Queues forming at turnstiles should be closely monitored by police and stewards.

It is recommended that mounted officers, where available, are used ... There is often frustration at turnstiles if queues remain after the game has started. Orderly control will minimise risks.'

'It is emphasised that stewards should ensure that all sections of the terraces and stands are filled to capacity before allowing access to further sections where possible. This will require monitoring turnstile totalisers and the use of public address systems in some instances. This operation is greatly assisted by the compartmentalisation of grounds, each compartment being filled in sequence.' These guidelines seemed to suggest that the strategy of letting fans 'find their own level' was not recommended, in fact, the South Yorkshire Police Standing Instructions appeared to suggest that the opposite was true. Duckenfield told the court that he 'could not be specific as to whether he was familiar with that.'

Sir Goldring continued to sum up the evidence of Mr Duckenfield, 'This is the South Yorkshire Police major incident manual, which contains, among other things, as you will recall, at internal page seven, the alert, the use of the word "Catastrophe". This is the document, just to remind you of it.'

Mr Duckenfield was asked whether he had read it. He said he could not say he had read the manual prior to 15 April. He said 'he may have done. He would have been aware that the police were in overall control of the response to a major incident.'

Duckenfield was asked about his familiarity with The Green Guide (guide to safety at sports grounds), a set of guidelines initially compiled by Lord Wheatley, and commissioned by the government in the wake of the Ibrox disaster. The first edition was published in 1973, and it was updated after the Bradford fire disaster in 1985. Duckenfield said he would have been familiar with it. Duckenfield was then asked about paragraph twenty-nine of the Green Guide which read: 'To draw up in consultation with the emergency services contingency plans, including arrangements with police for stopping an event ... ' etc., including 'coping with exceptionally large numbers of spectators arriving at the ground.' A further reference was read: 'Contingency plans should be made to deal with situation where the available entrances at a ground have proved insufficient to stop unduly large crowds from gathering outside... '

He was asked whether 'he knew about the entry rate, the notional entry rate of 750 people per hour in paragraph 47 of the Green Guide.' The coroner recalled, 'Mr Duckenfield said he didn't know whether he would have been aware of the notional maximum turnstile throughput of 750 people per hour. He said he did not think he should necessarily have been aware of that figure, or presumably his understanding of the Sheffield Wednesday figure of 1,000 per hour.' This notional rate related to the maths used to calculate how many people could enter through a turnstile, per hour. Lord Taylor, in his interim report, mentioned this as a serious flaw saying, 'The mathematics are elementary. Both the police and the club should have realised that the Leppings Lane turnstiles and the waiting area outside them would be under strain to admit all the Liverpool supporters in time. Success depended on the spectators arriving at a steady rate from an early hour and upon the maximum turnstile rate being maintained. In fact neither of these requirements, which are inter-linked, was fulfilled. That they might not be so was in my view foreseeable.'

Goldring reminded the jury, 'Mr Duckenfield said he did not know of the Freeman tactic of closing off the tunnel,' when the central pens became full, and that, 'He did not know, he said, the tunnel was closed in 1988.' He agreed that closure or control of the tunnel by the police might be common sense if the pens were becoming full to capacity. He agreed with Mr Greenwood's evidence that it would be an 'obvious expedience'.

With regards to the view Duckenfield and his colleagues had from the police control box, he described it [the view from the police control box] in terms of, 'A diminishing view ... I am not minimising our responsibility, and I am not saying that we didn't have a good view, what I am saying is that others above and below those pens, in my view, would have a better view.' He [Duckenfield] agreed it was clear, unobstructed and elevated. There were cameras and monitors. Mr Bichard could control three of the cameras. He could direct, he agreed, their line of sight.

Although at one point he said he was sure he knew that a zoom facility existed for the cameras, Mr Duckenfield later said he 'was not sure that a zoom facility existed for the cameras.'

Duckenfield was shown footage from police camera five, between 14:20 p.m. and 14:22 p.m., and he agreed that it showed 'an excellent view'. Duckenfield said that he would have perhaps been about two feet from the screen in the police control box.

Duckenfield was shown video footage made by a television programme called First Tuesday shot in February 1990. The court was shown these clips, the first from police camera one and the second shot using police camera three. The coroner reminded the court about what Mr Duckenfield said having seen the video footage in court: 'Mr Duckenfield said, members of the jury, that his visits to the police control box would not give him any real impression of the pens filling and the density of the crowd.'

The video footage was shot using the police cameras and shown on the monitors situated in the police control box. The video footage was played to the court, who could see that the camera could pan and tilt, and also zoom. Mr Weatherby, representing some of the families, put it to Mr Duckenfield, 'We can see the capability of the camera. We have seen a lot of the footage; it can move left and right, it can pan and tilt, and it can zoom. You get a very good image through that monitor in the control box. Yes?' Duckenfield replied, 'Yes , sir'. Mr Duckenfield was then shown footage shot from camera three, which was in colour, and could also pan and tilt, and zoom. Mr Weatherby said, 'Again, the camera can move, it can move left and right, you can point it down to the Spion Kop area, as we have seen when Ms Lambert showed you footage … So it can pan around the ground. It is in colour. The colour may not be as good as modern colour, but it is pretty good, Mr Duckenfield, isn't it?' Mr Duckenfield answered, 'It is, sir.' Mr Weatherby continued, 'It has got an amazing zoom, hasn't it?' Duckenfield agreed again, 'It has'. Mr Weatherby said, 'So from your position in the control box, you could have looked, with great closeness, at the front of those pens or the whole of those pens, or whatever you wanted to, couldn't you, Mr Duckenfield?' Once again, Duckenfield agreed, 'Yes, sir.'

Mr Weatherby seemed to be trying to show the court that Mr Duckenfield had a very good view of the pens on 15 April 1989, and should have been able to tell that the central pens were full before he gave the order to open the gate.

However, as Sir Goldring reminded the court, 'Because of his [Duckenfield's] inexperience, he did not know the difference between a crowded and an over full pen.' When asked if he should have given the order to close access to the tunnel after giving the order to open exit Gate C, Goldring recalled the evidence, 'Question: Do you think that such an instruction is something that could reasonably have been expected of you? Answer: "If ... I had been a knowledgeable, experienced Match Commander at Hillsborough, it should have been expected of me to know that. But sadly I wasn't."'

The coroner asked for video footage to be shown to the jury which showed video footage shot at about 14:47 p.m. on the day, and it showed the camera picture pan and zoom. Duckenfield told the court that he didn't recall asking Mr Bichard to pan and zoom, but the coroner said, 'Obviously this footage shows, does it not, the camera panning and zooming, obviously operated by PC Bichard.' He was then shown some BBC footage from a similar time, and the coroner reminded the jury that it was from a BBC camera in the South Stand, and so not the view that Mr Duckenfield would have had from the police control box. Duckenfield was asked in relation to the footage whether he would have thought it dangerous to allow further fans to enter the central pens at about 14.47.30 p.m., the time of this footage. He said, 'on what he saw and what crossed his mind at that time, no.'

Duckenfield was shown further BBC footage shot at about 14:49 p.m. and once again he said 'he did not think the pens were overcrowded'. However, by his own admission, because of his 'inexperience', 'he did not know the difference between a crowded and an over full pen'.

The coroner moved on to the moment when Duckenfield gave the order to open the gate. Duckenfield's evidence was read to the court: 'Mr Duckenfield said that he thought there were two requests from Mr Marshall. On the second, Mr Marshall said,

"If you don't open the gates, someone's going to get killed". Mr Duckenfield said that was, "A shocking almost terrifying moment to feel we'd got to that situation. I was thinking about where were they going to, and what have you, and I think he came back with another request, and Mr Murray said to me, and I shall remember distinctly, because of our radio problems, he'd got a personal radio in his hand and he held it in his hand and said, Mr Duckenfield, are you going to open the gates? And I remember saying to him quite clearly, Mr Murray, if people are going to die, I have no option but to open the gates."'

Duckenfield admitted that, after giving the order to open the gate, he gave no subsequent order to block access to the tunnel after opening exit Gate C: 'I think that probably at this stage, I won't say I was in a state of shock at that stage, but I was certainly in a surprised state still, that we had got to that stage where we had got to open the gates to save lives.' He told the court that he had not considered where the fans might go, or that they might go through the central tunnel into the central pens.

The coroner then recounted a series of questions that had been put to Chief Superintendent David Duckenfield:

'Question: "Do you think, as the Match Commander, the consequences of the decision you made, and in particular thought as to where the fans might go from the inner concourse, is something that you should have considered?"

Answer: "I think it's fair to say that that is arguably one of the biggest regrets of my life, that I did not foresee where fans would go when they came in through the gates".

Question: "Do you think you should have done?"

Answer: "If I'd been a fully competent, experienced, knowledgeable Match Commander with the experience, should we say, of Mr Mole or Mr Freeman, I no doubt would have thought about it. But I wasn't in their position".

Question: "Understanding ... your limited experience ... is it not a basic principle of policing and, indeed ... in

Answer: "I accept that ..."

Question: "Why do you think you didn't consider the consequences on 15 April?" Answer: "I think it's fair to say that I was overcome by the enormity of the situation and the decision I had to make, and, as a result of that, that is probably very hard to admit, as a result of that, I was so overcome, probably with the emotion of us having got into that situation, that my mind, for a moment, went blank."

Question: "Did you panic?"

Answer: " ... There is every possibility, but I think others should judge me, but ... I don't know what the alternative is to panic. There was certainly no shouting or ranting or raving, but there was certainly, I can't describe it any other way than a very, very difficult moment for me."'

Police Constable Huckstep had originally been stationed outside the turnstiles, but when he went into the ground he was under the impression that there had been a pitch invasion. The PC's evidence to the court, however, was that, 'It was quite clear early on it was not so.' PC Huckstep assisted in helping people out of pen three in what he described as 'a funnel of police officers taking people out of the gate of pen three.'

Sergeant Payne was in charge of serial sixteen and went onto the pitch at around 3.07 p.m., also under the mistaken belief that there had been a pitch invasion but as the coroner told the jury, 'As he approached the Leppings Lane end he quickly realised something serious had happened.' He said he set about trying to help.

Police Constable Lang belonged to serial fourteen and he heard a shout that there was a pitch invasion, so along with many other officers, he ran into the ground. His evidence was that as he got closer to the terraces, he saw 'an excessively large number of people in the central pen.'

Police Constable Ramsden was another of the officers who went onto the pitch. In his evidence he described the scenes at the Leppings Lane end of the ground as 'complete and utter turmoil,' and said that 'He could not see anybody taking control. He said control was needed.' Ramsden spoke about the state of the police officers in attendance, especially the younger ones, 'A number of the younger bobbies, he said, seemed to be in a state of shock, unable to do anything effective; traumatised for a brief time. He said people froze. Mr Ramsden said, as the situation developed, some officers were crying and obviously shocked.'

Sergeant Miller was also outside the ground when the shout for a pitch invasion was heard, and so he made his way inside the stadium. He told the court that it took him 'perhaps a minute to realise it was not a pitch invasion'. Miller had been at Hillsborough in 1981, when Spurs fans suffered crush injuries at the Leppings Lane end of the ground, and he said that 'he thought he was probably influenced in realising it was a crush by what he had seen at the 1981 semi-final'. Others, he said, 'Were taking longer to realise there was an unfolding disaster.'

Sir Goldring continued to refresh the memory of the jury about Miller's evidence: 'It took some officers longer to respond, he said, than they should have done. Chief Superintendent Nesbit, he said, ordered him to take his serial and help form a cordon across the pitch, which he did. He remained with the cordon, he said, until the pitch emptied. He said he questioned that order. He asked whether they should not be helping. He was particularly frustrated, he said, because he had had first aid training and it could not be put to use. On the cordon, he did not see any fighting or any trouble. In his statement, he had referred to fans shouting obscenities. He agreed they did so because they were upset and traumatised and frustrated about the lack of police response.'

Some officers who were involved in the rescue operation had talked of a small minority of supporters being aggressive, abusive and in some cases violent towards officers in the immediate aftermath, but Sergeant Miller's assertion that these actions were because fans were traumatised seems to make sense. It is hard to imagine how you would feel if you were to see a line of police officers standing across the centre of the pitch, not helping with the rescue efforts after you yourself had just been through hell and yet you were still trying to help your fellow fans as best you could. After all, Sergeant Miller said himself that he was frustrated that his first aid training was not being put to better use. As Liverpool supporter, Steve Hart, said when he encountered this thin blue line of inactivity '... The next thing I know we've put him on a board and we're running across the pitch with him. As we were running across the pitch, we came across a line of police standing there, and I remember screaming at them because they were just doing nothing!' From the police point of view, many were still labouring under the misapprehension that misbehaviour was causing the chaos, and indeed in the early moments the Nottingham Forest fans were by all accounts chanting offensive remarks towards the Liverpool fans who were in peril at the other end of the ground. Forest fans didn't at that stage know the enormity of the situation of course.

Sir Goldring reminded the court of the evidence of Superintendent Chapman: 'He said that he entered the ground in response to the order for all officers to attend. He said that from the perimeter track between the North Stand and the Spion Kop he saw "a heavy contingent of police officers containing what appeared to be some form of pitch invasion and disorder ... I observed the Nottingham Forest supporters on the Spion Kop and it was immediately apparent that their mood was hostile with supporters chanting, clapping and making violent gestures directed towards the Leppings Lane end ... I concluded that it was necessary to retain a contingent of officers at the Spion Kop end to defuse the situation and prevent any possibility of a pitch invasion." He said a line of officers was formed on the perimeter track in front of the Kop. He described the atmosphere as "electric" and said "the noise level was such that I could not hear any clear radio messages other than intermittent and distorted transmissions." He said that two or three spectators "made their way from the Leppings Lane end towards the Spion Kop, gesticulating and provoking a similar and very hostile response from officers to usher them back towards the Leppings Lane end."'

David Senior was a St John Ambulance volunteer and was stationed beneath the North Stand and Spion Kop. His summarised evidence was that from that area, he saw fans climbing over the perimeter fences: 'It appeared as though the police were trying to push them back, as though it could be like a pitch invasion.' His colleague sent a message on his radio saying that they needed assistance, and Mr Senior went down to the corner where his colleagues were situated. Sir Goldring told the court, 'A policeman pulled him towards the fence. He said, "It looks as though we have got some fatalities down here." Mr Senior thought the match was still going on. He said he saw quite a lot of fans who had been pushed towards the fence, "They were all laid out in a trough at the bottom, underneath the wall."' Once he realised the severity of the situation, David Senior radioed for all St John Ambulance personnel to come to the Leppings Lane end to assist. Mr Senior told the court that he received no instructions as to what to do. He then tried to help casualties as best he could, moving from one to another if he was satisfied that a casualty could not be helped.

Divisional Superintendent of St John Ambulance, Mr Towler, was at Hillsborough with his son who was a cadet, and they were both situated in the north-west corner of the stadium when, at about 2.55 p.m., they were called to the area behind the goal at the Leppings Lane [west] end. When he arrived he saw people pushed up against the fence at the front of the central pens. Mr Towler told the court that he heard people behind them say 'let them out' and he described the expressions of those pushed against the fence as 'absolute fear' and he said he could 'hear the older people shouting "get them out, get them out."' Mr Towler attended to some of the first supporters to escape through the small gate in the front fence between the terrace and the pitch. Sir Goldring told the court what Mr Towler had said in court, 'He went among them, checking their consciousness and their breathing. He said that everyone he attended to there was conscious, without life-threatening or serious injuries amongst that particular cohort of fans. They had been squashed and winded, he said.'

After a while, Mr Towler came across his first casualty, at around 3.15 p.m. He told the court that 'he checked one young male casualty for breathing and pulse, and found that there was none.' At this point, he realised that something was very seriously wrong, he said. He carried out CPR, along with a police officer. They were unable to make any progress, and so carried this person to the first aid room, where they left him in the care of SYMAS officers. Thereafter, he provided care to different casualties at different parts of the pitch. He did not know the gymnasium was the casualty clearing area. Mr Towler said he saw no fans who appeared to be drunk. The vast majority, he said, were supportive, helpful and trying as hard as the emergency services. The efforts of the police officers were exactly the same as the St John Ambulance members.

The first of only two ambulances to make it onto the pitch was driven by Frank Godley and it arrived onto the pitch at around 3.15 p.m. The court was shown video footage of the ambulance arriving behind the goal at the Leppings Lane end goal, and then the Coroner reminded the jury about Frank Goldley's evidence: 'Mr Godley said that a police officer had approached him whilst he was in the north-west corner of the pitch and asked him to drive onto the pitch. The officer said words to the effect that it was "bad out there." When he arrived at the goal he described it as "very crowded" and that there was what he thought was a police inspector with a megaphone asking the crowd to get back.' The coroner told the jury that they 'might think that might have been Superintendent Greenwood' who they had seen on video footage in that area and at that time previously. Godley said that he opened the back doors of the ambulance and somebody came up to him who was having difficulty breathing so he gave him some oxygen. He gave an oxygen bottle to someone who said he was a doctor. Godley gave CPR to a young man on the floor next to the ambulance, but there was no response. Goldring continued: 'He removed, as he thought, two bodies from the back of the ambulance. A doctor, and we know it was Dr Phillips, wanted him to take a casualty straight to hospital. We know, members of the jury, that that was Gary Currie, the young man who survived.' Frank Godley eventually drove off the pitch as the second ambulance was entering the pitch at around 3.36 p.m. having spent around twenty minutes on the pitch. Godley did not know that the stadium's gymnasium was a casualty clearing area.

Sir Goldring reminded the jury that they had heard from 'a number of St John volunteers who had been in the first aid room'. Ms Bower-Lissaman recalled receiving a radio message, which was sent by John Towler, and was to the effect that people were being crushed. That message was timed at 3.03-3.04 p.m. The first patient that they treated in the first aid room was a young boy who told them 'people were being crushed and killed'. There was soon not enough room in the small first aid room for the number of casualties that were arriving. Sheila Shelton was working in the first aid room and her evidence, a statement dated May 1989, was read to the court by the coroner: 'She spoke of dealing with five or six casualties in the first aid room. More were being brought to the corridor outside. She was told at one stage by Joan Saxton about five people who had died. She described how upset she was at being told by a doctor that three people who were outside, who looked "full of life", as she put it, were in fact dead. More casualties were being brought to the corridor outside. She said, did Mrs Shelton, that they didn't have any labels to affix to the casualties, so she may have checked the same casualty more than once. She said the two oxygen cylinders in the ambulances were rapidly exhausted.'

The next evidence to be summarised for the jury by Sir John Goldring was that of the South Yorkshire Metropolitan Service (SYMAS). Sir Goldring drew the attention of the jury to the SYMAS major incident plan. The introduction of the plan read: 'A major incident is a situation that we can never predict, it can occur at any place at any time. The object of this plan is to enable us to deal with any incident in an organised, professional way, by each and every member sticking to their own job and knowing exactly what their role is.' The definition was set out as, 'A major incident/catastrophe is any situation whereby the normal day-to-day running of the service is impeded due to the number of casualties requiring treatment and transportation, creating the need for extra operational resources from our own or other services.' The objective of the major incident plan as described in the plan itself was, 'To instigate a methodical plan of action, and to organise the ambulance service resources to provide: (a) sufficient resources for the effective handling, treatment and transportation of casualties; (b) to provide and set up an efficient control and communications system; (c) to ensure a minimum disruption of the normal day-to-day service; and (d) establish a close liaison with other emergency services.' With regards to specific duties, the first crew on the scene were given specific roles to play in the event of a major incident: 'Duties of first crew on scene ... The ambulance attendant or leading ambulanceman who is first on scene at an incident will assume the responsibilities for: (1)The initial assessment of the situation; (2)The instigation of the ambulance service major incident plan; (3) The management and organisation of the ambulance personnel until relieved by a more senior officer.'

The jury was reminded of a meeting that took place on 16 July 1986 to discuss the Bradford fire, and what the SYMAS would do if it were to ever happen in South Yorkshire. All the emergency services were present. According to Mr Wilkinson of the SYMAS, it was suggested that ambulance officers should be stationed at the Hillsborough Stadium, but Sheffield Wednesday Football Club were happy with the current arrangement of having volunteer St John Ambulance officers present instead. The coroner said, 'Tickets for SYMAS officers were in fact set aside from then on. The seats were high up in the south stand, which Mr Wilkinson explained was for the reason of a better view, access to a telephone, and allowing easier exit out the stands to the gymnasium...' Mr Page noted that the agreement for tickets for SYMAS officers at Hillsborough was a 'good start', and that other requests for SYMAS presence at football grounds had been unsuccessful. After the meeting, Mr Wilkinson and the other emergency services were given a tour of the Hillsborough ground by Mr Ward, the club's groundsman.

After the tour, Mr Wilkinson, Mr Ward and other SYMAS officers had a conversation with Sheffield Wednesday's club physiotherapist, Alan Smith, and the provision of ambulances was discussed. Mr Wilkinson's evidence pertaining to that conversation was, 'I do recollect the conversation, and we broached that we would want to put ambulances into the ground and have them ready so, if there was a major incident, we could start the process much quicker in relation to being able to respond ... I said there would be costs associated to it and we never got past that. Wilkinson said they never got down to precise figures because Mr Smith, the physiotherapist, said that the club was happy with "the status quo". He did not want to move away from that.'

Talking about the role of first responders to an incident at Hillsborough or any other venue for that matter, Mr Wilkinson had given evidence about what they should and should not do. Sir Goldring summarised that evidence by saying, 'The first responders, the first responders to the major incident, in other words, should stick to their role and not become involved in providing care. Their job, he said, was to make an assessment of the situation and remain "the eyes and ears" of control until relieved by more senior officers.' He said that, 'However great the temptation may be, the first responders should not get involved in caring for casualties. It was important that, as quickly as possible, the scale of the incident is established and the level of resources needed.' He said that, 'Until that information is sent to control, nothing is happening to support the scene. So it's absolutely crucial. Control can then instigate the plan.'

Mr Page, of SYMAS, agreed with a number of propositions that were put to him during evidence. They were that 'instigating or declaring a major incident was more than a mere formality,' as a clear declaration of a major incident would ensure that 'a number of steps would be taken, principally by those in control, ambulance control.' These steps included dispatching the major incident vehicle which had more equipment including a mass of airways, cutting equipment, oxygen and Entonox for pain relief. It carried old-fashioned stretchers. It should contain a number of personal radios that were charged. It could be used as a 'control communications hub on site: a first point of contact.' Summarising Mr Page's evidence, Sir Goldring also told the jury that, 'It was important that the hospital was notified as soon as possible of a major incident, and the number and nature of casualties, so they were able to mobilise resources.'

One of the first responders on the scene for SYMAS on April 15, 1989 was station officer Paul Eason who was stationed inside the stadium. Video and photographic evidence shows Mr Eason behind the goal, and so within a few feet of the central pens. Video evidence showed Mr Eason in front of the central pens at around 3.06 p.m. Eason said that he had assumed that the problems were some sort of crowd disturbance, and that he didn't look into the pens to investigate. The coroner summarised the evidence of Mr Page who said of Mr Eason and Mr Higgins, 'They should have gone and communicated with the police and got the information. He was there referring to the police facing the pens. He would have expected them also, he said, to speak to the St John Ambulance officers. He would expect them to be able to recognise the more senior police officers from the more junior. It would not be unreasonable to expect the police to alert ambulance personnel that a medical emergency was developing or had occurred.'

Despite attending at the Leppings Lane end of the ground at around 3.06 p.m., it wasn't until 3.22 p.m. that Eason declared it a major incident. The coroner reminded the court that 'Mr Page agreed that Mr Eason's failure to make a declaration until 3.22 p.m. was, as he believed, a very serious failing.'

There was so much more evidence that was heard and summarised by the coroner, and digested by the jury, but, as mentioned at the beginning of this chapter, it would take a whole book to properly chronicle such a long and complex case. After hearing evidence for more than two years, on Wednesday 6 April 2016 the jury was sent out by Sir John Goldring to consider their deliberations on the fourteen questions that were set out at the outset of the summing-up process. Sir Goldring told the jury that they must 'Put emotion to one side. Do not make critical findings unless the facts justify them. On the other hand, do not shrink from making such findings if they do.'

A few weeks after being sent out to consider the answers to the fourteen key questions listed at the beginning of this chapter, the jury came back and told the coroner that they had reached a verdict on thirteen of the fourteen questions, but needed further help with the last question. Then, the following week, on Monday 25 April 2016, the jury advised the coroner that they had made their decisions. On Tuesday 27 April, the court in Warrington was packed with families, survivors, and the press. The jury was due to deliver their determinations at 11 a.m., and thousands followed the story as it broke online.

At just past 11 a.m. on Tuesday 27th April 2016, a hushed court was waiting with hope in their hearts as the jury filed into court. Sir John Goldring bid them a good morning and explained that he would read the questions and ask the foreperson to read their answers. This is what happened next:

Question one:
'Do you agree with the following statement: On April 15 1989, ninety-six people died in the disaster as a result of crushing in the central pens of the Leppings Lane terrace, following the admission of a large number of supporters to the stadium through the exit gates.

Jury's answer: 'Yes'.

Question two:
'Was there any error or omission in police planning and preparation for the semi-final on April 15 1989, which caused or contributed to the dangerous situation that developed on the day of the match?'

Jury's answer: 'Yes. The jury feels that there were major omissions in the 1989 operational order, including: specific instructions for managing the crowds outside the lane turnstiles; specific instructions as to how the pens were to be filled and monitored; specific instructions as to who would be responsible for the monitoring of the pens.'

Question three:
'Was there any error or omission in policing on the day of the match, which caused or contributed to a dangerous situation developing at the Leppings Lane turnstiles?'

Jury's answer: 'Yes. Police response to the increasing crowds at Leppings Lane was slow and uncoordinated. The road closure and sweep of fans exacerbated the situation. No filter cordons were placed in Leppings Lane. No contingency plans were made for the sudden arrival of a large number of fans. Attempts to close the perimeter gates were made too late.'

Question four:
'Was there any error or omission by commanding officers, which caused or contributed to the crush on the terrace?'

Jury's answer: 'Yes. Commanding officers should have ordered the closure of the central tunnel before the opening of Gate C was requested, as pens three and four were full. Commanding officers should have requested the number of fans still to enter the stadium after 2.30 p.m. Commanding officers failed to recognise that pens three and four were at capacity before Gate C was opened. Commanding officers failed to order the closure of the tunnel as Gate C was opened.'

Question five:
'When the order was given to open the exit gates at the Leppings Lane end of the stadium, was there any error or omission by the commanding officers in the control box which caused or contributed to the crush on the terrace?'

Jury's answer: ' Yes. Commanding officers did not inform officers in the inner concourse prior to the opening of Gate C. Commanding officers failed to consider where the incoming fans would go. Commanding officers failed to order the closure of the central tunnel prior to the opening of Gate C.'

Question six:
'Are you satisfied, so that you are sure, that those who died in the disaster were unlawfully killed?'

Jury's answer: 'Yes.' [This is the only question which required a majority decision in order to reach a verdict. Seven of the nine jurors decided that the ninety-six were unlawfully killed.]

Question seven:
'Was there any behaviour on the part of the football supporters which caused or contributed to the dangerous situation at the Leppings Lane turnstiles?'

Jury's answer: 'No.'

'Was there any behaviour on the part of football supporters which MAY have caused or contributed to the dangerous situation at the Leppings Lane turnstiles?'

Jury's answer: 'No.'

Question eight:
'Were there any features of the design, construction and layout of the stadium, which you consider were dangerous or defective, and which caused or contributed to the disaster?

Jury's answer: 'Yes. Design and layout of the crush barriers in pens three and four were not fully compliant with the Green Guide. The removal of barrier 144 and the partial removal of barrier 136 would have exacerbated the waterfall effect of pressure towards the front of the pens. The lack of dedicated turnstiles for individual pens meant that capacities could not be monitored. There were too few turnstiles for a capacity crowd. Signage to the side pens was inadequate.'

Question nine:
'Was there any error or omission in the safety certification and oversight of Hillsborough Stadium that caused or contributed to the disaster?'

Jury's answer: 'Yes. The safety certificate was never amended to reflect the changes at the Leppings Lane end of the stadium. Therefore, capacity figures were never updated. The capacity figures for the Leppings Lane terraces were incorrectly calculated when the safety certificate was first issued. The safety certificate had not been reissued since 1966.'

Question ten:
'Was there any error or omission by Sheffield Wednesday and its staff in the management of the stadium and/or preparation for the semi-final match on April 15 1989, which caused or contributed to the dangerous situation that developed on the day of the match?'

Jury's answer: 'Yes. The club did not approve the plans for dedicated turnstiles for each pen. The club did not agree any contingency plans with the police. There was inadequate signage and inaccurate, misleading information on the semi-final tickets.'

Question eleven:
'Was there any error or omission by Sheffield Wednesday and its staff on April 15 1989, which caused or contributed to the dangerous situation that developed at the Leppings Lane turnstiles and in the west terrace?'

Jury's answer: 'No.'

'Was there any error or omission by Sheffield Wednesday Football Club (and its staff) on 15 April 1989 which MAY have caused or contributed to the dangerous situation that developed at the Leppings Lane turnstiles and in the west terrace?'

Jury's answer: 'Yes. Club officials were aware of the huge numbers of fans still outside the Leppings Lane turnstiles at 2.40 p.m. They should have requested a delayed kick-off at this point.'

Question twelve:
'Should Eastwood and Partners (structural engineers) have done more to detect and advise on any unsafe or unsatisfactory features of Hillsborough Stadium, which caused or contributed to the disaster?'

Jury's answer: 'Yes. Eastwoods did not make their own calculations when they became consultants for Sheffield Wednesday Football Club. Therefore, the initial capacity figures and all subsequent calculations were incorrect. Eastwoods failed to recalculate capacity figures each time changes were made to the terraces. Eastwoods failed to update the safety certificate after 1986. Eastwoods failed to recognise that the removal of barrier 144 and the partial removal of barrier 136 could result in a dangerous situation in the pens.'

Question thirteen:
After the crush in the west terrace had begun to develop, was there any error or omission by the police, which caused or contributed to the loss of lives in the disaster?'

Jury's answer: 'Yes. The police delayed calling a major incident, so the appropriate emergency responses were delayed. There was a lack of coordination, communication, command and control which delayed or prevented appropriate responses.'

Question fourteen:
'After the crush in the west terrace had begun to develop, was there any error or omission by the ambulance service (SYMAS), which caused or contributed to the loss of lives in the disaster?'

Jury's answer: 'Yes. SYMAS officers at the scene failed to ascertain the nature of the problem at Leppings Lane. The failure to recognise and call a major incident led to delays in responses to the emergency.'

The fresh inquests had made available a significant body of video footage from 15 April 1989 that had been shown to the jury over the course of the two years, and it undoubtedly helped them see some of the key points of the day. The video helped the jury understand that the build-up of fans in Leppings Lane was not a sudden, late surge of supporters. Rather it was a steady growth from 2 p.m., that caused officers to close the road from 2.17 p.m., and that was not filtered or managed, so an obvious bottleneck occurred in the small concourse area outside the turnstiles.

The match-day ticket had printed instructions for supporters to be in their place by 2.45 p.m., so a crowd outside that started to build at around 2.17 p.m. was understandable and foreseeable at a game due to kick-off at 3 p.m. The outer perimeter gates were mostly open, and were not used to filter the fans into the cramped area outside the turnstiles, as had been done in previous years. The video showed, and officers admitted, that the dangerous bottleneck of fans in the small area outside the turnstiles had caused chaos, but that no misbehaviour by the fans was visible on the video footage. I think it is fair to say that if the AV footage had shown a 'tanked-up mob' arriving late, and pushing their way forwards from behind then the South Yorkshire Police and their council would have shown it.

Once the police had 'lost control' of the situation outside they were forced to open a large exit gate to allow unfiltered access to thousands of supporters. The video evidence seen by the jury once again showed that these fans did not storm the stadium. They walked in, together, as a mass of people and went in the only obvious direction, which was through a long, dark tunnel immediately in front of Gate C. Above the tunnel there was a large sign that read 'STANDING' and at the end of the tunnel supporters entering through Gate C could see the pitch. Due to changes in the layout of the Leppings Lane terraces over the years, the tunnel that once fed the entire standing Leppings Lane terrace now only fed the two, small central pens behind the goal. The tunnel was dark and sloping forwards towards the back of those pens, and the jury heard evidence that once you started to walk down that tunnel shoulder to shoulder with so many others, it was almost impossible to stop and go back. The jury had heard from police officers, fans, and many other people who had given evidence to say that the central pens were already packed when the order to open Gate C was given.

Tragically, Chief Superintendent David Duckenfield, the Match Commander, did not appear to recognise the danger and with his admitted lack of experience, he didn't think about where the supporters would go after they entered through Gate C into the inner concourse area. Hundreds of fans poured down the tunnel into already, fatally, packed pens, and a 'vice like' crush ensued. The jury heard that police officers were slow to recognise that people were in trouble in the pens, and many viewed the fact that people were climbing out as a potential pitch invasion for too long, and so reacted too late to the plight of those in the pens.

These verdicts have set the record straight, and finally, after twenty-seven years allow the true story of that awful day to be put on record. But it is unlikely to be the end. The Independent Police Complaints Commission (IPCC), the Crown Prosecution Service (CPS), and Operation Resolve still have work to do to decide if those responsible for causing the disaster, and then covering up the facts for so long, should face court again. However, fuelled by love, the families of the ninety-six victim have finally won their battle for the truth. It is criminal that it has taken so long, and despite winning this battle they are still the losers in this tragic story. They lost mums and dads, sons and daughters, brothers and sisters, uncles and aunts, friends and lovers ... they lost something that can't be replaced. Their consolation is that now the whole world knows the real truth of what happened on 15 April 1989. The support the families have had from Liverpool supporters, the city of Liverpool, and many others over the years has been breathtaking. As Margaret Aspinall from the Hillsborough Family Support Group once said 'We Never Walked Alone'.

6

The 96

You'll Never Walk Alone

John Alfred Anderson (62)

Colin Mark Ashcroft (19)

James Gary Aspinall (18)

Kester Roger Marcus Ball (16)

Gerard Bernard Patrick Baron (67)

Simon Bell (17)

Barry Sidney Bennett (26)

David John Benson (22)

David William Birtle (22)

Tony Bland (22)

Paul David Brady (21)

Andrew Mark Brookes (26)

Carl Brown (18)

David Steven Brown (25)

Henry Thomas Burke (47)

Peter Andrew Burkett (24)

Paul William Carlile (19)

Raymond Thomas Chapman (50)

Gary Christopher Church (19)

Joseph Clark (29)

Paul Clark (18)

Gary Collins (22)

Stephen Paul Copoc (20)

Tracey Elizabeth Cox (23)

James Philip Delaney (19)

Christopher Barry Devonside (18)

Christopher Edwards (29)

Vincent Michael Fitzsimmons (34)

Thomas Steven Fox (21)

Jon-Paul Gilhooley (10)

Barry Glover (27)

Ian Thomas Glover (20)

Derrick George Godwin (24)

Roy Harry Hamilton (34)

Philip Hammond (14)

Eric Hankin (33)

Gary Harrison (27)

Stephen Francis Harrison (31)

Peter Andrew Harrison (15)

David Hawley (39)

James Robert Hennessy (29)

Paul Anthony Hewitson (26)

Carl Darren Hewitt (17)

Nicholas Michael Hewitt (16)

Sarah Louise Hicks (19)

Victoria Jane Hicks (15)

Gordon Rodney Horn (20)

Arthur Horrocks (41)

Thomas Howard (39)

Thomas Anthony Howard (14)

Eric George Hughes (42)

Alan Johnston (29)

Christine Anne Jones (27)

Gary Philip Jones (18)

Richard Jones (25)

Nicholas Peter Joynes (27)

Anthony Peter Kelly (29)

Michael David Kelly (38)

Carl David Lewis (18)

David William Mather (19)

Brian Christopher Matthews (38)

Francis Joseph McAllister (27)

John McBrien (18)

Marian Hazel McCabe (21)

Joseph Daniel McCarthy (21)

Peter McDonnell (21)

Alan McGlone (28)

Keith McGrath (17)

Paul Brian Murray (14)

Lee Nicol (14)

Stephen Francis O'Neill (17)

Jonathon Owens (18)

William Roy Pemberton (23)

Carl William Rimmer (21)

David George Rimmer (38)

Graham John Roberts (24)

Steven Joseph Robinson (17)

Henry Charles Rogers (17)

Colin Andrew Hugh William Sefton (23)

Inger Shah (38)

Paula Ann Smith (26)

Adam Edward Spearritt (14)

Philip John Steele (15)

David Leonard Thomas (23)

Patrick John Thompson (35)

Peter Reuben Thompson (30)

Stuart Paul William Thompson (17)

Peter Francis Tootle (21)

Christopher James Traynor (26)

Martin Kevin Traynor (16)

Kevin Tyrrell (15)

Colin Wafer (19)

Ian David Whelan (19)

Martin Kenneth Wild (29)

Kevin Daniel Williams (15)

Graham John Wright (17)

Acknowledgements

Thanks go to the many survivors and families who have provided 'the words' for this book. Likewise thanks to Dave Sinclair (www.flickr.com/ photos/dave_sinclair_liverpool_photos/) for permission to use several of his images, Margaret Aspinall and Sue Roberts of the Hillsborough Family Support Group (hsfg.co.uk) for agreeing to write the foreword, and the Press Association for the use of several images. Below are a number of sources that were used in the writing of this book:

The Taylor Report (Interim) on South Yorkshire Police website (http:// www.southyorks.police.uk/sites/default/files/Taylor%20 Interim%20Re port.pdf).

All of the quotations used within this book that are from police officers or FA officials are available in their witness statements, which can be found on the Hillsborough Independent Panel website (HIP). The main witness statements used are listed below but any other source can be found by searching on http://hillsborough.independent.gov. uk/. The majority of witness statements from Liverpool fans were taken in face-to-face interviews. The many accounts I received from Leeds fans were a result of an appeal online, and via the Yorkshire Evening Postand supplied to me as email accounts.

Chief Superintendent David Duckenfield witness statement on HIP website (http://hillsborough.independent.gov.uk/repository/ docs/ SYP000002130001.pdf).

Superintendent Bernard Murray witness statement on HIP website (http:// hillsborough.independent.gov.uk/repository/docs/ SYP000002070001.pdf).

Superintendent Roger Greenwood witness statement on HIP website (http://hillsborough.independent.gov.uk/repository/docs/SYP000004210001.pdf).

PC Illingworth witness statement on HIP website (http://hillsborough.independent.gov.uk/repository/docs/SYP000009690001.pdf).

Graham Kelly, Chief Executive of the Football Association. Witness statement on HIP website (http://hillsborough.independent.gov.uk/repository/docs/HOM000001380001.pdf).

Glen Kirton of the Football Association. Witness statement on HIP website (http://hillsborough.independent.gov.uk/repository/docs/HOM000001420001.pdf).

David Cameron apology on 12 September 2012. Parliament website (Daily Hansard) (http://www.publications.parliament.uk/pa/cm201213/cmhansrd/cm120912/debtext/120912-0001.htm).

Sheffield Wednesday Football Club apology after HIP report in September 2012 (http://www.swfc.co.uk/news/article/club-statement-363649.aspx).

Draft Incident Report – HSE – Barrier 124a from pen 3 (http://hillsborough.independent.gov.uk/repository/docs/HSE000000960001.pdf).

The maps of Hillsborough Stadium and the Leppings Lane terrace are reproduced from Lord Justice Taylor's interim report, under Crown Copyright and the Open Government Licence (http://hillsborough.independent.gov.uk/terms-conditions).